UNKNOWN PLEASURES

Also by Peter Hook

The Hacienda: How Not to Run a Club

UNKNOWN PLEASURES:

INSIDE JOY DIVISION

PETER HOOK

**SIMON &
SCHUSTER**

London · New York · Sydney · Toronto · New Delhi

A CBS COMPANY

First published in Great Britain by Simon & Schuster UK Ltd, 2012
A CBS COMPANY

ISBN: 978-0-85720-215-4 (Hardback)
ISBN: 978-0-85720-216-1 (Trade Paperback)

Typeset in the UK by M Rules
Printed and bound by CPI Group (UK) Ltd, Croydon, CR0 4YY

Dedicated, with love, to my mother Irene
and her sister, Jean.

CONTENTS

Introduction   xi
Prologue: January 1978   xiii

Part One: 'Insight'

'For seventeen days that's all we had: chicken and chips'   3
'You can take the boy out of Salford but you can't take
    Salford out of the boy'   10
'Barney would always eat on his own or in the bath' _   17
'Oh, fuck, it's Steve Harley'   23
Timeline One: May 1948–April 1976   27

Part Two: 'Disorder'

'Normal band, normal night, few people watching, clap-clap,
    very good'   35
'Is that a bass guitar?'   39
'He was just a kid with "Hate" on his coat'   44
'He was one of us'   49
'I can't actually think of anything less "us" than a wet-towel fight' 53
'The twats were flicking the Vs up'   61
'Apart from the odd pint pot in the gob it was a good gig'   68
'Even the shit ones were pretty good'   73
'I told him exactly where he could stick his vibrators'   79
Timeline Two: June 1976–December 1977   87

Part Three: 'Transmission'

'It was like *The X Factor* for punks'   97
'We need to get rid of this Nazi artwork'   103
'The biggest rain of spit I've ever seen in my life'   120
Timeline Three: January 1978–December 1978   125

Part Four: 'Love Will Tear Us Apart'

'Peter's fell off his chair again'   137
'Fuck. Martin's got a boot full of stolen car radios'   140
'It sounds like a fucking helicopter'   147
'He was looking for that spark'   150
'Not that I'd change anything'   160
'Stop fucking moaning, Hooky'   167
'I just went for a piss'   170
'You shouldn't trust a word I say'   173
'Bring it on'   179
'Turned out to be horse meat'   185
'He's possessed by the devil, that twat'   191
Unknown Pleasures Track by Track   199
Timeline Four: January–December 1979   208

Part Five: 'Ceremony'

'A right mother hen'   235
'We carried on'   240
'He thought we were pricks – and how right he was'   244
'His mum got the blood out by washing it in a bath
  of salt water'   254
'We were so excited about going to America'   263
'I never said goodbye'   267

Epilogue   273
Closer Track by Track   275
Timeline Five: January1980–October 1981   281

Acknowledgements   301
Index   305

This book is the truth, the whole truth, and nothing but the truth … as I remember it!

Peter Hook, 2012

INTRODUCTION

It's a strange life. Normally I don't include any other people in my writing. Everyone remembers the same things completely differently. The contradictions really confuse you and spoil everything, making you question yourself and what happened. I proved it to myself by letting a very close friend see what I had written. He replied with a great comment: 'What's the point of all this?'

So, answers on a postcard, please.

Hooky

X

PROLOGUE

January 1978

Our first gig as Joy Division and it ended in a fight. Typical.

Not our first gig. Before that we'd been called Warsaw but, for reasons I'll explain later, we couldn't carry on being called Warsaw so we'd had to think of a new name. Boys in Bondage was one of the many suggestions and we very nearly went with another, the Slaves of Venus, which just goes to show how desperate we were getting.

It was Ian who suggested Joy Division. He found it in a book he was reading, *House of Dolls*, by Ka-Tzetnik 135633. He then passed it round for all of us to read. In the book, 'Joy Divisions' was the name given to groups of Jewish women kept in the concentration camps for the sexual pleasure of the Nazi soldiers. The oppressed, not the oppressors. Which in a punky, 'No Future' sort of way was exactly what we were trying to say with the name. It was a bit like Slaves of Venus, except not crap.

So that was decided: we were Joy Division. Little did we know what we were letting ourselves in for, that for years people would be asking us, 'Are you Nazis?'

'No. We're not fucking Nazis. We're from Salford.'

So anyway, we had this gig at Pips Discotheque (formerly Nice 'N' Easy) on Fennel Street in Manchester. It was our first official gig as Joy Division, though it had been advertised as Warsaw (the name change came over Christmas), and we were pretty excited come the night – me especially, because that day I'd been out and bought a brand-new guitar.

I'd been paranoid about my old one since recording our EP *An Ideal for Living*. Barney had told me it was out of tune between the F and the G. I didn't know what that meant but it sounded serious. So I'd saved up for a new one, a Hondo II, Rickenbacker Stereo Copy (I beat the guy down from £99 to £95) and tonight was its debut. Not only that but I had a lot of mates coming to see us – the Salford lot, we'll call them: Alex Parker and his brother, Ian, Twinny, and all the lads from the Flemish Weaver on Salford Precinct, my local.

Before the show started Ian Curtis had been listening to *Trans-Europe Express* by Kraftwerk over the PA. He loved that record. He must have given it to the DJ to play as our intro music, and I'm not sure if he was planning to get up on stage from the dance floor, or what he was intending to do really, but he was on the dance floor and he was sort of kicking broken glass around as *Trans-Europe Express* was playing. Kind of kicking it and moving round to the music at the same time.

We already knew Ian was driven, and recently we'd been seeing how volatile he could sometimes be. He was going through a phase of acting up a bit, shall we say. A frontman thing, of course, and partly his Iggy Pop fascination, but also frustration – frustration that we weren't getting anywhere, that other Manchester bands were doing better than us, getting more gigs than us. The Drones had an album out. The Fall, the Panik and Slaughter & the Dogs all had singles out, and their records weren't all muffled and shit-sounding like ours. To cap it all, here we were, our first gig as Joy Division, and only about thirty people had turned up – twenty of them my mates.

All of this got to me, Steve and Bernard, too, of course, but Ian had it worse than we did. Probably because we all lived with our parents but he was married, so maybe the group felt more like real life for him somehow, more like something he *had* to make work.

Or perhaps I'm talking out my arse. Maybe Ian was just kicking glass because he was pissed and felt like it. Not that it mattered anyway: the bouncer didn't care whether Ian was developing his stage persona or acting out his career frustration or what. He just saw a twat kicking broken glass. He stormed over, grabbed him by the scruff of the neck, marched him to the door and threw him out.

Great. Someone came and told us; so, instead of going on, the three of us had to go to the door and beg the bouncer to let him back in.

He was going, 'Fuck off, he's a wanker kicking broken glass round …' and we were going, 'Yeah, but that wanker's our singer, mate – he's the singer of our band – you've got to let him in. Come on, mate …'

Eventually, and after much begging, the bouncer relented and let Ian back in, and at last we got on stage, about twenty minutes late, looked out into the crowd – if you can call it that – and there were all my mates right at the front going, like, 'Hiya, Hooky. Are you all right, Hooky?' grinning at me and giving me the thumbs-up. I was thinking that it was nice of them to turn up, but the grinning and thumbs-upping I could have done without. In Joy Division we were very serious. We were more into scowling.

Meanwhile Barney was giving me daggers, like, 'Your mates better behave themselves.' Ian as well, the cheeky bastards.

Then Ian went, 'Right, we're here now. We're Joy Division and this is … "'Exercise One'"," and I struck a pose with my brand-new Hondo II and hit the first note of the first song, an open E.

Except that instead of the first note of 'Exercise One' there was a massive *boing* sound, and everyone looked at me.

Oh, fuck. The string had flipped off the guitar. I pushed it back over the nut so it clicked into the hole and hit it again.

Boing.

It jumped out again.

Fuck, fuck, fuck-a-duck.

It was a fault on the guitar, honest. I had to hold the string in with my thumb and my finger as I was playing. I was just getting to the point of mastering that when I looked down and saw Alex Parker, who was a very good friend of mine, and his brother Ian all of a sudden start fighting.

No worries, I thought. *The rest of them'll sort that out.* Sure enough, a load more of the Flemish Weaver mob waded in to split them up. But then more punches were thrown, one of them went crashing to the floor and instead of the fight stopping it got worse, gradually escalating until *all* of my mates were involved, a huge mass punch-up. Like a giant ball of them rolling up and down in front of us as we were playing. Oh my God! The rest of the band were looking at them and then at me and giving me daggers as this big ball of fighting blokes rolled across the front of us and then back again. Of course the bouncer who'd thrown Ian out was nowhere to be seen, and they were just left to roll about, so we just kept on playing. Flat as fuck but the band played on.

But then it escalated. These other kids kept running forward from the back, starting on my mates, lashing out at them as they rolled past. Which of course wound me up. So I started kicking these kids from the stage.

'Don't fucking kick my mate, y'bastard!'

'Hey, la, pack it in!'

'Bleedin' Scousers!'

So there I was, kicking them in the head, trying to play 'Exercise One' while trying to hold my string in, the rest of the band really pissed off with me for bringing along my daft scally mates. *Shit!*

At last the bouncer reappeared. He had a bunch of mates with him and they started knocking heads together, kicked out the Flemish Weaver lot and then the Scousers, which left us finishing the gig to an empty room, me holding my string, Ian, Barney and Steve all looking at me like they wanted to throttle me. It was terrible, absolutely fucking awful. Our first gig as Joy Division and we didn't play another one for almost two months, which back then seemed like a long, long time. Definitely the worst thing in the world.

Like I say. Little did we know, eh?

PART ONE

'Insight'

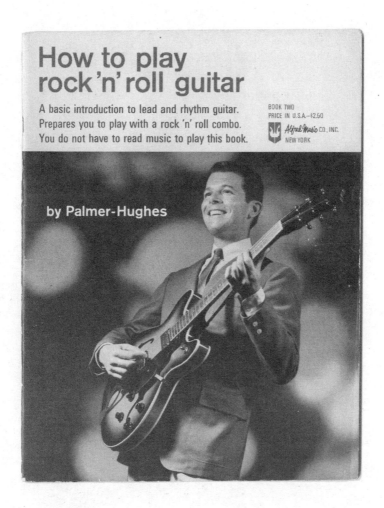

'For seventeen days that's all we had: chicken and chips'

I was born at about four o'clock in the afternoon at Hope Hospital, Salford on 13 February 1956 – and no, not Friday the thirteenth; it was a Monday.

Mum: Irene Acton. She was stubborn, obstinate, had a will of iron. A typical Northern mum, in other words. Dad: John (Jack) Woodhead. He was a driver for Frederick Hampson Glassworks in Salford, whose building was one of the few left standing when the council demolished Salford and rebuilt it from scratch in the seventies. I still drive past it all the time.

My first memory is of being in a pram on the pier at Blackpool with someone feeding me chips; I think it was my Auntie Jean. Not long after that my mum and dad split up and got divorced, the paperwork citing 'cruelty to the petitioner' – my mother. He was beating her up, of course. It was standard Salford practice for men to get pissed and knock their wives about in those days. But the final straw was when he started seeing this other woman. My mum hated him for that. She hated him till the day she died. Even though she met Bill, married him and was with him for forty years – *forty years* – she hated my father's guts, even after he died. Wouldn't hear his name mentioned. That's the kind of woman she was.

After they split up, me, Mum and my younger brother, Chris, went to live with our gran; and, once my mum finished paying for the front-room carpet in the old house because she couldn't trust Jack to pay (she didn't want the money-lenders to think she was unreliable – she was very proud), we were for a while a pretty normal single-parent working-class family: two-up, two-down, outside toilet, coal hole, living in Jane Street, Langworthy, in wonderful, dirty old Salford. When I saw *Control*, all those years later, I didn't even notice it was in black and white because it was exactly what my childhood had looked and felt like: dark and smoggy and brown, the colour of a wet cardboard box, which was how all of Manchester looked in those days.

There was nothing to do for us kids, apart from mooch around kicking a tin or poking a lolly stick into a bit of hot tar. The whole of Salford was our playground: we were let out in the morning and told to be back for tea. I remember getting lost and being brought home by the coppers a couple of times. The first time we seemed to have toys was the Christmas Bill came along, when I would have been five. He was courting my mum so of course he inundated me and our Chris with gifts. I remember coming down on Christmas morning, and the presents – I'd never seen anything like it in my life: he'd bought me and our kid a pedal car each and loads more besides. He spoilt us rotten that Christmas, for the first and last time. After that it was back to an orange and a few nuts.

Bill was Ernest William Hook. I thought he was single when he met my mum but I found out years later that he'd been married before and had kids, two daughters, of his own. I only found out one afternoon after a match: United, of course. I used to get a programme then take it to Bill's dad, Granddad Hook, a lovely old bloke who used to have a second-hand clothes stall on Salford Market with his wife. She'd died and he now lived on the Precinct after the slum clearance. There was a picture of two young girls on his sideboard. Innocently I asked . . .

'Who are they, Granddad?'

'Your dad's other family,' he replied. It still seems strange they were never mentioned.

In the beginning, when he was courting my mum, Bill was really nice. Me and our kid once poured a cup of tea in his petrol tank one afternoon (jealous, I suppose, because we were used to having Mum to ourselves) and he didn't even batter us! Just told us off. But over the years his hidden/ignored family made more sense, because he soon became a bit of a misery. He could be a real horrible fucker sometimes, especially at Christmas. His catchphrase used to be, 'If I'm suffering we're all suffering' – and he meant it. I still use it now to wind my kids up.

His saving grace was his money, I suppose. He was a highly skilled glass fitter. You know those machines they use for blowing glass, to make bottles and jars and all that? His job was to fix them and he went all over the world to do it: Singapore, India, the Caribbean – he was a proper seasoned traveller and the only guy on our street with a car, a 2.5 Riley RMB four-door that me and our kid put the tea in. He got us a telly, too, which again was the only one on our street. People used to queue up to watch it; we were suddenly popular. That's another of my earliest memories: me and Chris, after we'd been put to bed, creeping out and sitting at the top of the stairs listening to *Coronation Street*.

I was enrolled at Stowell Memorial School and loved it. I was happy. Mum and Bill got married — we stayed at home with Granny that day — and not long after that it was announced that he'd been offered a new job. So we were moving. The job was with Jamaica Glassworks and that's where we were going: we were moving to Jamaica.

In 1962, this was. Bill went on ahead, and a few days later me, Mum, Chris and all our worldly goods travelled down to Southampton, me clinging on to a plastic bag of toy soldiers. There was a very big storm and because of the bad weather we had to get a tug out to the boat. We were all petrified by the size of waves, the noise of the engines and the sailors bawling at us as they hauled us aboard the ship. Then when it came to my turn the plastic bag tore and my soldiers all spilt out into the stormy sea, leaving me holding the tattered bag.

Then there was the crossing. Oh my God.

You have to bear in mind that my mother, right up until the day she died, was the most conservative eater imaginable. She could hardly bear to eat anything that came from south of Salford. So when we ended up on an Italian cruise liner going to Jamaica she was freaked out because there was only one thing she could eat, which meant there was only one thing me and our kid could eat, too: chicken and chips. I still love chicken and chips now, funnily enough — dry, with a bit of salt and lots of pepper — but God only knows why because it never fails to remind me of being on that ship. For seventeen days that's all we had: chicken and chips. At the kids' dinner we'd watch the ice statues being carved and the huge cakes being laid out for the adult sitting later, but my mum said we couldn't have any cake because they were dirty.

Our Chris was only three. He was a screamer, not a sleeper, and it felt like he screamed all the way to the West Indies. This made us very unpopular — especially in the afternoons, when everyone was trying to snooze on deck. On top of that we were all seasick and hardly came out of the cabin (apart from one notable exception when, running down the corridor, I fell and smashed my nose, blood everywhere). We stopped at some fantastic places, though: Bilbao, Madeira, the Canary Islands and Trinidad. But still we never ate, and always made it back on board for the old chicken and chips. The journey seemed to take forever, but – apart from Chris nearly falling overboard as we docked because he'd seen Bill on the dockside – we arrived safely.

Our accommodation in Jamaica was a rented detached bungalow: three bedrooms and an inside toilet – the first place I ever lived with an inside toilet. All marble floors. One day these two black guys came to the door and asked if they could milk our calabash tree, and in return they'd make maracas for me and our kid. Proper maracas are made out of the fruit of a calabash tree – they empty out the middle bit, put stones inside and there you go. So Mum was like, 'Yeah whatever,' and these guys tore into the tree, threw down all the fruit, made us two pairs of maracas – one for me and one for our kid – and fucked off.

Later, all hell broke loose. The tree must have been full of spiders and that night the house was overrun with them, fucking hundreds of them, all over. They were huge, and I bet they were poisonous too. Man eaters, definitely. Bill was racing round killing them while me, Mum and our kid stood on the table screaming. We then beat a retreat to the bedroom, where Bill used a shoe to whack the spiders scuttling under the door as we all stood there wailing. I'm not joking! It was like a horror film. I'm getting the heebie-jeebies now just thinking about it. Hate spiders still – no *I'm a Celebrity ... Get Me Out of Here!* for me (although I did get asked to audition last year, funnily enough).

Not long after that we moved to 31 Phoenix Avenue, Kingston, which was also a detached bungalow, with fantastic, beautiful grounds where pineapples grew. It too had an inside toilet, and more beautiful marble floors – it even came with staff. We were sent to a private school, Surbiton Preparatory, which was terrifying. The teachers would scream at us to do joined-up writing and spell, which at six you didn't do in Salford. But we soon settled in and as a great bonus it was too hot in the afternoons to work so school finished at 2.30pm. All in all it should have been pretty idyllic, except that things had started to get a bit shit around that time: firstly between my mum and Bill and secondly in Jamaica, where the locals had got fed up with the Chinese and whites running all the businesses and had started to turf them out – literally storming into shops, chucking out the owners and taking over. At the same time a lot of houses were getting robbed, people were being mugged in the street and there were riots not far from where we lived in Kingston so there was a dangerous air about the place. You'd be on

the street watching the cops beat the shit out of the thieves, cha
them down, and when they caught them sitting on them and giving
them a good pistol-whipping.

Bill stopped coming home. He was spending a lot of time drinking
in the club at the glassworks after his shifts. He was a twat to us but a
great friend to everyone else, and one of the only white guys at work
who mixed with the black guys. He'd go out drinking with the white
guys then carry on with the black guys and reckoned that was why
ours was the only house on our street that was never robbed. At night
my mum would sit on the veranda with a crate of Red Stripe, waiting
for him to come home, getting drunker and angrier, and when he
eventually arrived back they'd have a screaming row. Me and our kid
would cower behind the sofa, praying for him to die, while they
charged around the house screaming at each other and smashing the
place to smithereens. He'd beat her up; she'd attack him with her high
heel, giving as good as she got; and by the time they'd finished the
house would look like a bomb had hit it. The next morning the maid
would put it all back together again, so it was nice and tidy for the next
fight.

You can't have everything, though. Mum and Bill knocking lumps out
of each other was a small price to pay for the fantastic weather, posh
house, car and money. Plus Mum worked for the Jamaica Tourist Board,
so we used to get free tickets to all the resorts and hang around in
country clubs. You know how I said that life had been black and white
in Salford? Well in Jamaica it was definitely in colour.

So what did we do? We returned to Salford.

She was homesick, Mum. That was the problem. She hated the food
and she missed her mother and sister. So when Bill's contract came up
for renewal she persuaded him to move back to Salford, which must
have caused some mega-arguments, because of course he wanted to
stay on in Jamaica. There were rumours about an American woman. I
remember one night my mum drunkenly pushing me into our blue
Ford Prefect and setting off, bread knife in hand, to kill them both.
Trouble was, she couldn't drive – and I don't know if you've ever tried
to learn to drive while holding a bread knife in one hand and a cigarette
in the other, but it's pretty difficult. Luckily, after hopping through a
couple of intersections, she thought better of it and hopped us home.
I always wonder why she never took our Chris, lucky bugger.

When it came to moving she got her own way, though, (and, knowing my mum, I don't expect that outcome was ever in doubt) and Bill gave in, probably thinking he'd be able to find a good job back in Manchester. There were a lot of glassworks around and at least they'd saved up enough from working in Jamaica so we were well-off financially.

Or we would have been, but for the fact that on the day we were due to fly home (first time on a plane for me) we were paid a visit by a couple of cops and a 'tax inspector' who claimed that Bill had 'mis-paid' his taxes. They knew he had the money – he'd drawn it out of the bank to return home – and they weren't going to let us leave until he paid them. These guys basically screwed all of Bill's savings out of him, and we came home with nothing.

This was the summer of 1966. I was ten. Everyone else was going mad about England winning the World Cup as we returned from Jamaica, where we'd been for nearly four years, in our posh house with its marble floors, inside toilet and maids, to a two-up, two-down in Salford with an outside toilet and a very unhappy stepdad who never got another job in glass again and who got more and more bitter about it as the years went on.

We moved to back to Granny's for a while but soon went to Ordsall, just down the road, to 32 Rothwell Street, right by the park passage. They paid £300 or so for it. I went to Regent Road Primary, a mixed school, where my Auntie Jean was a dinner lady, which was great, because not only did I get tons of blancmange but also I'd returned from Jamaica as a bit of an outsider and needed all the allies I could get. In Jamaica the kids were much more advanced than I was, and I'd had to catch up. That meant that I'd returned miles ahead of the other kids back here in Salford. Now I was given a bollocking for doing joined-up writing. It was great: I could really take it easy. I had quite a good time at Regent Road. Again all of Salford was my playground and, apart from a few jibes about my big nose and a crippling shyness with girls, I was quite well behaved and enjoyed myself.

I'm sure that was the reason I passed the Eleven Plus – because I was so well educated compared to the other kids – and in those days you had to be bright to get into grammar school. The way it went back then was that if you failed the Eleven Plus you went to the secondary school, which was where the thickos went, or to the technical college if you were borderline, or the grammar if you were bright. There was no way in hell a thick bastard like me would have got in without an advantage.

I went to Salford Grammar School. This was where I met Barney Dickin (to become Sumner). Eventually we would start Joy Division together, and then New Order. So I've got Jamaica to thank for a life-long love of chicken and chips and a lifelong fear of spiders – but also, in a funny kind of way, for all of that too. How different things could have been if I'd stayed. Would I have suited dreads and reggae?

'You can take the boy out of Salford but you can't take Salford out of the boy'

I met Barney in that first year at Salford Grammar. He still gets really annoyed when I call him Barney.

'You're the only fucking person who calls me Barney. Everyone else calls me Bernard,' he bleats. But at school they used to call him Barney Rubble – this even cropped up in an early Joy Division review – and his surname was Dickin so they took the piss out of him about that, too, as you can imagine. He changed it to Sumner after he finished school.

Barney wasn't in my class, though. He wasn't even in the same house. I was in Lancaster and he was in Gloucester, the other two being Warwick and York. There were a few lessons we shared, but not many. My first memory of him is standing outside the gym and him coming up, and I just went, 'All right?' and he went, 'All right?' and that was it; that was the first time we had any kind of contact. No indication that we'd be spending the rest of our lives together, in one way or another, and change the world of music not once but twice. Even then we didn't really become friends at first, not really until the third year, when we both became skinheads.

A pair of right bastards we were too. Always in trouble. I hate to admit it now, but I was a bit of bully. There was a pecking order and you had to keep to it. I mean, I wasn't the biggest – nowhere near, not by a long way – but I hung around with them and that kind of behaviour rubs off – peer pressure, as they say – and I did my bit. We all did. Plus, I was a thief. Oh my God, was I a thief.

It was quite normal where I lived, to steal, because basically we had nothing. Not that I'm excusing it, mind you. I mean, my mum had nothing and she was as honest as the day was long – she once found a ten-bob note on King Street and stood there for two hours to see if anybody came back looking for it. And I'm certainly not claiming that I became a tea-leaf because I didn't get any affection from my parents, because nobody got affection in those days. But there it was. I was one. A thief.

10

Got nabbed for it, too, loads of times. Always getting beaten up by the coppers. Back then, if you got caught shoplifting, you got a good kicking from the police and you didn't do it again. Well, you did do it again, but you know what I mean – we didn't have to go to court and all that bollocks. The coppers just used to beat the shit out of you. Nowadays they're kittens, aren't they? Waste of time.

I remember once we'd done this bookies over, which – before you chuck this book away in disgust – isn't quite as bad as it sounds. It's not like we barged in there with sawn-offs and stockings on our heads; there was never any of that, never any violence – we were only thirteen after all. No, it was just that Salford at that time was being redeveloped: all the houses were being emptied, so what you had was a lot of crofts – which are bomb sites from the war, where a building's been blown up and then cleared – and derelict houses. There was one particular row of empty houses with a bookies (or bookmaker's or betting office, whichever you like) at the end of it. So what we did, me and my mates, was get some tools from somewhere and just break through the wall. It took us about a week to chip away enough bricks to make a hole big enough to crawl through, but that didn't matter because there was nothing else to do. I mean, we were bored to death; we'd do anything for a bit of excitement, and we'd had enough of lighting bonfires and larking about in the empty houses. So we spent about a week carving out this hole, then squeezed through – only to find that the bookies was more or less empty. Later we were in the doorway of another shop, just messing about, as you do, and the police came screaming up. We scattered and they chased us. I ran down a back alley, pulling over all the dustbins behind me so the coppers were tripping up on them. But when I came out of the alley at the other end another copper tripped *me* up and sent me flying. He picked me up, put me in the van, kicked the shit out of me, took me to the station and did it again. I think I confessed to every crime ever committed in Salford that night. Then I got another battering off my mam when she had to come and get me. Ouch.

We stole from the Canada Dry warehouse. Used to wriggle through open windows into the factory at night and pass out a load of stuff. Next day I'd go into school with tins of cola and lemonade, sell them for 5p each, then treat everyone to the chippy at dinnertime. Shops, too, of course. In those days shops were in people's houses: you'd go in, the bell would tinkle and some creaky old dear would get up from the front room and shuffle into the shop, and by the time they appeared half the stock would have disappeared. I'd sell it at school. 'Cakes, Biscuits. What do you want? Pens? I've got hundreds of pens.'

You know what? It was the same being in a group. Just goes to show that you can take the boy out of Salford but you can't take Salford out of the boy, because we were *terrible* for nicking things in Joy Division and New Order. We used to go to these wonderful gigs with all this beautiful stuff backstage and nick it all. Now you've got bands like the Happy Mondays, or Oasis (in the early days), who had big scally reputations, but they had the same background as us: just working class thieves. You never had anything so you took it. Same attitude to music: you've got to start somewhere. The difference was that nobody expected that sort of behaviour from us in Joy Division or New Order because we had the arty intellectual image. These days I restrict it to hotels.

Back at school, the thievery lasted only a couple of years, until I got interested in girls. Meanwhile, me and Barney had become mates. He was funny. He's got this really northern, evil sense of humour and he loves playing practical jokes (can't take them, mind, as you'll discover), and together we were bad lads. Like I said, we were both skinheads by then and we used to hang around with the school hard-nuts. His best mate, Baz Benson, was the cock of our school and my best mate from Regent Road, Dave Ward, was cock of the technical school, which was just across the playing fields from Salford Grammar. They'd take people's dinner money and buy shit with it, get into fights, terrorize the teachers, all of that. We never used to do our homework. Fuck that, we just took it off the swots in the morning, gave them a cuff and copied it in the cloakroom.

We went back to school, me and Barney, years later. We were doing an article for the *NME* and the photographer was going on about how it would be great to get some pictures of us at our old school. So we were like, 'Right, mate,' and went and picked this guy up and drove over to Salford Grammar. But for some reason he hadn't organized it properly. I think he may have phoned up the cleaner or something, who would have been like, 'Who's the group? No Order? Are they famous? "Blue Monday"? Never heard of it. Oh, bring 'em along anyway.'

So we turned up, me and Barney in our leather jackets, biker boots on –1982 or 1983, this was, so we were still pretty punky. But however weird we looked was nothing compared to how weird we felt trooping up to the gates of our old school. It had become a comprehensive by then but otherwise hadn't changed at all: there were still the same grand old 1960s buildings, and they still had all the old prize cups in the cases, the wood panelling and pictures of all the head boys on the walls. What blew our minds was how it all looked the same except so much smaller. We were like, 'Fucking hell, this is wild being back here.' It even smelt the same.

We reached the headmaster's office and the guy from *NME* said to the secretary, 'Oh hello, I've got Peter Hook and Bernard Sumner here from the successful group New Order, and they're old boys from the school. We just wondered if it was possible to take their pictures in the hall for the *New Musical Express*, the biggest music paper in England.'

She was nice enough, quite excited really, and said, 'If you wait one second I'll just ask the headmaster.' And she disappeared off into his office. Then all of a sudden we heard, '*What?* That pair of dickheads!' Then the office door flew open and out burst our old geography teacher, Dave Cain, now the headmaster, roaring at us: 'You pair of bastards!'

Oh dear – we used to make his life a misery.

'Get out!' he screamed at us. 'Get out, you pair of twats!'

And you know what? Straight away we were schoolkids again. It was like going back in a time machine. In a flash we were out of there, the head on our tails, clattering along the old wooden corridors in our jackboots. Not a word of a lie: we had to run off the premises, laughing hysterically, kicked out by our old geography teacher.

Not to be outdone, we skulked back when the coast was clear; the *NME* guy going slowly nuts because he needed to get his picture. Outside the school was a board with the name of the school on it. The photographer thought this board would make a nice image, so he positioned us near it, one either side, and got ready to take his picture. But the head must have been keeping watch, because all of a sudden we heard, '*Oi, you!* I thought I told you pair of bastards to fuck off!'

Again he came charging out. Again we legged it. The *NME* guy was still pointing his camera at the sign but we were off, so he still couldn't take the picture he wanted – all he managed to get was a Polaroid, which I still have. We ended up doing the proper photoshoot near Barney's old flat in Greengate, Broughton.

Anyway. Just before I left school, in 1973, I was sent to see the careers teacher, who said, 'So what do you want to do?'

'I want to be in a group.' I think I'd seen Led Zeppelin the night before or something ...

He rolled his eyes, reached across the desk and cuffed me round the head. Then, as I sat there rubbing my sore head, he said, 'Do you want to get your hands dirty or not?'

And I went, 'Well, not really.'

'All right then,' he sighed. 'Obviously you want to go and work in an office. Well, we've got either Salford Town Hall or Manchester Town Hall. Which is it to be?'

Well I lived in Salford, so I went for an interview at Salford Town Hall. Now don't forget I was a complete prick at school – I'd done no work whatsoever, and the only exam I was likely to pass was English. So when the guy at Salford Town Hall said to me, 'Are you going to pass your O Levels?' I said, 'No, not really. I think I might get one or two if I'm lucky, but I don't think I'll get the others.'

'Right – get out, y'bastard,' he said, and threw me out.

So off I went off to Manchester Town Hall, where the guy said to me, 'Are you going to pass your O Levels?'

And I went, 'Yeah, course I am. Going to get 'em all. Six guaranteed. No problem.'

And he said, 'Right, okay, you've got the job.'

Bloody hell, that was easy.

I got a Grade 6 in English lit. at O Level – a pass, *just* – but that was it. I even failed technical drawing, my favourite subject. The teacher, Cup Cake we called him, a right daft old dodderer, hadn't realized that there were two papers and gave us the second one right before the time ran out. When we complained he just said, 'Tough.' Barney did art. They always said that if you were awake you passed art, so he got two O Levels – art and English – and I got only one, because I didn't do art. This became just one of many on-going rivalries between us.

I'd had a job before. When I was fourteen my Auntie Jean got me work cleaning offices in Quay House in Manchester. I worked for a company called Whipclean and many of my friends joined me. It was a valuable part of our education, working with all the old saucy women – Auntie Jean even had the dubious honour of being the first woman I ever heard swear. That was a great job: £1.75 a week for ten hours' work; it gave me the money to be a well-dressed suedehead. But this job at Manchester Town Hall was my first proper job. I got £8 a week. My room was 234, where I worked under an old guy called Mr Wilson who used to smoke a pipe all day. Quite ironic, really, considering the part a certain other Mr Wilson was to play in my life.

'What would you like me to do, Mr Wilson?' I'd ask.

He'd puff away on his pipe and say, 'Just sit down and don't bother me, Peter.'

So that's what I did. I'd just sit there all day doing nothing, not bothering Mr Wilson.

It was while I was at the Town Hall that I had a mind-blowing experience at the Lesser Free Trade Hall – although it's probably not the one you're thinking of. It was the night of the Christmas party and my workmates had been winding me up about it all week because it was my first office do. Telling me all the horror stories about what so-and-so had got up to last year. I was sixteen. After work they took me and a couple of the other office juniors to the pub, forcing pints of mild down us until my head was spinning. I remember arriving at the Lesser Free Trade Hall for our big Christmas buffet, making it down the steps and into a corner of the room, but that's as far as it got because I was so pissed by then that I collapsed. How long I lay there I don't know. The next thing I knew, my workmates were carrying me out, holding me aloft like some kind of Viking burial, but only as far as the stairs for some reason. There they dumped me and I just lay upside down on the stone steps, puking, the stairwell revolving slowly around me. Then gradually I became aware of feet around my head and someone saying, 'Who's this?' When I focused I could see it was the Lord Mayor.

'Oh, that's Peter Hook from the conveyancing department,' said the town clerk, and then he helped the Mayor and his wife step over me, carefully avoiding my puddle of sick, so they could go and have their Christmas meal. Later two of my workmates helped me home.

'Where do you live, son?' one asked.

'Just around the corner,' I mumbled back, and the poor sods ended up carrying me all the way back to our house in Ordsall, an hour away, me telling them, 'Just around the corner ...' the whole way home.

'Where is it, son? Fucking hell.'

'Just around the corner ...' They propped me against my front door, knocked then ran away so I fell in when the door opened. My mam went mad.

So that was my first experience of the Lesser Free Trade Hall. Amazingly, I kept my job: went right on back to spending my days not bothering Mr Wilson.

At nights I used to hang around with Bernard. Both of us had scooters but Barney got his first; they'd changed the licence age from sixteen to seventeen and he lied about his age to get his. My birthday being in February meant I had to wait a year. We were both gradually getting into music: starting with soul and reggae, moving into pop. Barney's scooter was adorned with stick-on letters spelling 'Santana', his favourite group, and I had 'Abraxas' on mine, the name of their second album, and we used to ride around Langworthy Road on our Santana-themed scooters, looking for girls to chat up.

So there I was: working by day, pissing around and going out at night. Brilliant. Couldn't last, though; those O Levels I told them I was going to pass came back to haunt me. Ironically I was doing my job really well and I'd been put in for a raise, but the raise meant I got noticed by the personnel department, who realized I hadn't passed my exams. I tried to re-take them at night after work, with no success; I'd basically come up with a great scam where I got paid for sitting exams I never turned up for. So they asked me to leave. No hurry, they said, but I knew I was going to have to go sooner or later. Typically, I was too busy enjoying myself messing about with the lads to bother about exams, and in the end it was David Essex who showed me the way out.

Fucking David Essex.

'Barney would always eat on his own or in the bath'

I'd gone to see *That'll Be the Day*, starring David Essex and Ringo Starr, at the Carlton in Salford with Danny McQueeney, Deano, Greg Wood and Gordon Benbow, all mates from school. The film was great. If you haven't seen it, David Essex plays this likely lad who works on the fairs, works at Butlin's, shags around, has a right laugh then goes off to be a rock star. Now you've got to understand that, at that age, what I wanted was to shag around and be a rock star, and probably in that order if I'm honest, so that was it for me: I wanted that life. So I persuaded my mates that they wanted it, too – that we should all give up our jobs to go and work at Butlin's.

The whole lot of us applied. They used to hold open interviews at the Midland Hotel in Manchester; you'd just phone up, go along and smile.

'Have you got a criminal record?' they asked.

'No,' I said, nose growing.

'Right, okay. What do you want to do at Butlin's? Do you want to be a Redcoat?'

I didn't want to be a Redcoat. I'm quite shy, believe it or not, so I opted to work in the kitchens. Next they asked which Butlin's I wanted to work at. Beforehand we'd all decided to say Pwllheli, and if not that then Blackpool.

As it turned out I didn't get either of those. None of us did. We got Clacton-on-Sea.

But it didn't matter. And, even though none of us knew where it was, and never thought to look, we were so excited about getting the job and pleased that all five of us were together that we thought, 'Great!'; we quit our jobs, didn't tell our parents till the Sunday before, and then Monday were on the coach to Clacton.

Where it was nothing like *That'll Be the Day*. Where it was a nightmare from start to finish.

For a start it was scruffy and run-down – the bit where the staff lived was, at least – and there were only two chalets between the five of us, so one of us had to sleep on the floor. Then there were the other staff, who were the biggest bunch of bastards I've ever come across. We soon realized they were all in gangs. There was a Cockney gang and a Geordie gang, who of course hated each other's guts and were always fighting. At night it was like the Wild West. Then you'd wake up in the morning and there'd be not only trails of blood everywhere but also all these guys kicking out last night's conquests, these poor young girls they'd managed to lure back to their chalets; daughters of the punters — sometimes the wives.

In the kitchen I was with the biggest bunch of tossers you can imagine. I turned up to find I was working for this Scottish guy who stank of booze all the time. First thing he had me doing was scrubbing a set of steps that were caked in filth. The next thing he said was to get on the food line and dole out celery hearts for the punters' lunch.

'Right,' I said, 'I'll just go and wash my hands ...'

He spat. 'Don't be so fucking stupid. Don't answer me back and get on the fucking line.'

Meanwhile the Cockney bastards who worked there came up with a couple of great games. For instance, if you left your light on, they'd put a dustbin through your chalet window. (They couldn't rob you if the light was on, you see: didn't know if you were in or not.) They'd pour hot fat on the floor in front of the huge rotating ovens, too; then they'd make me take out the roasted chickens, hundreds of them, and place bets on me going arse over tit. Also, when we were working the food line, they'd take turns throwing tomatoes at the back of our heads. All the time I'd be thinking, 'What the fuck has gone wrong here?' This was supposed to be my escape from the nine-to-five, my *That'll Be the Day* life. I was missing Mr Wilson. The drudge was better than this. *Anything* was better than this.

On our third night in the camp, Thursday, we were getting ourselves dressed up to go out in the hope of copping off like David fucking Essex, when a guy from a chalet nearby said to me, 'Is that a leather jacket, mate? Fucking hell, you're not going to have that for two minutes. Someone'll chin you and take it off you. Hide it now!'

Off it came and we slunk away to the Western bar. All five of us were having the same miserable experience so we sat swapping horror stories about the work and generally bemoaning our lot when this *huge* fight broke out. It was the kitchen Cockneys against the Geordies. God knows what started it but it completely went off, this huge punch-up in the middle of the bar, punters running for cover, everyone screaming and finally these Cockney guys picking up one of the Geordies and heaving him straight through the bar's plate-glass window. They just left him hanging through the broken window, half in, half out, and sat themselves down and carried on drinking.

We were out of there, scuttling back to our chalets. We sat together in one of them for security, shaking like shitting dogs and going, 'We've got to get out of here – we've got to get out.'

Then we heard a commotion from outside: two Cockneys, pissed. By now it was about two o'clock in the morning and next thing you know it was all going off again. A couple of Geordies ambushed them right outside our chalet, and for a while they were absolutely kicking the shit out of these two Cockneys. But then all the rest of the Cockneys came round the corner, caught the two Geordies and started kicking the shit out of *them*. At one point they had hold of this Geordie and were slamming his head on the wall of our chalet; meanwhile we were all inside, teeth chattering like Shaggy and Scooby Doo, still going, 'Oh God, we've *got* to get out of here.' We were only seventeen, remember.

In the end we all just slept where we were. When we got up the next morning there was blood everywhere outside our chalets and that was it: we decided there and then that we'd had enough and went and quit.

At the same time, 500 punters checked out because of the fight, and the police arrived to try to find out who had thrown the Geordie through the window of the Western bar – poor bloke was in intensive care. Co-operating fully with the investigation, we told the cops that we hadn't seen a thing and were tucked up in our beds. All we wanted to do was work our week in hand and get the fuck out of Dodge – and when eventually we did, let me tell you, I have never been so happy to get on a coach in my life.

On return to Manchester a job in sewage would have been preferable to Butlin's but, thanks to Danny McQueeney, I got a brilliant job doing shift work at the Co-Op Tea Warehouse on Ordsall Lane. Where my duties included sitting on my arse and occasionally falling asleep in a lovely warm, wonderful-smelling tea warehouse. Every time I sniff a teabag I'm right back there. It was well-paid, too. I was there for six weeks and was minted, absolutely minted, until my mum said to me, 'You can't work in the Co-Op Tea Warehouse, our Peter, it's beneath you.'

I didn't bother arguing. She already worked for the Manchester Ship Canal Company, in King Street, and I think she persuaded them to interview me for a job at their Chester Road conveyancing office. I got the job, just near where the Haçienda ended up years later. My first day there my new boss, Peter Brierley, said to me, 'You're lucky, you are: this desk that you're getting, that used to be George Best's desk.' Apparently he'd worked there before he went full-time at United, as part of his apprenticeship.

Actually, I've got a George Best story for you. This occurred much later, when I was married to Caroline Aherne, who played Mrs Merton on telly. Me and her is a whole other story and we're not going into it here – or anywhere, come to think of it (well, maybe in the New Order book) – but the point is we took a holiday to Spain, and were out one evening at a bar, and in the bar opposite was George Best with a load of blokes and a girl, who was very, very, drunk. She was lolling around all over the place, out of her tiny head, and the guys with George were taking turns feeling her up.

Watching this, me and Mrs Merton really got the hump. So Mrs Merton said to me, 'You know him, go over and stop them.'

Now New Order had done the theme tune for the TV programme that Tony Wilson had presented about George Best and Rodney Marsh. He'd told us that Granada had no money for a theme tune and asked if we'd do it for free, which we duly did. That's all it was.

I said, 'Well, I don't *know* him, do I? We did the theme for the programme, but I don't *know* him.'

'Well go over and say hello to him anyway. That'll make him ashamed and he'll stop.'

To be honest they'd settled down a bit by then but Mrs Merton was still mithering on at me, so in the end we both went over and I said, 'Hello, George.'

He turned round, so drunk he was swaying on his feet and trying to focus, and he slurred, 'Yeah?'

I said, 'My name's Peter Hook from New Order. We did the theme music to *Best & Marsh* – you know, the programme on Granada.'

And he went, 'Yeah, I know,' and turned away and blanked me. It was so embarrassing. I just looked and felt like a complete twat. Then Mrs Merton started mouthing off and I had to drag her away. In the meantime they started messing about with this girl again. So in the end we rescued her, pulled her away, and these kids who were with George Best started getting a bit uppity: 'What the fuck are you doing?'

I was like, 'Fuck off, mate. She's pissed; she needs to go home. She shouldn't be here.'

George Best was completely oblivious to all this. Never meet your heroes.

So anyway, it's a small world. I got George Best's job at the Manchester Ship Canal Company, then later I joined a band and ended up wanting to chin him. But back then I was pleased as punch to have got his job.

I was still living in Ordsall and could walk to work. They soon moved the department to the Dock Office on Trafford Road, which was even nearer, so for about a year everything was great. Like I've already said, though, the council was redeveloping and they started to knock down all the houses in Ordsall, wanting to move everyone out to a new development called Ellor Street, near the Precinct in Salford.

All my friends moved to Ellor Street, which was all high-rise seventies flats and a new shopping precinct all built out of concrete. It was fucking rotten, horrible, like a concrete wasteland. And this was when it first opened.

So, my mother, God rest her soul, wouldn't move there. Me and our kid were gutted because all of our mates had moved but she wouldn't budge, not even when the bulldozers moved in and we were the pretty much the last house standing in Ordsall – just ours and an empty one either side to prop it up. They kept offering her places in Ellor Street to try to get rid of us, but she wouldn't go into a flat. She wouldn't have it. All the flats they showed her she said were shitholes. The whole of Ellor Street she said was a shithole. Mind you, she was right: it was a shithole. But all my mates lived in that shithole and I wanted to live there too. I remember persuading her to at least have a look at one flat; we drove to see it but on the wall at the entrance to the flats there was sprayed the legend 'Glasgow Rangers will die tonite!' I don't know if it was the bad spelling that most offended her but she made Bill turn straight round and she never went back.

21

We lived like that for about six months, on our own like the weird family in a surreal film. The buses had stopped running – there was no traffic at all. To get anywhere we had to walk across a wasteland that had once been full of houses. Until at last my mum got an offer to relocate to another overspill area, Little Hulton. They'd offered her a three-bedroomed house in Brookhurst Lane with its own gardens, front and back, *and* an inside toilet. Didn't have heating, mind, but otherwise it was fantastic and she took it on the spot.

So we moved to Little Hulton, and all my mates were in Salford. Twenty miles, which seemed a long way at seventeen with no car. Nightmare. This was when I started spending a lot of time at Barney's, because getting back to Little Hulton was so difficult. Most weekends I'd get the bus to his in Broughton on a Friday after work. Then we'd hang around in Pips or Man Alive in town, getting pissed and trying to chat up girls even though we were useless. We'd sober up all Saturday and go out again that night, to Tiffany's, Rotters or Rowntrees Sound, again in town, getting pissed and trying to chat up girls, back to his house again, me sleeping on the floor. We'd laze around all Sunday morning, fuck around in the afternoon, and then I'd get the last bus home.

It's not for me to talk about Barney's situation, but let's just say that for one reason or another it wasn't your average home life. He was quite indulged by his mum and dad. They didn't exactly have pots of money but anything he wanted, he got – or seemed to: scooter, clothes, later an electric guitar, amp, etc.

The only room in the house that had any character was his. With his posters on the wall and his stuff lying around it looked like a proper lived-in room, whereas the rest of the house was strangely neat and tidy. No newspapers hanging around, the telly never on – no, well, *life* to it, really – and Barney would always eat on his own or in the bath. He was forever eating then falling asleep in the bath and waking up to find bits of his dinner floating around him. 'I fucking fell asleep again,' he'd moan. 'Fucking dinner ended up in the bath.' We would also spend a lot of time across the canal at his gran and granddad's, the Sumners; they were lovely and waited on him hand and foot.

I was twenty, then, in early 1976, not long before the Sex Pistols came to Manchester for the first time.

22

'Oh, fuck, it's Steve Harley'

I'd started getting interested in pop music around twelve or thirteen, when, like every other kid back in those days, I was glued to *Top of the Pops* every week. Then somebody gave me a reel-to-reel tape recorder that already had a load of music on it, and I used to listen to that over and over again – stuff like 'Chirpy Chirpy Cheep Cheep'. Still, though, nothing could eclipse *Top of the Pops*, which I lived for. You forget now, what with MTV, YouTube, and the fact that music's shovelled into your ears in every shop, restaurant and supermarket, but back then *Top of the Pops* was the only way you could get to see pop music being per-formed. For a kid from Salford it was mind-blowing to see Deep Purple doing 'Black Night', Sabbath ripping through 'Paranoid', Family doing 'The Weavers Answer', Marc Bolan, Bowie... Like having a window on a wonderful other world, even if they were miming. And it annoyed your parents.

As I got older I became a skinhead and from that discovered reggae: the Upsetters, the Pioneers, Desmond Dekker, Dave & Ansel Collins. It wasn't until the fourth year that I got my first record player, though, when I bought one from Martin Gresty, who needed some quick cash. I don't think his mum even knew he was selling her Dansette, to be honest, but I gave him eleven quid for it, which was all the money I had and a fortune in those days. Of course that meant I couldn't afford to buy any records, which my mother thought was hilarious. So I nicked some. There was a shop on Langworthy Road that used to have old ex-jukebox singles for sale in a box outside and I swiped a couple sight unseen, just to have something to play on my Dansette. When I got round the corner to take a look at my haul I wasn't exactly overjoyed: 'Ruby, Don't Take Your Love to Town' by Kenny Rogers and 'The Green Manalishi' by Fleetwood Mac. I'd never heard of either. Still, at least I finally had something to listen to. Or so I thought. Turned out I couldn't play them – being ex-jukebox they had no middles – and it took me another week to steal one! Years later I appeared on that BBC pro-gramme *The One Show*, talking about the first record I ever bought: I told them it was 'Ruby, Don't Take Your Love to Town'; I didn't tell them that I'd nicked it, though.

But when I *really* got into music – when the bug didn't so much bite as take a huge fuck-off chunk out of my leg – was on holiday in Rhyl. This was just before I left the Town Hall for Butlin's: 1973, it would have been. There was me, Deano, Stuart Houghton, Danny Lee and Greg Wood, I think, five of us in a four-berth caravan. Christ it was freezing, and there was no electricity – there were gas mantles for lights – but it was the first proper holiday I'd ever had, and we spent it roaming the streets of Rhyl and listening to Radio Luxembourg in the caravan. They kept playing a song called 'Sebastian' by Cockney Rebel. That was it for me. For the first time, I listened to a record and really thought, *Wow.* Why, I don't know. Because it was different, I suppose; it seemed so different. It had a slow orchestral start and built to a climax – it was very long, too, which was something unheard of for a pop record back then. It just grabbed me – grabbed my attention and held it. Strange how we would emulate it with 'Blue Monday' years later.

When I got back off holiday I bought the single. It was nine minutes long and you had to turn the record over halfway through, which just sort of added to the experience: it was part of the ritual of playing it, gave the song a dramatic pause and made me like the record even more. After that I became a fan of Cockney Rebel and bought their first LP, *The Human Menagerie* – a great record. They became my gateway to music. Before this when I'd watched *Top of the Pops* I'd just goggled at it, but now it was like I was part of it; I understood it. Bowie, Roxy, Ian Dury – I started to get them now.

Years later I was at an awards ceremony with New Order getting an award for 'Blue Monday'. I'd given up drinking by then, so I was straight as an arrow when Steve Harley strolled up to me, and I thought, *Oh, fuck, it's Steve Harley out of Cockney Rebel.*

He went, 'Hello, Peter, how are you?'

And I thought, *Not only is it Steve Harley, but he knows who I am and he's dead fucking nice.*

He went, 'Oh, it's so lovely to meet you. I believe that our first record was one of your inspirations?'

I was like, 'Yeah, yeah, it was,' and ran away. Just couldn't deal with it. Left him standing there looking around and no doubt thinking, *That was fucking bizarre.* But it wasn't as bizarre for him as it was for me. 'Sebastian' had got me into the whole thing. If it hadn't been for Steve Harley I wouldn't have been standing at that awards ceremony talking to Steve Harley. Very, very weird, that was.

After that – Rhyl, I mean, not the awards – I started reading *NME* and *Sounds.* Then we began going to gigs. Saw Led Zeppelin, Cockney Rebel, of course, and half of Deep Purple's set before Barney made us leave because he had a toothache. It wasn't just him who had to leave: it was all of us. He's always got away with fucking murder, that one.

I first read about the Sex Pistols in April 1976, on another holiday. Me, Stuart Houghton, Danny Lee and Danny McQueeney decided to go to Torquay and Newquay in my new car, a Mark Ten Jag 420G, registration KFR 666F (funny how I can remember all the numbers) – the same model the Krays had – that I'd bought for £325. We weren't staying anywhere, just sleeping in the car. Needless to say it was tough, but enjoyable; we got on well – it was one of those holidays I'll never forget. The tyres were knackered and we couldn't go more than fifty miles an hour – took us hours and hours to get there. But one thing I do remember was sitting in a car park in Newquay at about seven in the morning, still pissed from the night before, reading *Melody Maker.* It had the Sex Pistols in it, and there was a picture of them taken at their gig at the Nashville Rooms where a huge fight had broken out. Sitting there in the car park in Cornwall, with the sun coming up and all my mates snoring in the Jag, I had ... Well, I suppose you could say I had another David Essex moment, an *epiphany.*

First off I was intrigued by the idea of a group who seemed, I don't know, *human* compared to bands like Led Zeppelin and Deep Purple, who seemed, to a working-class tosser from Salford, so out of my league they might as well have lived on another planet. I mean, I'd never have looked at Led Zep and thought, *I'm going to be the next John Paul Jones.* He was like some kind of god up there. I loved the music. I loved watching it. But the idea of emulating them was ludicrous.

The Sex Pistols, though: they looked like working-class tossers *too*, which automatically made them completely different to anything I'd seen in music before. I was a great fan of James Dean; I'd seen *Giant* and *Rebel Without a Cause.* And now I felt a connection between him,

25

these *punks* and me. That real snotty, rebellious, arrogant-kid type of thing, only not in glossy-looking 1950s America but in grey old 1970s Britain. The Pistols were the link somehow. And the fact that they had a reputation for fighting at every gig and were part of this movement – this *punk* movement ...

I was like, *I have got to see this lot.*

TIMELINE ONE:
MAY 1948–APRIL 1976

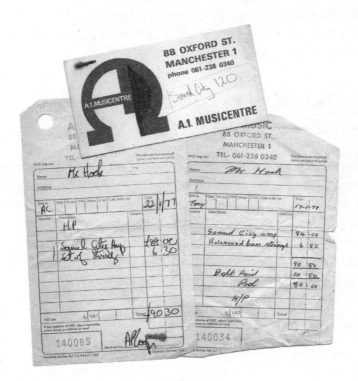

31 May 1948

Martin Hannett born, Miles Platting, Manchester.

From an early age Hannett showed an aptitude for mathematics and science, interests he would carry through to his musical theory. Gaining a chemistry degree from Manchester's UMIST, he played bass for Greasy Bear before forming the Invisible Girls, the backing band for John Cooper Clarke and, in later years, Pauline Murray and Nico. Together with Tosh Ryan he helped set up the musician's collective

Music Force, then Rabid Records, the home of Slaughter & the Dogs. Styling himself Martin Zero, he went on to produce the Buzzcocks' *Spiral Scratch* EP, the first release on the independent New Hormones label run by the Buzzcocks' manager Richard Boon. He produced Slaughter & the Dogs' debut single, 'Cranked Up Really High', then worked with Chris Sievey (later known as Frank Sidebottom) and his band the Freshies, before scoring a Top Three hit producing Graham Fellows' 'Jilted John' in July 1978. (Indeed, Hannett can be seen playing bass on a *Top of the Pops* performance of that song.) Shortly afterwards he produced Joy Division for the first time.

26 April (he asked me not to put the year in)

Alan Erasmus born, Didsbury.

Erasmus and Tony Wilson became friendly when they met at a Christmas party and bonded over a spliff. For a while Erasmus managed Fast Breeder but parted company with them and instead sought out Wilson, the two joining forces to put together a new band, the Durutti Column. The flat Erasmus shared with best friend Charles Sturridge (a Granada director who went on to make *Brideshead Revisited*) was at 86a Palatine Road, and doubled up as the Factory HQ.

20 February 1950

Tony Wilson born, Salford.

Wilson attended the De La Salle Grammar School in Salford, developing a love of drama and literature thanks to a performance of *Hamlet* at Stratford-upon-Avon. At seventeen he worked as an English and drama teacher at the Blue Coat School in Oldham; he then attended Cambridge, graduating with an English degree in 1971. After working for ITN as a trainee reporter he returned to Manchester in 1973, joining Granada and presenting *Granada Reports* as well as the music programme *So It Goes*. However, the end of *So It Goes* left Wilson pondering ways in which he could continue and extend his involvement in the music business ...

15 January 1953

Rob Gretton born; raised Newall Green, Wythenshawe.

A fierce Manchester City fan, Gretton worked as an insurance clerk before leaving the job to work on a kibbutz with girlfriend Lesley Gilbert. He returned to the UK in 1976 and became involved in the emerging Manchester punk scene, working with Slaughter & the Dogs then the Panik.

9 October 1955

Peter Saville born; raised Hale, Manchester.

Saville attended St Ambrose College before studying graphic design at Manchester Polytechnic. Envious of contemporaries Linder Sterling and Malcolm Garrett, who had already made their names designing for the Buzzcocks and Magazine, and learning of the soon-to-open Factory club, Saville approached Tony Wilson at a Patti Smith concert. Not long afterwards the pair met in the canteen at Granada, where Saville showed Wilson a book of Jan Tschichold typography …

4 January 1956

Bernard Sumner born; raised Lower Broughton, Salford.

Sumner attended the Salford Grammar School, where he met Peter Hook.

13 February 1956

Peter Hook born.

15 July 1956

Ian Curtis born, Stretford, Manchester.

Early academic prowess saw Curtis admitted to the King's School, Macclesfield; while there he met Deborah (Debbie) Woodruff. He was also friendly with Helen Atkinson Wood, who later found fame playing Mrs Miggins in *Blackadder*, and gave her his copy of *The Man Who Sold the World*. He passed seven O Levels but dropped out of school midway through studying for his A Levels to begin a job at Rare Records in Manchester. He became engaged to Debbie on 17 April 1974. After a spell running a record stall, he took jobs in the civil service, eventually settling in Oldham after his marriage in 1975. Still dreaming of a career in the music business, Ian placed an advert in the music press, signing himself 'Rusty', which attracted the services of guitarist Iain Gray.

13 December 1956

Deborah Woodruff born, Liverpool.

Having left Liverpool when she was three, Deborah's parents set up home in Macclesfield, where she attended Macclesfield High School for Girls, a 'sister' school to the King's School. She became acquainted with Ian in 1972 when she was seeing his friend Tony Nuttall. When she and Tony split, she agreed to go on a date with Ian, to see David Bowie at the Hardrock Concert Theatre in Manchester. Soon they were a couple. Deborah was Ian's second serious girlfriend.

12 October 1957

Annik Honoré born, southern Belgium.

To satisfy a voracious musical appetite, Annik travelled to gigs throughout Europe, seeing Siouxsie & the Banshees more than 100 times, as well as Patti Smith, the Clash, Generation X, Iggy Pop and David Bowie. Like Ian Curtis, her favourite album was Bowie's *Low*. Annik became involved with the fanzine *En Attendant*, and then made plans to move to London. In the meantime she saw Joy Division for the first time at the Nashville Rooms on 13 August 1979, having travelled from Belgium especially to see them, and two weeks later interviewed the entire band at the Walthamstow flat Dave Pils shared with his girlfriend, Jasmine. By September that year Annik was living in London, in Parsons Green, and working at the Belgian Embassy.

28 October 1957

Stephen Morris born, Macclesfield.

Morris attended the King's School, Macclesfield but was expelled for drinking cough syrup. Morris had drummed with the Sunshine Valley Dance Band, a group of school friends, and worked for his father's firm, G Clifford Morris, a local plumbers' merchants. He spotted two adverts in the window of Jones' Music Store in Macclesfield: 'Drummer wanted for punk band the Fall' and 'Drummer wanted for local punk band Warsaw'. Luckily for him he responded to the advert with the local phone number.

23 August 1975

Ian Curtis and Debbie Woodruff marry, Henbury.

23 April 1976

The Sex Pistols play the Nashville Rooms, London.

It was by all accounts an unremarkable concert until Vivienne Westwood decided to 'liven things up' by slapping a female audience member. The girl's boyfriend rushed to help her, at which point Malcolm McLaren came to the aid of Vivienne, then the band to the aid of them both. All of which was captured in what were to become iconic images of the Pistols and reported in the *Melody Maker* and the *NME* (in a piece written by a pre-Pet Shop Boys Neil Tennant), marking the beginning of the Pistols' notoriety and the aura of violence that was to accompany them from then on.

PART TWO

'Disorder'

'Normal band, normal night, few people watching, clap-clap, very good'

Inspired by the Velvet Underground, friends Howard Devoto and Pete Shelley had formed a band, taking their name from a headline in Time Out that read: 'Feeling a Buzz, Cocks?' Having made a pilgrimage to see the Sex Pistols in High Wycombe, they resolved to stage the Pistols in Manchester — with themselves supporting. A gig was scheduled for 4 June 1976, at Manchester's Lesser Free Trade Hall — although, as it turned out, the Buzzcocks were not ready to play and support was instead provided by rock band Solstice.

Very few attended. Fifty at most. Yet the concert has been immortalized in two films (24 Hour Party People and Control), is the subject of a book (I Swear I Was There: the Gig That Changed the World, by David Nolan) and is popularly believed to have been the wellspring for years of musical innovation that was to follow, not just in Manchester but globally: in punk, post-punk and ultimately dance-music culture.

Among those who were definitely at the gig were Peter Hook and Bernard Dickin, who went on to form Warsaw/Joy Division/New Order; Steven Morrissey, later of the Smiths; Mark E. Smith, later of the Fall; Mick Hucknall, later of Frantic Elevators then Simply Red; John the Postman; photographer Kevin Cummins; and writer Paul Morley. They and others went away inspired: bands were formed, fanzines published, wardrobes overhauled — and the word about the Pistols was spread, so that the next concert, on 20 July, also at the Lesser Free Trade Hall, was far better attended. Most of those at the first gig returned, along with Ian Curtis and producer Martin Hannett.

I've always read the *Manchester Evening News* cover to cover, ever since I was a kid. Don't ask me why. Same with watching *Coronation Street*; it's just something I've always done. Home is Becky and the kids, *Corrie* and the *MEN*.

Reading the small ads in the *MEN* was how I found out that the Pistols were playing at the Lesser Free Trade Hall, 50p a ticket.

Now my mates – and I mean this in the nicest possible way – have always been dead normal, so they weren't interested. But I'd been going to gigs with Terry and Bernard and (apart from the infamous toothache incident) having a laugh, so I phoned Bernard up.

'The Sex Pistols are on – do you want to go and see them?'

He went, 'Who?'

I said, 'Oh, it's this group. They have fights at every gig and it's really funny. Come on, it's only 50p.'

'Yeah, all right, then.'

Terry was up for it too, so it ended up being me, him, Barney and Sue Barlow, who was Barney's fiancé. I think they'd met at Gresty's house when he was sixteen or so. They'd been going out for a few years and used to fight like cat and dog. With the possible exception of Debbie and Ian, they had the most tempestuous, argumentative relationship I've ever known in my life. *And* they ended up getting married ...

So that was it anyway, the group of us who went and saw the Sex Pistols at Lesser Free Trade Hall. A night that turned out to be the most important of my life – or one of them at least – but that started out just like any other: me and Terry making the trip in Terry's car; Barney and Sue arriving on his motorbike; the four of us meeting up then ambling along to the ticket office.

There to greet us was Malcolm McLaren, dressed head to toe in black leather – leather jacket, leather trousers and leather boots – with a shock of bright-orange hair, a manic grin and the air of a circus ringmaster, though there was hardly anyone else around. We were like, *Wow*. He looked so wild, from another planet even. The four of us were in our normal gear: flared jeans, penny collars and velvet jackets with big lapels, all of that. Look at the photographs of the gig and you can see that everybody in the audience was dressed the same way, like a *Top of the Pops* audience. There were no punks yet. So Malcolm – he looked like an alien to us. Thinking about it, he must have been the first punk I ever saw in the flesh.

Wide-eyed we paid him, went in and down the stairs into the Lesser Free Trade Hall (the same stairs I'd laid down on many years before). At the back of the hall was the stage and set out in front of it were chairs, on either side of a central walkway, just like it was in *24 Four Hour Party People* – although I don't remember many sitting down like they are in the film. I don't think there was a bar that night, so we just stood around, waiting.

The support band were called Solstice, and their best number was a twenty-minute cover version of 'Nantucket Sleighride'. The original, by Mountain, was one of my favourite records at the time so we knew it really well, and we were like, 'This is great. Just like the record.'

Still, though, nothing out of the ordinary. Normal band, normal night, few people watching, clap-clap, very good, off they went.

The Sex Pistols' gear was set up and then, without further ceremony, they came on: Johnny Rotten, Glen Matlock, Steve Jones and Paul Cook. Steve Jones was wearing a boiler suit and the rest of them looked like they'd just vandalized an Oxfam shop. Rotten had on this torn-open yellow sweater and he glared out into the audience like he wanted to kill each and every one of us, one at a time, before the band struck up into something that might have been 'Did You No Wrong' but you couldn't tell because it was so loud and dirty and distorted.

I remember feeling as though I'd been sitting in a darkened room all of my life – comfortable and warm and safe and quiet – then all of a sudden someone had kicked the door in, and it had burst open to let in an intense bright light and this even more intense *noise*, showing me another world, another life, a way out. I was immediately no longer comfortable and safe, but that didn't matter because it felt great. I felt alive. It was the weirdest sensation. It wasn't just me feeling it, either – we were all like that. We just stood there, stock still, watching the Pistols. Absolutely, utterly, gobsmacked.

I was thinking two things. Two things that I suppose you'd have to say came together to create my future – my whole life from then on.

The first was: *I could do that.*

Because, fucking hell, what a racket. I mean, they were just dreadful; well, the *sound* was dreadful. Now the other band didn't sound that bad. They sounded *normal*. But it was almost as though the Pistols' sound guy had deliberately made them sound awful, or they had terrible equipment on purpose, because it was all feeding back, fuzzed-up, just a complete din. A wall of noise. I didn't recognize a tune, not a note, and considering they were playing so many cover versions – the Monkees, the Who – I surely would have recognized something had it not sounded so shit.

So, in fact, sound-wise it was as much the sound guy who inspired us all as it was the Sex Pistols, who were, as much as I hate to say it, a pretty standard rock band musically. I'm not saying it's a bad thing that they played straightforward down-the-line rock 'n' roll, but it didn't make them special.

No. What made them special, without a shadow of a doubt, was Johnny Rotten. The tunes were only a part of the package – and probably the least important part of it, if I'm honest. Close your eyes and like I say you had a conventional pub-rock band with a soundman who either didn't have a clue or was being very clever indeed. But who was going to close their eyes when he, Johnny Rotten, was standing there? Sneering and snarling at you, looking at you like he hated you, hated being there, hated everyone. What he embodied was the *attitude* of the Pistols, the attitude of punk. Through him they expressed what we wanted to express, which was complete nihilism. You know the way you feel when you're a teenager, all that confusion about the future that turns to arrogance and then rebellion, like, 'Fuck off, we don't fucking care, we're shit, we don't care'? He had all of that and more.

And, God bless him, whatever he had, he gave a bit of it to us, because that was the second thing I felt, after *I can do that*. It was: *I want to do that*. No. *I fucking need to do that*.

Tony Wilson said he was there, of course, but I didn't see him, which is weird because he was very famous in Manchester then; he was Tony Wilson off the telly. Mick Hucknall was there, and Mark E. Smith and everyone, but of course we didn't know anybody – all that would come later. The only people we knew there were each other: me and Terry, Barney and Sue. I don't know what Sue made of it all, mind you; I'd love to know now. But me, Barney and Terry were being converted.

The Pistols were on for only about half an hour and when they finished we filed out quietly with our minds blown, absolutely utterly speechless, and it just sort of dawned on me then – that was it. That was what I wanted to do: tell everyone to Fuck Off.

'Is that a bass guitar?'

On the way home that night we decided to form a band. If they can do it, we said, meaning the Pistols, then so can we.

We decided to follow the rules of punk …

Rule one: act like the Sex Pistols.
Rule two: look like the Sex Pistols. One guitar, one bass.

Terry volunteered to be the singer. Barney had been given a guitar and a little red practice amp for Christmas, which made him the guitarist, so I thought, 'Right, I'll get a bass.'

Of course I'm pleased it worked out like that because I ended up learning the bass guitar, really making it my own and developing a very distinctive style, whereas (who knows?) if I'd tried learning the guitar I might just have been a bog-standard rhythm guitarist. It's one of the strange things about writing a book like this, actually. You start seeing your life as series of chance happenings that somehow come together to make you what you are. You start thinking, *What if I hadn't come back from Jamaica? What if I hadn't bought that week's* Melody Maker *or seen the advert for the Sex Pistols in the* Manchester Evening News? *What if Barney's parents had bought him a Johnny Seven for his birthday instead of a guitar.*

But they didn't. They bought him a guitar so I became a bassist. The very next day I borrowed £40 off my mam, and got the bus to Mazel's on London Road, Piccadilly, in Manchester. I had no idea how much guitars cost. But I think Barney's was about £40. Mazel Radio was one of those shops that always felt dark, it was that filled with weird indecipherable stock. (I used to go there with Terry for fun most weekends.) It was an Aladdin's cave stuffed with transistors, valves, accumulators, TVs, radios – all kinds of electrical doo-dahs.

And cheap guitars.

'Can I have one of those, please?' I said, pointing at them.

'Well, what kind do you want, son?' said the bloke behind the counter.

'A bass one.'

And he went, 'Well, how about this one?'

'Is that a bass guitar?

'Yeah.'

'That'll do.'

So I bought my first guitar, which I've still got: a Gibson EB-0 copy. No make on it. They tried to sell me a case but after bus fare I didn't have enough money so I took it home in a black bin liner they fished out from behind the counter. Very punk.

Barney had been playing a bit so he showed me a couple of notes. He'd go, 'Hold your finger there then move your finger to there. Move your finger back ...'

We were off. Not long later, we got books on how to play: the Palmer-Hughes *Book of Rock 'n' Roll Guitar* and *Rock 'n' Roll Bass Guitar*. Mine came with stickers for the neck of the bass so you knew where to put your fingers. When the stickers wore off with sweat, I painted them on with Tippex. We'd be sitting round practising, with Barney shouting out the chords, like, 'Play A, A, A, A, and then we'll change to G, G, G, G.' I'd practise by myself, too, but it was far more interesting learning together than it was playing on your own at home.

Teaching myself meant I ended up learning it wrong, though, because I picked up the bad habit of playing with three fingers. A teacher would have made me play with four, but the Palmer-Hughes *Book of Rock 'n' Roll Bass Guitar* didn't talk back so I started off – and have ended up – a three-fingered bass player; and having to hold down my little finger as I play makes me slower. Saying that, I suppose it also gave me my style, which is slower and more melodic compared to most bassists'. It's a different way of playing, and it came through learning badly.

We began by practising in Barney's gran's front room. I told you she was a lovely lady. She had an old stereogram record player, and Barney, who was always good with electronics, wired up our guitar leads to the two input wires on the needle cartridge so we could play through it. It worked as well. I mean, it sounded fucking diabolical, and if we both played at the same time you couldn't hear anything but a wall of noise, but it worked. So we'd made it, we'd arrived – right up until his gran discovered that we'd wrecked her stereo and went berserk and threw us out. Then we ran down Alfred Street laughing.

But we didn't care. We were punks. We raided Oxfam and cut up the clothes we stole; I spiked up my hair and took the dog collar off the dog to wear. My mam went mad yet again. At first we were just copying the look from *Melody Maker* and *NME*, and wearing what the London punks were wearing, but pretty soon we were developing our own style. Barney discovered the Scout shop on New Mount Street and started wearing a more military look (typical of him, he wanted to be a neat-and-tidy punk) while I used masking tape on my blue blazer to put stripes on it, and we both sprayed prison arrows on our clothes.

You used to get shouted at in the street for dressing like that; you were given the right leper treatment. I mean, these days nobody would bat an eyelid, but back then it was really shocking to see these kids walking round with hair in spikes and their clothes cut up. Which was, of course, why we did it – we wanted to be shocking; we wanted people staring at us. We loved that our mums hated it and that we had to get changed on the bus. It was all part of being a punk.

This was it for us: we'd get the guitars out, play around for a bit, go out so that people in the street could treat us like lepers, then come back and play around on the guitars some more. It was great.

The next punk happening in Manchester was the Pistols' second gig, on 20 July, also at the Lesser Free Trade Hall. Apart from the venue it was completely different: for a start, we were punks now and knew what to expect from the band; plus there were a lot more people there, not only because the word had spread in Manchester but also because the Pistols, unless I'm very much mistaken, had brought a coachload with them, which was exciting straight away. At that time if you put a group of Cockneys and a group of Mancs into a municipal building at the same time, a fight was bound to break out – which it did.

We were in the bar talking to these kids who were from Manchester. They'd come over to us, one of them going, 'Hey, are you fucking Cockneys or what?' all up in our faces.

And we went, 'No, fuck off, mate, we're from Salford.'

'Oh, right. Well, we're from Wythenshawe. We're a group.'

'Oh, right. We're a group, too. Sort of.'

'Well, we're Slaughter & the Dogs. We're supporting tonight.'

Wow – it was Slaughter & the Dogs; and this bloke's name was Mick Rossi, the guitarist. Slaughter & the Dogs were one of the earliest punk bands in Manchester – it was them and the Buzzcocks, who were also playing that night.

'What's your group called?' said Mick Rossi.

We looked at each other. 'Dunno. We haven't got a name yet.'

Didn't have a name. Didn't have songs. Didn't have a lead singer unless you counted Terry, which – after a couple of disastrous practice sessions – we didn't. But still, we were a band.

'Right, the Cockneys are here,' said Rossi. 'We're having the Cockneys, we're fucking having them.'

And this was the support band. So there was a hell of an atmosphere right from the beginning and, true to form, there was as much fighting as there was pogoing and moshing, everyone rolling around the room. It was more good-natured than you might have expected, but, even so, pretty chaotic and, because it was all going off, a lot more exciting than the first gig. At the first gig it all went off on stage. At the second gig it all went off in the audience *and* on stage.

Looking back, I don't know which of the gigs was the most important in terms of the influence it had. A lot of people say the second because there were more people there, the Pistols were better known and punks had started to get going in the city, but for me and Barney it was the first because that's when we decided to form the group. Overall I think you'd have to say they were both as important as each other. I mean, after those two gigs, bands had formed and venues were putting them on and there was a group of us who soaked up whatever punk we could. That autumn we saw the Stranglers at the Squat on Devas Street; in September, Eater played the first-ever gig, at Houldsworth Hall on Deansgate. Eater were supported by the Buzzcocks, who played at just about every gig in Manchester and were also doing a lot to help other punk bands find their feet. They'd encouraged us; their manager, Richard Boon, had come up with our first name, the Stiff Kittens, and later we found out that Ian had been in touch with them too. Together with the Drones and Slaughter & the Dogs they were the backbones of the punk scene and helped make Manchester the major punk city after London. They all played regularly at the Squat and at a gay bar on Dale Street called the Ranch, owned by Foo Foo Lamar, as well as at the Electric Circus in Collyhurst Street, which quickly became the city's main punk venue.

Debbie Curtis remembers Ian talking to me and Barney at that second Pistols gig. (He wasn't there for the first one, which he was always a bit pissed off about, but he brought Debbie along to the second.) Maybe we did share a few words that night but he certainly didn't really register with me then. The first time I remember Ian making an impact was at the Electric Circus, for the third Pistols gig. He had 'Hate' written on his jacket in orange fluorescent paint. I liked him straight away.

'He was just a kid with "Hate" on his coat'

The Electric Circus was an older, normal rock venue, in that it was a redbrick building, with a pointed roof like a church. The front door opened into one big, dark room with a high ceiling. The bar was on the right-hand side and there was a balcony, which I never saw open. In fact, the only reason I knew it had a balcony was that I was mooching around one night – this was later, when we were Warsaw – and somehow we got on to it, and there sat the Drones' PA.

By that time the Drones were like Slaughter & the Dogs – real fucking mouthy, football-hooligan types, and we hated them. I mean, with the exception of the Buzzcocks, who were like the father figures of Manchester punk, all the bands hated one another and were forever trying to get one over on each other, and Slaughter & the Dogs and the Drones were the worst of the lot. The second time the Pistols played the Lesser Free Trade Hall, Slaughter & the Dogs had their own posters made up that had their name above the Pistols' and missed out the Buzzcocks altogether. That's the kind of thing I'm talking about. Horrible twats. They made us look like angels. The Drones were just as bad. So ... Well, let's just say something happened to their equipment. Something nasty.

All of which is a roundabout way of saying that, once we'd put our knobs away, I knew there was a balcony in the Electric Circus.

Even before the Pistols played there the Circus was a big punk venue; and because there was only that and the Ranch, which was a punk club on Thursday nights, you got to start recognizing all the punks because they were going to the same two places on the same nights. The people who stuck out tended to be the well-known ones, like the Buzzcocks and Slaughter & the Dogs, or the guys with big personalities – people like John the Postman, the noisy bastard. Me and Barney were pretty quiet. We'd just stand on the side-lines and not get noticed, but you'd see the faces and you'd let on. 'All right, mate, how are you?' something like that. People got to know you.

The night of that third Pistols gig there was a really lively atmosphere, to say the least. You've got to bear in mind that this was 9 December 1976, a week or so after the Pistols had done their *Today*-programme interview, when they'd gone on teatime TV and told Bill Grundy he was a 'fucking rotter'. Next day it was all over the papers – 'The Filth and the Fury!' – and suddenly the Pistols were public enemy number one. They were about to go on their Anarchy tour with the Damned (who ended up getting thrown off it, for some reason), the Clash and Johnny Thunders & the Heartbreakers, and because of the outcry most of the gigs were cancelled. Seventeen of the twenty-four dates were stopped by local councils. Among those that went ahead were two at the Electric Circus, and consequently a lot more people came along. The place was fucking rammed.

Even so, we recognized Ian. He stood out. Me and Barney were at the top of some stairs looking down and he came up the stairs with his donkey jacket on and we got talking to him because we'd seen him around. What were our first words to him? Fucked if I can remember. 'Didn't I see you at the Squat?' something like that. I'm not sure we even found out his name that night, to be honest. He was just a kid with 'Hate' on his coat, just a normal kid. Of course, we were all punks, so we must have looked pretty wild compared to everybody else but he looked normal compared to us. He was nice. Softly spoken. Sharp sense of humour. Of the two portrayals of him on film, I prefer the one in *24 Hour Party People*. The guy in *Control*, Sam Riley, played him as being much more arty and conventionally pretty than he was in real life, whereas Sean Harris in *24 Hour Party People* had a bit more of the real-life Ian's edginess and intensity. Neither were perfect and neither were totally off the mark, but for my money Harris was the more accurate.

It was at that same Pistols gig that we spoke to a guy from *Sounds*, who quoted us in his report of the gig – our very first national write-up.

The sentiments [that the Pistols were great] were echoed by most every kid I spoke to – they were certainly all in the process of forming bands. Stiff Kittens (Hooky, Terry, Wroey and Bernard, who has the final word) being the most grotesque offering.
Pete Silverton, *Sounds*, 18 December 1976

'Grotesque', eh? Cheers, mate. Wroey was someone Barney had met in Broughton, a friend of his cousin Grimmie. We were trying him out as singer at the time, which is why he got a mention in *Sounds*. Like most of our singers he didn't last and we added him to a growing pile of rejects. The problem wasn't that they were terrible as such, just that they were the wrong sort of terrible. I mean, we just needed someone to sound horrible and shit – we were a punk band after all – but they weren't right for it. For some reason they couldn't do proper singing or horrible and shit singing, just awful singing, but not in a good way. I suppose it's one of those star-quality things. You recognize it when you see it.

Our search was taking too long. So we decided to advertise for a singer with a notice on the board in Virgin Records in Piccadilly, and in response got the biggest bunch of weirdoes you've ever met in your life. Barney went to meet a couple of them on his own, and we saw a few together, but none of them really stuck out. Getting a bit frustrated, we decided to ask Martin Gresty from school because he was the wackiest person we'd ever met in our lives. Fucking mental, he was, absolute psycho, but in a nice way, the terror of the school. We thought he'd be ideal as a punk singer. We went round to his house, just near Langworthy Road, and knocked on his door.

'Is Martin there?' we asked when his mother answered the door.

'Sorry, love, he's gone out plane-spotting.'

Turned out the scourge of Salford Grammar had calmed down. He was a plane-spotter now. Not trains but planes: he joined coach trips to different airports to spot planes. Very weird. (I mean, how hard can it be to spot a plane at an airport?) Anyway, we gave our numbers to his mum but Nidder (as we called him) never got in touch. Too busy spotting planes, probably. Which was a shame because I'm sure his lunatic tendencies would have been reawakened by being in the group. Plus he and Barney would have had mad fights. At school they used to wind each other up like crazy, and every Friday night they'd have a fight. We'd all go and watch them in the park but we'd be bored because they were so evenly matched – we'd be like, 'Oh come on, lads, it's five o'clock, we want to go home ...' Anyway, it wasn't to be.

Then Danny Lee, my mate from Sorbus Close, tried out for the singer, but he wasn't much cop. Then Wroey tried his hand but he wasn't much cop either.

In the meantime we were becoming more and more friendly with Ian. We started seeing him out more often and we'd recognize him because he'd either be wearing his jacket with 'Hate' on it or his mackintosh, which he wore when he came straight from work. We'd found out his name, that he was from Oldham and married, which came as a bit of a shock – not that he was from Oldham, but that he was married. I mean, *married*. We'd only just left school. Or it felt like we had.

He'd got a band together as well. That was the thing about that period. We'd all been inspired. We were all desperate to get on and do it. Ian had returned from a punk festival in France, having seen Iggy and the Damned, all fired up about doing his own stuff. So far he'd managed to recruit a drummer and a guitarist and, like us, had been getting help (advice mainly) from Richard Boon and Pete Shelley.

We wanted a singer and a drummer but Ian had a drummer and a guitarist, so – remembering the rules of punk – we couldn't join up, even though we desperately needed a singer and he desperately needed a bassist. We had to follow the rules.

We'd meet in the pub. 'Hiya, mate. How are you? How's it going? How's the band?'

'Oh, me drummer's left.'

Ian's drummer was Martin Jackson, a very good drummer. We ended up trying to get him for Warsaw but he said no and went to play for Magazine initially then ended up with Swing Out Sister, among others. I bet he still kicks himself now.

So anyway, he'd left Ian.

'Still got me guitarist, though,' said Ian. That was Iain Gray, a big mate of Ian's and another familiar face on the punk scene. He'd been at the first Pistols gig.

There are two schools of thought on how Ian ended up joining us. The first is that Ian answered another advert we put in Virgin Records, but that's not what I remember. (Saying that, there are a lot of things I don't remember ...) The way I thought it happened was that the next time we saw Ian, at the last Sex Pistols gig at the Electric Circus, we said to him, 'All right, mate. How's it going? How's the group? You still got Iain as your guitarist?'

'Nah, he's fucked off.'

And we had a Eureka moment. 'Well, come in with us, then. You can sing for us.'

Either way, the result was the same: we had our lead singer. We met the Saturday after the gig and took him with us for a scramble round Ashworth Valley in Rochdale, getting him well and truly wet and covered in mud. A great way to audition singers; I highly recommend it.

But back to that fourth and last Pistols gig. It was a virtual riot, the kind of night you look back on and wonder how the fuck you escaped with your life. Like I said, the Damned were off the tour, so the Buzzcocks opened instead, followed by the Clash, Johnny Thunders & the Heartbreakers, and then the Pistols, who'd been kicked out of not one but two Manchester hotels earlier that day. It was absolutely packed, inside and out, a riot outside and a riot inside. Loads of football fans had come looking for a fight and the Pistols played under a hail of gob and bottles, with constant fights taking place in front of the stage. Even in the queue outside you risked life and limb, with the kids on the flats raining bottles and bricks down from the roofs on to the punks below. They'd even gone to the trouble of taking the spikes out of the railings round the Electric Circus beforehand, to use as ammunition. After the gig it was bedlam outside, with the punks getting hammered left, right and centre. We flagged down a passing cop car and asked for help getting past these lunatics and the copper said, 'Run behind the van and we'll escort you to your cars.' We all trooped behind, but as he set off he put his foot right down and sped off – leaving us at the mercy of the mob. The bastard. Luckily Terry's car was nearby so we dived in and scarpered.

Looking back I wonder if that last Pistols gig at the Electric Circus was the night that the allure of punk started to fade for some of us. Once you get football fans coming – the twats who just want to spit and throw bottles – it's time to move on, and people like the Buzzcocks and then us, Magazine, the Fall and Cabaret Voltaire were eventually able to find a way forward. We'd already decided that the name the Stiff Kittens was too 'cartoon punk' and were looking for something else. Also, we'd started writing some songs. We still needed a drummer, though. Terry tried for that, too, but alas it wasn't going to be him.

'He was one of us'

Even though Terry was a bit shy and awkward in company, and all our school mates picked on him, we liked him all the same. Whereas my other mates preferred to stay in the pubs in Salford, Terry was into Bowie and Roxy and he introduced us both to the discos in town, Pips or Time & Place. Plus he was there right at the beginning. He was there for the Pistols, and he was in on the conversations about starting the group. He was one of us.

Like I say, I thought we'd given him a go as the singer and it didn't work. He disputes that, but agrees that he then tried his hand at guitarist and that didn't work. Then he became the drummer. By that time we'd recruited Steve, but Terry kept up with the lessons for himself. So he became the manager and he wasn't very good at that, either. No killer instinct – he was too nice. Then he became the sound guy, and he was shit at being a sound guy, too, because Harry DeMac had taught him – as a joke, presumably – to turn things up with the 'gain pots' on the desk instead of the faders (ask your roadie), which resulted in some pretty wild mixes. (Saying that, if you listen to the tapes now they sound great. Quite a few have been released to much acclaim.)

After we found OZ PA, a local Manchester sound company, Terry became our roadie, eventually becoming New Order's tour manager, and we had a great time. He was my oldest friend and my sounding post for the start of my moaning about Barney. We were always very close; Barney hated this and he took it out on Terry sometimes. I remember at the sound-check for one New Order gig, in the Midwest somewhere, some kid gave Terry four Es, saying, 'Give them to the band, buddy!'

We shared them out, but Barney, who didn't do sound-checks at that time so wasn't even there, somehow found out and demanded Terry be sacked for it. I wouldn't mind but American E is shit anyway; it wasn't worth moaning about, especially with the amount we were earning then – something like a million dollars per gig with merchandizing – and we were carrying ounces of coke! Me and Rob told Barney to fuck off and he stormed out after the gig.

So anyway, by 1989 Barney had had enough of him. They hated each other. The Barney-and-Terry hate was even more intense than the me-and-Barney hate – and Barney threatened to leave New Order many times if Terry didn't go. Eventually Terry moved to Los Angeles. With the advent of technology he reckoned he could work from any- where so why not somewhere sunny? Thirteen years he'd worked with us by this point: through thick and thin, a loyal colleague and friend – still is, hopefully.

I mean, the trouble was that he started off as our lead singer and went right down the ladder, or up the ladder, all the way to the bottom or the top depending on how you think. It was actually Terry who dis- covered distortion for us. Ian had a small WEM amp and two columns of ten-inch speakers he used for his vocals. Terry didn't have an amp that day so plugged in to the WEM while Ian wasn't singing … Oh my God, it sounded like choirs of angels, distorted choirs of angels: heav- enly. Barney elbowed him out of the way immediately, saying, 'You and Ian use mine!'

Barney discovered distortion.

Still, things certainly improved and we started practising more reg- ularly at night, often going straight from work. I was working at the Ship Canal; Ian was working at the Employment Exchange in Macclesfield and Barney was at Cosgrove Hall Films helping to make cartoons for ITV. His job was to colour them in, although he used to tell the girls he was a graphic artist. It was a cool place to work, actually, much more relaxed than the Town Hall. They let us practice there in the early days; it was one of the many places we used when we pinged around from place to place. It used to be very difficult to find rehearsal rooms. Every pub you'd go in you'd say, 'We're a band and we're just looking for a rehearsal room.'

And they'd say, 'Oh right. Why don't you rehearse in the main room and you can play your songs and the punters will love it.'

Which sounded horrific to us. 'Oh no, you wouldn't like us …'

So we got a lot of offers but not many that were suitable, and we ended up shuttling around: the Albert pub in Macclesfield; Bernard's gran's front room; the Swan in Salford, which the landlady let us use for free if we bought a pie and a pint; disused mills and warehouses all over the place, where we used to go and drag gear up and down stairs then set up and play in the freezing cold. None of them were fully fledged rehearsal rooms apart from the Big Alex, where twelve bands practised at once and you couldn't concentrate because it was like being in an engine room. You'd have a reggae band going on, a heavy-metal band sawing away. To try to compete, Ian had to go and buy himself the WEM PA system.

Up till then he'd just been hollering, which didn't bother us because it sounded like the Sex Pistols, which is what we aspired to: that volume and attitude. Our first songs were like that, all just punk-copy songs. We had one called 'BL' – bleedin' 'ell – which was about Danny Lee's sister Belinda, who I went out with and who broke my heart. I wrote it and Ian used to sing it, God bless him. I wrote 'At a Later Date' and 'Novelty', too – I was writing a lot of lyrics at work because I was bored. I could get rid of the whole month's work in a week, so all I had to do for the other three weeks was go up and down the canal collecting the rent, piss about, fall asleep in the file room and write lyrics. Most of them were terrible but Ian was so nice and gracious like that he used to sing them anyway. Then we'd do one of his songs and it sounded so much better – and that was before we even knew what he was saying. What was obvious about Ian was that he was pouring everything into it; he wasn't playing at being in a band. My lyrics were just words on a page whereas his were coming from somewhere else, his soul.

We were getting to know him a bit better, too. When we first met him he and Debbie lived in Oldham, but they sold up – either because she wanted to move back to Macclesfield or they just weren't getting on in Oldham, whatever. But while they sorted out the house in Macc he lived at his gran's in Stretford. Me and Barney would go round there to practise and usually go out to gigs and, as he was spending so much time with us ... Well, I suppose you'd have to say we corrupted him a bit. Like, when we first met him he was a married man and behaved like one. If a fit girl walked by on the street, me and Barney would look but Ian wouldn't give her a second glance. He was just that bit more of a gentleman than we were, I suppose you'd have to say. Well, a *lot* more of a gentleman.

But he didn't stay that way for long. Soon enough he was behaving the same way: if a fit girl walked down the street, he'd be looking too. But that was his personality, though I'm not sure I realized this at the time. (Probably didn't, if I'm honest.) But looking back that's exactly what he was: a people pleaser; he could be whatever you wanted him to be. A poetic, sensitive, tortured soul, the Ian Curtis of the myth – he was definitely that. But he could also be one of the lads – he *was* one of the lads, as far as we were concerned. That was the people pleaser in him, the mirror. He adapted the way he behaved depending on who he was with. We all do a bit, of course, but with Ian the shift was quite dramatic. Nobody was better at moving between different groups of people than he was. But I also think this was an aspect of his personality that ended up being very damaging to him. He had three personas he was trying to juggle: he had his married-man persona, at home with the wife, the laddish side and the cerebral, literary side. By the end he was juggling home life and band life, and had two women on the go. There were just too many Ians to cope with.

I've realized all this in the years since, of course. At the time I just thought he was a great guy. And he was a great frontman. You could tell.

Now, if only we could find a drummer.

'I can't actually think of anything less "us" than a wet-towel fight'

So we asked around for a drummer and when that drew a blank we tried advertising. Our first reply was from a student whose name I can't remember. We took him on but he really got on our tits, so even though he was an okay drummer we decided to get rid of him. Being a right pair of shits, me and Barney decided that the only way to ditch him was by telling him he was 'too good' for us.

We drove to Middleton College to give him the good news to his face – it's where Steve Coogan went, funnily enough, a famous college in the area – and made our way up to his dorm, only to find him and his mates flicking each other's bare arses with their towels. If we'd had any doubts about sacking him they were laid to rest at the sight of that, because offhand I can't actually think of anything less 'us' than a wet-towel fight.

Out of breath from his jolly larks he came bounding up to us: 'All right, lads! How's it going?'

'We think you're too good for us,' we said as rehearsed, heads down. 'You know, the sound we're going for, you know, it's ... And ... You're too ... Good.'

'Right,' he beamed and ran back to whipping his mates' arses with his towel while we sloped off to wrestle with the thorny issue of finding another drummer – an issue that was about to get even thornier: we had our first gig coming up.

When we'd started the group, me and Bernard had got in touch with Pete Shelley from the Buzzcocks. (I can't remember how – he must have given us his phone number.) We met him in a pub in Broughton where we picked his brains. We were a bit star-struck, a bit in awe of him because he was in a band and they were like Manchester punk royalty, but mainly we were just pleased that he'd agreed to see us, because in those days there were no books on starting a band. You couldn't go on a course or look it up on the Internet. Being in a group gave you instant social-leper status. It meant you were ostracized by your family and shunned by passing strangers in the street, and your workmates made no bones about what they thought of it all.

'Why do you want to be in a group? Fuck off, do some work why don't you?'

So to actually talk to someone with first-hand experience was very valuable. And, though the Manchester punk scene would go on to resemble a snake-pit of petty jealousy, backbiting and rivalry, the Buzzcocks and especially Pete seemed above all that. Right from the word go they were about being inclusive – the proper punk ethos. It was just the rest of us who squabbled like kids over a bag of sweets.

Because we'd met up with Pete, and because Pete was a nice, gracious guy, he'd ask me and Bernard how it was going. We told him that Ian was really working out as a lead singer, which was good because Pete knew Ian, too, and Pete asked us if we'd like a support slot with the Buzzcocks, and even though we still didn't have a name that we all liked, and we were 'between drummers', we virtually bit his hand off. This was it. This was what we were getting ready for.

The first thing we did was work on the look. I went shopping with Terry at the Army & Navy Store on Tib Street, where a black plastic cap set me back 50p.

'You have to have a gimmick, our Peter,' as my mother always said. These were probably her only words of advice about the band other than, 'You should give it all up and settle down.' (I remember once arriving late for my Sunday lunch at home because I'd been doing an interview for the *NME* in town. When I told her I thought she'd go mad: dinner was ruined. Instead she burst out crying, hugged me and said, 'At last. You're getting a proper job!' That was in 1986.) But it wasn't bad advice as it goes and that was my gimmick at first: the cap and a moustache. Terry, who by now was trying his hand at being our manager/roadie, got his tank commander's goggles; Barney no doubt invested in a fresh supply of Scout clothes from the Scout shop, and of course Ian had his own Ian thing going on. One thing they got dead right in *Control*, actually, was how Ian looked. He didn't go in for the jackboots (ex-German army, £3.50 a pair from Tib Street; wore them for years) or the tank hats or Scout stuff. He was just Ian, and he was always much cooler than us without really trying to be. Just was.

Next we needed a new name, Stiff Kittens being too 'London punk'. We chose Warsaw. Just like that. For any group the name's your most important thing, definitely as important as the music, and I've always found it tough to choose one. But Warsaw was a piece of piss, far easier than any of the name changes that came later. We picked it because it was cold and austere. It was either that or Berlin, and because we all liked 'Warszawa', the track on Bowie's *Low*, we chose that. Too late for Richard Boon, though: the Buzzcocks' manager had been screaming at us for a name but by the time we eventually we came up with Warsaw it was too late, or so he said, and he'd gone with Stiff Kittens on the poster. This annoyed us and kind of led to us falling out with the Buzzcocks a bit – because we would have been very, well, *vocal* about our annoyance.

But we still didn't have a drummer. For a while it looked like we might have to cancel the gig or maybe even go back to the wet-towel kid, but in the end we got a guy called Tony Tabac, who we recruited a night or two before the gig. Nothing like cutting it fine; it was straight in at the deep end for him. Quite a nice guy he was, too, and a good drummer. I remember his audition: a bit meat-and-potatoes, but good – and he'd decorated his bass drum with all kinds of shit, like dimps and fag packets, which we liked because it looked punky.

On 29 May 1977, at the Electric Circus, the band played their first-ever gig, supporting Penetration and the Buzzcocks. Tony Wilson was in the audience, as well as Paul Morley, who by this time was writing for the NME and was impressed by Warsaw's 'twinkling evil charm'. 'The bass player had a moustache,' he later wrote. 'I like them and will like them more in six months' time.' Photographer Kevin Cummins was also there, as well as Steve Shy of local fanzine Shy Talk; John the Postman, who led the crowd in a rendition of 'Louie Louie' at the end of the night; and punk poet John Cooper Clarke, who performed after Warsaw.

I remember driving there in the afternoon, and I remember getting there and loading the gear in. I don't remember the sound check. We had one, I think, but we had no idea what to do because we'd never done one before. No one had the foggiest.

Not knowing what to do made it exciting, though. Like, now, everybody's got a stage manager and a sound guy, lights, etc. The bands know all about sound-checks and levels, equipment and all that. Now they even have music schools to teach you that kind of stuff. Back then you knew fuck all. You didn't have anyone professional, just your mates, who, like you, were clueless; you had a disco PA and a sleepy barmaid. It's something I find quite sad about groups today, funnily enough, the careerism of it all. I saw this programme once, a 'battle of the bands' sort of thing. It had Alex James from Blur on it and Lauren Laverne and some twat from a record company, and they'd sit there saying what they thought of the band: 'Your bass player's shit and your image needs work; lose the harmonica player.'

All the bands just stood there and took it, going, 'Cheers, man, we'll go off and do that.'

I couldn't believe it. I joined a band to tell everyone to fuck off, and if somebody said to me, 'Your image is shit,' I'd have gone, 'Fuck off, knob-head!' And if someone had said, 'Your music's shit,' I would have nutted them. That to me is what's lacking in groups. They've missed out that growing-up stage of being bloody-minded and fucking clueless. You have to have ultimate self-belief. You have to believe right from the word go that you're great and that the rest of the world has to catch up with you. Of us lot, Ian was the best at that. He believed in Joy Division completely. If any of us got downhearted it was always him who would gee us up and get us going again. He'd put you back on track.

Anyway back to our first gig. Clueless or not, we got set up. The changing rooms were in the old projection rooms. (Not that we ever changed clothes as such – in fact we used to look down on bands who did. I bet those bands on the Alex James programme 'change' ...) I remember walking down the steps to the stage, and Ian saying, 'We're not Stiff Kittens. We're Warsaw,' and that was it – we were off – and I can't remember a thing more about it because I was so frightened. When we came off we felt we'd done okay and there was a lot of relief that we'd got through it, that first step of playing in front of people. Because it's the weirdest sensation: I mean, I find it pretty weird even when I do it now, to be honest ...

Warsaw's next gig was on 31 May at Rafters on Oxford Street, supporting the Heartbreakers, who were fronted by Johnny Thunders, an ex-member of proto-punks the New York Dolls. The Heartbreakers had arrived in the

UK in time to ride the punk wave and found themselves much admired by the English groups. Their heroin use, however, was legendary.

Getting that gig was a massive thrill. You've got to remember that in those days we played just to play. It didn't matter that we weren't getting paid: we did it anyway, and fucking loved it. I'd get so worked up before a gig that I had to run off the excitement. There was that much adrenalin in me I just had to get rid of it somehow and I'd set off running like Forest fuckin' Gump. And supporting Johnny Thunders was mega because, well, he was Johnny Thunders out of the New York Dolls; I was a huge fan. He was American. The Heartbreakers were the first group we'd met who we didn't already know, which made them otherworldly, as far as we were concerned.

So when we got in to Rafters in the afternoon, loaded our gear in raring to go, dead excited to be meeting the Heartbreakers, we were very surprised to find them all laid out on the seats. Sparkled, comatose, passed out.

We stood there looking at them, mouths hanging open, thinking, 'Oh my God! How you can be in a group and be *asleep*?' There's me, so excited to be doing a gig I was charging about. There's the Heartbreakers, so hungover or smacked-up or whatever, just laying there. We couldn't believe it.

What's more, it became our problem, because we had to wait until they'd sound-checked before we could do anything, and it took something like four hours for them to get their shit together. They had road crew, but the road crew were just as wasted, and it was like the lot of them were running on half speed, like watching punk skeletons staggering in slow motion, and as a result we never got to sound check. When they eventually played they were almost as much of a shambles on stage as they'd been during the afternoon. During their set they played 'Chinese Rocks', which was their big hit, three times. I was looking at the crowd, thinking, *You're pissed off? We've had to put up with this all day.*

So it was a bit disillusioning, really, because we'd thought it would be like before, with the Buzzcocks, where everybody was dead excited and enthusiastic and planning on changing the world. But it wasn't. These guys could barely stay awake let alone change the world. It was a relief to get back to 'our world' for our next gig.

This was where Barney's infamous sleeping bag made its first appearance. We had been invited by Penetration to support them, the Adverts and Harry Hack & the Big G at Newcastle Town Hall. It was the first time we'd used borrowed equipment, meaning we had to walk on, plug in and play, so we sounded dreadful, and I think also the first time we got paid. Twenty quid. I'd asked Danny McQueeney to drive us up there in his three-and-a-half-ton van, which just had three seats in the front. Obviously there was me, Barney, Ian, Tony, Terry and Danny, which makes six; so this meant that three of us had to go in the back, one of them being me. Now, if you've never been in the back of a three-and-a-half-ton van all the way from Manchester to Newcastle, let me tell you, it's like being locked in a box. A freezing box. Newcastle's a long way. It was hell. So, when the gig ended and Danny announced that he was too pissed to drive back (and none of us was insured to drive), we weren't too fussed about postponing the hellish journey back and staying the night.

Until it got cold, that is. Really. Fucking. Cold. One minute we were milling around outside the van where we'd parked – under the big Tyne Bridge, just by the docks – still a bit pissed and having a laugh. Next thing you know, about 4am, the temperature had dropped and we were diving in the van for any shred of warmth. Then we watched in amazement as Bernard first got a deckchair out, and next wrapped a scarf around his neck and put a hat on. Then pulled out a sleeping bag, wriggled into it and settled himself into his chair for the night. Slack-jawed, we were, green with envy and turning blue with the cold, wishing that we'd thought of bringing warm clothes and wondering why Barney had thought of it.

We couldn't put the heater on. There was only just enough fuel to get us back as it was. So for the rest of the night we took turns trying to kip in the cab, where it was warmest, and Barney sat there, snug as a bug and twice as smug, while we froze. Whoever it was who said that 'no man is an island' never met Bernard.

Around this time we played at the Squat in Devas Street. The Squat was in an almost derelict building in the middle of wasteland off Oxford Road. It had been part of the Royal Manchester College of Music but it became a punk venue, only a really rough one – really dingy – where you could just turn up and play, and there would always be more people from bands than there were audience in there. We played with the Drones, the Negatives, the Fall and the Worst, a real gathering of Manchester punks that was, for the Stuff the Jubilee festival. Suddenly it felt like we were part of something. Us, the Fall, the Worst: after the Buzzcocks and Slaughter & the Dogs we were the next wave of punk bands and we'd be following each other around for years.

Word was beginning to spread about Warsaw, with the second Squat gig, on 25 June, reviewed for Sounds *by Tony Moon, who wrote, '[Warsaw] have slightly better gear than the Worst and since they have done a couple more gigs are a bit tighter. Tony Tabac is on drums […] he only joined a few weeks ago. Pete Hook is on bass/plastic cap, Barney Rubble is on guitar and Ian Curtis is the voice. Lotsa action and jumping in the air […] to […] 'Tension', 'The Kill'.'*

Bernard never referred to himself as Barney Rubble and it's unclear where that name originated outside of Salford Grammar. The gig would also be Tony Tabac's last, as he was arrested shortly afterwards.

Tony, it turned out, was a bit of an entrepreneur, which got him in big trouble, taking his mind off drumming and resulting in his parents clamping down on him completely. I remember going to his house to practise once, and the family were obviously very well-to-do, very posh: they had games machines, pinball machines in the living area, all shit like that, and we were like, *Wow.* It was the nicest house I'd ever seen. Huge. He had his own room and everything, which was unusual back then. His sister was dead fit as well, and he'd written 'Warsaw' on the bass-drum skin next to the dimps and fag packets, which we all thought was *dead* fucking cool: 'Whoa, look, we've made it. We've got our name on a bass drum.' All in all, what with the cool house and the fit sister and the fact that he was obviously into the band, we were pretty sad to lose him.

So we got another drummer. A small, thin guy by the name of Steve Brotherdale. Again a meat-and-potatoes drummer, but not bad apart from he'd always be banging on the ride cymbal. It's a fucking hateful sound, the ride cymbal; used to drive us mad. Me and Barney used to run over and swipe it off him. Plus he had his girlfriend with him all the time. Even while we were rehearsing this poor cow was sat there. And he was horrible to her, which rubbed us up the wrong way into the bargain. We were always falling out with him about it. I chucked him out of the car once in the middle of Piccadilly, on the way home one night, closely followed by his drums. Told him to fuck right off.

He was with us when we next played at Rafters (on 30 June), though, where we first came across Martin Hannett and Alan Erasmus, and saw a new side to Ian. A bit of a worrying side.

'The twats were flicking the Vs up at us'

The gig had been organized by Martin Hannett, who by then had formed a promotions company called Music Force. We were supposed to be headlining but when we got there the other band were sound-checking first. This was Fast Breeder. They were from South Manchester and they were shit, absolute fucking rubbish. They went, 'No, no, no: we're headlining; we're headlining!' and we were going, 'No, no: we're headlining; fuck off. We arranged it with Martin Hannett!' and before you know it we were all having a massive row, us lot saying we should be sound-checking first because we were on last, them lot saying the same, all squaring up to each other. Well, me and Ian were, while the rest of the group stayed out of it, which was pretty much how it went for the rest of our career, come to think of it. Only Ian ever got involved in arguing and then only if he'd had a few.

Anyway, me and Ian were squaring up to them, secretly shitting it because they were much bigger than us, when their manager got involved. A black guy wearing a flat cap, he looked quite tasty and we were thinking, 'We'd better be careful here . . .' and it turned out to be Alan Erasmus, who later became a partner in Factory and who was indeed very tasty. I think he threatened to throw Peter Saville out of a window once. Can't blame him for that, though: Peter can be very annoying sometimes.

To our immense credit we didn't back down and, with neither side budging, we decided to phone the promoter, Martin. I went to the back, where the payphone was, called and found him very laid back about it all, like he'd been smoking, just going, 'You know what, it doesn't make much difference really,' which was easy for him to say. There was pride at stake here.

I went back and said, 'Right, Martin's just confirmed. We're headlining.'

Then some twat from Fast Breeder went, 'I'm not having that. I'm not having that!' And he stormed off to the phone, came back and said, 'Martin says that *we're* headlining.'

So Ian went back to the payphone to try Martin again, but by this time he'd stopped answering; so we carried on arguing until they eventually backed down – or seemed to – and agreed that we were headlining so we should sound-check. So we did. Then they set up their gear. But what they did – and this is a trick I've seen repeated many times since, a really sneaky one – they did their sound-check then fucked off, leaving their gear on stage.

They were supposed to be on at half-nine. Support band: half past nine. That's the way it goes. But at half nine they weren't there. Their roadies were assuring us that the band were on their way but it was all a ruse. In the end they came back really late – about the time of the headline slot, funnily enough, so it looked like they were headlining – did their set and by the time they came off most of the audience had gone home. The twats were flicking the Vs up at us as they packed up.

By now the place was nearly empty. One of the few left was a punk girl called Iris with her friend Pauline. I'd seen them around, and I'd been talking to them while we were waiting for Fast Breeder to turn up. We got together that night, started going out, ended up having two lovely kids and stayed together for ten years. Saying that, I was away for eight-and-a-half of them.

Anyway, while I was chatting up the future mother of my kids, Ian had been knocking the beers back. All of us were fucked off at being kept waiting, but he was the only one who showed it by getting pissed. Really pissed, he was. So pissed that a couple of songs into the set he suddenly jumped off the stage and upended a table. Glasses went everywhere. We played on. Maybe he'd come back ... Then he tipped up another table. He'd stopped singing, of course: too busy going berserk. He picked up a third table, smashed it on the dance floor and the top sliced off, sending shards of it everywhere that nearly hit Iris.

Still we played on. We were looking at each, like, 'What the fuck? He seemed so nice ...' as Ian threw himself to the floor and began writhing around in the broken glass, cutting himself in the process. Any remaining audience members were either scared half to death or laughing at him, while we were just freaked out. This was our mate going mental here. In the end he returned to the stage and we finished the gig, watching as what was left of the crowd scarpered rather than risk another outburst. Nobody fancied being pelted with more broken glass or bits of broken table. It was one of our worst gigs ever.

Looking back, I think there was a bit of showmanship involved. Ian was really into Iggy and was always pushing us in that direction musically. But I think this was a time that he took on the physicality of Iggy too, prompted partly by him being pissed and partly by this huge fall-out with Fast Breeder. Even so – even knowing where it was all coming from – it was a massive shock to see him like that. We'd witness other examples of it, of course, when he'd lose his temper – usually when he was pissed – and start screaming and shouting. But that was the first time.

That was Steve Brotherdale's first gig with us – what an initiation. His second was at Tiffany's in Leicester, when he blotted his copybook with us all by coming to the front of the stage, bringing his high-hat with him, and then playing said high-hat. Ian just looked at him with his gob hanging open then told him to get the fuck back, which he did. But the writing was on the wall from that moment on.

He was still with us for our very first recording session: the Warsaw demo, which we did at Pennine Sound Studios, a converted church on Ripponden Road in Oldham. We'd pooled what money we had to buy some recording time and in we went, green as you like. Paul the engineer walked us through the process: he'd mic it all up, sound-check and we'd record it all in one take, no overdubs. He listened back. 'Great. There's your master, lads.' Five tracks – 'Inside the Line', 'Gutz for Garters', 'At a Later Date', 'The Kill' and 'You're No Good for Me' – all done in three or four hours, which was all we could afford.

'Inside the Line' and 'The Kill' were Ian's; 'Gutz for Garters', 'At a Later Date' and 'You're No Good for Me' were mine. Listening back now you can hear what a punk band we were then. 'You're No Good for Me' in particular was proper sub-Buzzcocks rubbish. Just about the only indication to our future sound was 'The Kill', which we later re-recorded during the *Unknown Pleasures* sessions, when it sounded very different indeed. Overall, the demos were the sound of a band still finding its feet, but 'The Kill' still showed that we were getting somewhere. More importantly, for the time being at least, we now had demo tapes we could use to try to get lots more gigs outside of Manchester.

Terry, still our manager, had the job of copying the demos and sending them out to venues. The idea was that he'd ring the venue a bit later, find out what they thought of the tape and see if they'd give us a spot. 'All right, it's Terry Mason, manager of Warsaw – just wondered what you thought of the demo I sent you?' That sort of thing.

But every time he rang someone he was getting the same reaction.

'Terrible.'

'Absolutely shit, mate.'

'Fuckin' awful.'

So Terry was saying to us, 'No one wants you, lads. They all say you're shit,' which we couldn't understand because other groups who were much shitter than us (like the Drones, for example) were getting gigs out of town. Us? Nothing.

So I said to Terry, 'Terry, give us one of them tapes and let me have a listen to it, and make sure it's all right.'

He went, 'All right, Hooky, here y'go,' and fished one of out his jacket, one of those tapes you get – or used to get – in a pack of three; TDK, something like that. I put it on in the car and it started off okay. Bit muffled, a little distant, but you could hear my bass, Barney sawing away, Steve Brotherdale doing the business, Ian doing his punky singing – yet to fully develop his baritone, of course; still doing the punky shouting back then but sounding great. We're sounding like a band, a good band. The kind of band you'd want playing at your venue, surely ...

Then suddenly I heard the theme tune to *Coronation Street* drown it all out. And next I hear this voice, Terry's mum, Eileen, saying, 'Come on now, Terry, your tea's ready ...'

Now back then the only way you could record tape-to-tape was by using two little flat cassette players, put speaker-to-speaker, which was what Terry had been doing. But the dozy bugger had been recording them while he was watching telly and waiting for his mum to do his tea. No wonder no one wanted to book us.

So Terry stopped being our manager and became our road manager, or head roadie or whatever, and we started doing the managing ourselves. We sent out new demo tapes, made some calls and sure enough we got some bookings – the first being for Eric's in Liverpool. Result. Except our drummer upped and left.

Rob Gretton was a high-profile member of the Manchester music scene. He'd missed the two Pistols concerts, having been on a kibbutz in Israel with long-term partner Lesley Gilbert, but on his return became involved with

Slaughter & the Dogs and helped to finance their first single, 'Cranked Up Really High' (produced by Martin Hannett, then working as Martin Zero). Next he produced a fanzine, Manchester Rains, before setting up Rainy City Records, which released the one and only EP by the Panik, It Won't Sell. He had also promoted Siouxsie & the Banshees at the Oaks in Chorlton.

We didn't yet know Rob, but he was already doing us a favour in a weird kind of way – because for some insane reason the Panik asked Steve Brotherdale to join them and off he went. They were a lot punkier than us, and he was a hard, fast drummer, so he suited them, plus he thought they had more potential than we did. He probably regrets leaving us – well, he *must* regret leaving us – but looking back I don't think he would have lasted anyway. He was the right drummer for that phase of the band, but not for the sound we were moving towards.

Anyway, off he went to join the Panik and I barely saw him after that. He stayed around, because after the Panik he joined a band called V2. After V2 faded away, well, I went in a McDonald's about ten years ago, ordered a quarter pounder (no ketchup, no cheese) and medium fries, and the guy serving me went, 'Hooky?'

And I went, 'Yeah?'

He said, 'Don't you remember me? Steve Brotherdale.'

There he was. Let that be a lesson to you.

The next I heard of him was in 2009 in the *Manchester Evening News*, when he was banged up for stalking his ex-wife, sad to say.

Anyway – we needed a new drummer. What a ball-ache.

We placed more ads. Put one in Virgin Records in Piccadilly, where we used to buy our records, and Ian put one up in Jones Music Store in Macclesfield, which was where Steve saw it.

Steve was Stephen Morris. He contacted the number on the advert and arranged an audition, which took place in a classroom at the Abraham Moss Centre in Cheetham Hill, a community centre we were using for rehearsals at the time.

The first thing we noticed about him was that he was dressed like a geography teacher, right down to the patches on the elbows of his jacket. The second thing: that he was nervous as hell. Smoking. Shaking. Me and Barney were looking at each other, like, *Oh my God, he's a shivering wreck.*

Still. After we'd shifted tables, we set up our gear and cranked up. You know exactly what I'm going to say now: he was mega, an absolute revelation. He had all that power that we were looking for but with a texture we hadn't heard before. Most drummers just hammer it out. Steve was *playing* the drums. You could tell he'd been playing with a jazz trio, because it was as though he'd somehow combined the feel and intricacy of jazz with the power and energy of rock and punk. We were over the moon. At last, we had a drummer: a drummer straight from the drummer genie who was not only brilliant but also had his own kit and his own car. Steve worked for his dad's plumbing firm, G Clifford Morris in Macclesfield, so he was on a good wage, and the car came with the job. He seemed a nice bloke, too, very witty and dry, and if it pissed him off that Barney's mate Dr Silk called him Son of Forsyth because of his big chin – a nickname that stuck – well, he was gracious enough not to show it.

On the other hand, he was very closed-off. Musically we were fine: we clicked and went on to become one of the best rhythm sections in music history. But on the personal side I never got to know him properly, not in all the years we worked together. I'm very direct and he's not. I'm a working-class yobbo; he's an English eccentric. I like change; he doesn't.

It's quite funny really, because even at that early stage of the band we were all pretty distant from one another. Me and Barney – once best mates – had fallen out after a motorbiking holiday in the South of France we went on with Danny Lee and Stuart Houghton, when I'd ended up playing the middle man between the two sets of mates. That was bad enough, but the whole thing went tits-up when Stuart crashed his bike, spent all his money on medical bills and then, when his bike finally expired, needed cash to get home. Let's just say that, when it came to helping out, Barney wasn't very helpful: 'It's my holiday. Why should he spoil it?'

After that I couldn't really look at him the same way. When I got back I just hung out with Terry and Twinny – the roadies, in other words – because they were my mates. Twinny I'd met in the Flemish Weaver and got to know him over a beer. But then a couple of days later when I said hello at the bar he was really fucking rude, looked at me like I was off my head and told me to fuck off. I went back to my corner moaning about it to Greg Wood, like, 'That fucking Twinny's a weird one, isn't he? I had a good crack with him the other night and he'd just told me to do one.'

'Why do you think he's called Twinny?' said Greg. 'That's his twin, y'dickhead.'

Ah ...

He ended up being our roadie – the 'Karl' Twinny did, while 'Paul' Twinny became a good friend once I got to know him – and mostly I hung around with him and Terry and Platty on the Precinct. Barney ended up becoming quite close to Ian – when he and Sue did eventually get married, in October 1978, they invited Ian and Debbie but not me and Iris, which goes to show how far we'd drifted apart by then – and Steve, well, he was Steve, an island of Steve. He was with his girl-friend Stephanie until he got together with Gillian, and then it was Steve and Gillian, 'the other two'. That was pretty much how the alliances went for the rest of our careers together. I mean, I loved them as band-mates – I *loved* the group – thought they were great musicians and we really clicked as songwriters. But as people? As friends? Not really. We were individuals, me, Steve and Bernard. The glue that held us together, the driving force of the band, was Ian. Us three were con-centrating on just our bits, with him holding it all together. That's why we never really looked at his lyrics until after he'd died. It was because we were all just concentrating on doing our bit. Three little musical islands with Ian pulling us all together.

The story of how New Order began is for another time, but it was hard to write songs without Ian because the spot we looked to for help was empty. Rob Gretton was our manager by then, so he became the glue that held us together – as people, at least – but when he died of a heart attack in 1999, well, that left nobody. And it's been downhill ever since – until, at the time of writing, it's as bad as it could possibly be.

Joy Division and then New Order were ships that needed captains, but our captains kept on dying on us.

'Apart from the odd pint pot in the gob it was a good gig'

So our first gig with Steve was at Eric's, Liverpool, supporting X-Ray Spex, which you'd have to say marked a new phase of the band: new drummer, getting out of Manchester more. I later found out that the audience was full of members of Liverpool bands: Jayne Casey from Big in Japan, Pete Wylie out of the Mighty Wah! Ian McCulloch from Echo & the Bunnymen and Julian Cope from the Teardrop Explodes. It was there that we met Roger Eagle, a real legend in the North West, who used to promote the Twisted Wheel club in Manchester and had gone on to run Eric's. It was his idea to put us on twice, first in the late afternoon – a matinee show for kids, which we were delighted about because we really did love to play in those days – and then again in the evening. What's more, Roger gave us a crate of Brown Ale, our first-ever rider. None of us liked Brown Ale, but still – the fact that we had a rider was fantastic.

So it was great, the beginning of a brilliant relationship with Roger, who we really got on with, and with Eric's, one of my favourite-ever venues.

The next gig was Middlesbrough. Put on by someone else who would have a big effect later on in our career: Bob Last, who, along with his label Fast Records, would become a great supporter. Now back then, there was none of this, 'Oh, bloody hell, not another gig.' It was, 'Yeah, let's go.' Of course, we weren't used to playing outside Manchester so were all out of bed at the crack of dawn with excitement, me having to run off the adrenalin as usual, and us turning up about midday only to find the venue shut up and locked till five. Great.

We waited around, got in and did the sound-check. Then later when the venue opened it began to fill up with skinheads, thousands of 'em. Well, probably only thirty, but at the time it seemed like more, all milling around swilling beer. Then just before we went on the DJ put on an Adam & the Ants record, which had some kind of weird, mad amphetamine-like effect on them, like a bunch of six-year-olds drinking Coca-Cola at a birthday party. No kidding, they went berserk. It was if they wanted to get a full head of steam before the main event. Which was us, of course. As we came on and started playing, the skins surged to the front and immediately started slinging plastic pint pots at us. All of us apart from Steve were getting showered in plastic and beer (not much beer, mind – the pots were empty – but still) and I seemed to be getting the worse of it, with several bouncing off my head. One of these twats obviously had me right in his sights and I spent the whole night ducking. I was livid.

It didn't affect our playing, though. We were always the kind of band who performed best with the crowd against us. Apart from getting the odd plastic pint pot in the gob it was a good gig. Bob had been watching us play, and had seen this particular skinhead throwing pint pots at me all night, and afterwards he dragged him by the ear backstage. But the dressing room was L-shaped and I was at the bottom of the L, so he spoke to Bernard.

'This is that bastard who was throwing pots at Hooky all night. I've brought him to apologize.'

And Barney went, 'Oh, don't worry about that. It's all right, let him go' – without telling me; I was just sitting at the back oblivious to it all.

Next thing I knew Ian came back and said, 'Oh fucking hell, Hooky, that skin who was throwing pint pots at you all night – he's just been dragged back by the promoter to apologize.'

'Right, where is that *twat*? I'm going to rip his fucking head off.' Full of the usual bravado.

'Oh, Barney told him it was all right and to let him go,' says Ian. I went mad. Stormed up the dressing room and went off at Barney: 'You fucking what?' Started having a massive row with him, which was probably our first ever argument, after all those years. Even during the holiday in the South of France we'd never really argued; whenever he'd pissed me off I just used to seethe and bottle it all up. But that night, because my blood was up, I let rip at him and it opened the floodgates because from then we were *always* arguing, worse than a married couple.

In New Order he'd say, 'If you ever hit me, it's all over. You'll never see me again.' We never did come to blows. I sometimes wonder, though, if a good scrap might have been the answer, might have cleared the air.

Manchester's punk hub, the Electric Circus, no longer able to afford the big names and refused a food licence – and thus a late licence – by the council, was forced to shut in October. Among the bands performing on the final Saturday were Steel Pulse and the Drones. Warsaw opened the Sunday, while the Prefects, the Worst and the Fall all played, Howard Devoto debuted three songs from his new band, Magazine, and the Buzzcocks headlined, the night ending with a stage invasion and a 'Louie Louie' sing-along. Virgin Records sent a mobile studio to record the weekend for a ten-inch, Short Circuit: Live at the Electric Circus, *which was eventually released in June 1978. It featured 'At a Later Date' by Warsaw (though credited to Joy Division, the band having changed their name by then), the performance beginning with Bernard Sumner calling out, 'You all forgot Rudolf Hess.'*

I don't know the reason for him saying that. One theory is that we'd just played 'Warsaw', which was a song about Rudolf Hess. Well, it wasn't *about* Rudolf Hess as far as I know, but the lyrics quoted his prison number, 31G-350125, which Ian had used because Hess was in the news. A book had come out about him that Ian and Bernard had read, and there were people saying he should be let out because he'd served his time. It was very much a topical issue of the day. However, I don't know if we'd even written the song at that point, never mind played it.

Whatever the reason, Bernard must have been gearing himself up for it, and we got the shock of our lives when he did it because he didn't even have a microphone; he went over to grab Ian's mic to do it.

We'd regret all that later, of course. Because all it did was give more ammo – if you'll forgive the phrase – to those who said we were glorifying Nazis. But at the time we were just pleased to get on the record; whatever Barney said was nothing compared to that. We'd had a period of lying low a bit. There was the demo tape debacle, then Steve Brotherdale leaving, and Ian in particular was getting frustrated that we didn't seem to be getting anywhere. Other bands – the Panik, the Nosebleeds, the Drones, Slaughter & the Dogs – seemed to be overtaking us, which wound him up no end because he felt we were much better than they were. All of which meant that we turned up for the last night of the Electric Circus absolutely determined to get on the bill.

Trouble was, so was everybody else, and there was loads of in-fighting and backbiting going on. We felt we were being excluded. We didn't even know it was being recorded.

We couldn't even get through the front door. We had to use a lot of harsh language and threats to argue our way in and on to the bill, and we found out later that the Drones told the promoter to leave us off the bill and we almost didn't get to play. It ended up with us going on first; and when we played there was a cock-up in the sound truck. The sound engineer for some reason started recording halfway through 'Novelty', which is why only 'At a Later Date' appeared on the record when all the other artists got two tracks. As I said, I can't remember what else we played. But it was another example of the utter chaos that reigned supreme that night. A fucking shambles, it was, most of it orchestrated by the Drones and Slaughter & the Dogs, the bastards. Another unpleasant aspect of this was our first brush with publishing and a 'proper' publishing/record company. Virgin, Richard Branson's label, decided to sign the bands' publishing for the tracks featured on the record. Each band would get £200 advance on signing, a fortune then, and all bands would receive 10 per cent of the publishing. Now that didn't seem like a bad deal, 10 per cent each – good old Virgin – and we couldn't sign fast enough. Afterwards, though, we found out that what they meant was that *all bands* would receive 10 per cent in total, as in 2 per cent each. We got two pence in the pound for whatever Virgin earned on the sale of our track, signed away in perpetuity, as everything was in those days. If you're in a band, take my advice and get a lawyer, whatever stage you're at – in fact, it's even more important at the start. Don't ever sign your publishing away; you wrote the songs and they should always be yours. Those starting mistakes will haunt you till you die. (I have a ritual with my lawyer, Stephen Lea – lovely man. He shows me a piece of paper. I read it, say, 'What fucking idiot would sign something like that, Stephen?' He turns it over and says... 'It's you again, Hooky!')

The only joy where that record was concerned came after we got big, when it was reissued and stickered 'Featuring Joy Division'. Ah well, back to our tale.

Just our luck, we had to play with both bands again four days later, this time at Salford Technical College. Apparently this was the first time Martin Hannett saw us. All I remember was afterwards chatting up this girl who lived near Langworthy Road, and then it all going off between the Wythenshawe lads, who were with Slaughter & the Dogs, and the Salford lot, who'd steamed in to get them, and me, like a knight in shining armour, protecting this girl from all the violence. My first groupie.

Of course if a band gets a reputation for trouble then trouble's bound to follow; and when we played with Slaughter & the Dogs *again* the following night that went off in a riot, too, with all the Slaughter lot upstairs throwing bottles into the ruck downstairs. Later, after Rob became our manager, we got talking to him about that gig and he said, 'Oh fucking hell, yeah, that was me fighting and throwing the bottles off the top balcony.' He was their roadie for a while, of course, and no doubt loved all the mayhem that came with it. Their music, thankfully, wasn't built to last and it wasn't long before all that speeded-up punky stuff sounded absolutely prehistoric and we finally said goodbye to Slaughter & the Dogs and the Drones.

'Even the shit ones were pretty good'

I suppose you could say we were getting a bit fed up with our lack of forward motion. We'd looked at other bands with records out and decided that the only way was to release one of our own: to go DIY. We'd started taking turns to manage and when it was Ian's go he worked out that for us to press 1,000 or so records was going to cost about 600 quid. So he borrowed the money from the bank. I think he told them he was going to buy furniture for his new house. I don't think he told Debbie straight away, either. He saved that particular pleasure for later.

We booked the studio, which was Pennine in Oldham again, and Paul offered a one-stop-shop deal: you go into the studio, play, hand over the cash and in return they give you 1,000 singles, but with blank sleeves so you have to do the sleeve yourself – which of course Barney was going to do, being the graphic designer. Then you had to distribute the records.

In the meantime we got talking to Paul Morley one night. He was writing for the *NME* and had covered the last night of the Electric Circus for them, and we'd made his acquaintance around town, mainly at the Ranch. Although he had this strange art-band project called the Negatives, which annoyed us because we felt they were taking the piss, we asked if he fancied producing the EP for us. Couldn't hurt to have a prominent journalist on your side could it? He said yes so we arranged to meet him in town and take him up to Oldham. It just goes to show how green we were that it seemed like a good idea – he'd never produced a record before. The morning of the session we sat in St Ann's Square, the four of us, waiting for him to come. For two hours we sat there and he never turned up. Turned out he'd got pissed the night before and couldn't get out of bed. I don't think Paul would have helped much, to be honest, which he freely admits, but he's gutted about it now. He'd love to say he produced our first record.

At Pennine the session went well, apart from sussing out that my guitar was out of tune and had been the whole time I'd been playing. The neck was warped so it wouldn't stay in tune. The guitar – my £35 first guitar – was fucked.

I've never been able to tune. I'm tone deaf. Barney always did it for me, much to his delight. Like, if I knocked the guitar on stage and it went out of tune, he'd have to come over and retune it, with a big piss-take grin on his face, or I couldn't play. I'm telling you, the best moment in my musical life was when they invented a portable guitar tuner in a foot pedal. I went out and bought four. Fantastic, because you don't half feel like an idiot on stage when your band-mate has to come over and tune your guitar for you.

But anyway, when we were recording the EP, I was greeted with the news that my guitar was out of tune, which immediately ruined it for me because I was shitting myself. But we struggled through. We did 'No Love Lost', with Barney going, 'Ooh, it sounds a bit out, doesn't it? Hooky's guitar...' and me getting wound up but having to grit my teeth and let him retune it each time. After that we did 'Leaders of Men', 'Failures' and 'Warsaw', all of them Ian's songs – I'd pretty much given up on the songwriting by then. I knew when I was beat.

Listening back to the EP, you can really hear how we'd developed – although I'm still amazed how fast we played. Later on in our career I think we ended up playing some of the songs too slowly, funnily enough. Like on *Unknown Pleasures* 'New Dawn Fades' is too slow, if you ask me, and when I play it live now I speed it up a bit. But back then we were definitely playing like our arses were on fire. Still had that punk thing going on.

Lyrically, I was struck by 'No Love Lost', especially the spoken-word verse, an extract from *House of Dolls* (not the last time he found inspiration in that book, of course ...). But, like I say, I never paid too much attention to the lyrics at that time. I kind of knew that they were good, and that there was something really special about them, but mainly I just appreciated that they *sounded* good, and that Ian singing them *sounded* great and looked great. Which he did, he really did. I think you could point to that EP as being the moment that he truly began to find his feet in his writing and singing. All of the experiences he'd had with the band so far, watching other bands at work, reading, getting into Iggy and Throbbing Gristle, it was all coming together for him. It was shaping him into the writer that he became, which was arguably one of the best lyricists ever. His songs from that point were like having a conversation with a genius, sort of profound and impenetrable at the same time. I think that for a while he found it easy as well. The songs seemed to flow out of him and he didn't put a foot wrong after that point, didn't write a single bad lyric after *An Ideal for Living*, right up until his death. Whether we were feeding off him, or whether it was Steve joining or what, I don't know, but musically we were gelling so well, too. The songs were flooding out of us. Any one of us would be playing and it'd be, 'Oh, that's another great riff.' Ian would either memorize it and go home and come back with some lyrics for it, or he'd pull out scraps of paper from a carrier bag and start adapting them on the spot – and we'd have a song. A good one. I'm not being big-headed; I'm happy to say if a song is bad. I've done a few bad songs in my time. But there weren't any in Joy Division. Even the shit ones were pretty good.

Which was why the session turned out to be so easy: because we had the material, and we were working well together, and we didn't know enough about the recording process for it to be difficult. All four tracks were played live and the vocals were overdubbed at the end. I think he did them in one take, and then we sang the backing vocals together, me and Ian, and that was it.

I have a feeling it took a day. The engineer did us a mix and sent it off to be pressed. We were too inexperienced to be pains in the arse about it. We didn't say, 'Oh, it needs a bit more reverb on the snare drum,' because we didn't know enough to ask. God, we must have been so easy to work with.

All we had to do then was wait a couple of weeks for the record, during which time, of course, Barney designed the sleeve. And what did he do? Used a picture of a Hitler Youth member banging a drum. *Yet again* something else that would come back to haunt us. Saying that, I did like the sleeve a lot. He did 1,000 or so of them, printed on pieces of paper that we had to fold into four.

All we needed now were the records. The day they were delivered to the studio I drove to Oldham to pick them up, all 1,000 of them, then sped back as fast as I could to play it. Got home. Rushed upstairs. I was still using the same Dansette, the one I got off Gresty. I'd played all my records on it and now I was going to play *my own* record on it. Excited doesn't cover it: I was nearly wetting myself. I put on the record to play.

It sounded awful.

I thought, *Oh God, there must be something wrong with this one …*

So I whipped out another one and it was exactly the same. Got another one out: the same. Really, really quiet, like there was a wad of dust on the needle. I tried and failed with five of them before I gave up and rang Bernard.

'There's something wrong with the record,' I wailed at him. 'It just sounds fucking shit. It sounds terrible, really muffled and horrible.'

He said, 'Get on to the guy at Pennine, find out what's gone wrong.'

I phoned up Paul at Pennine. 'Hey, man, our record – it sounds shit. It's all muffled.'

And he went, 'Oh yes, it will do. You've made a mistake there.'

'What do you mean we've made a mistake? What mistake?'

'Well,' he said, 'because you've put four tracks on the EP, long tracks, the amount of time makes the grooves really narrow, and when the grooves are really narrow, the sound quality's really bad.'

I was like, 'Why didn't you tell us? You're the fucking engineer; you're supposed to say, "Don't put four tracks on, lads, it'll sound shit – just put two on."'

He went, 'Hey, hey, don't start fucking moaning at me, you dick.'

I said, 'Don't you fucking call me a dick. You're the dick. The fucking record sounds shit, you tosser.'

He hung up. Put the phone down.

Me and Bernard were panicking and I think it was him who suggested that, while the record sounded shit on my old Dansette, it might sound good on a big system. So off we went to Pips Discotheque. When punk got big, Pips had started punk nights alongside the Roxy nights. One of my favourite stories was when Roxy Music were playing at Belle Vue in Manchester and Mr Ferry, hearing about the infamous Roxy/Ferry room, decided to visit after the show, but when he got there the bouncers wouldn't let him in because he had jeans on. Me and Barney used to go quite a bit. One night they had a competition to win the Sex Pistols album and I won by correctly naming the lead singer. Still got the album at home.

The point was, they sort of knew our faces in Pips so we thought there was a good chance they'd play our EP for us. We handed it over to the DJ Dave Booth and patiently waited to hear it, then watched horrified as it cleared the floor, sounding just as bad as if not worse than it had on my Dansette. The big system didn't hide the terrible sound, it just amplified it. He took it off and handed it back.

I felt sick, like you feel when you've lost a lot of money. Ian had lied to the bank to pay for 1,000 singles that were virtually unplayable, and there was no question of dumping them because he needed to get the money back. We had to sell them. Going round to Steve's one night we found ourselves putting the vinyl into Barney's sleeves, knowing that we had to go out and flog a terrible-sounding record that would probably do us more harm than good. Knowing that people were going to buy it and not realize it was shit till they got home.

We were so demoralized that we barely even noticed how posh Steve's house was. He had a koi-carp pond in his drive and not one but two inside toilets, as well as central heating. Any other time we would have been ripping into him about it, but all we could do was sit there pushing the records into sleeves, putting the sleeves into plastic bags, having to be very quiet because his dad was having a nap. Steve's mum and dad were proper parents, like off the telly. I remember one night he had a cold so his mum locked away his drum kit to stop him coming to rehearsal. Of course he arrived anyway and ended up having to use Terry's kit, which kept falling apart as he was playing. He was forever stopping to put it back together again. Good practice for working with Martin, that was.

Anyway, we were sitting in his house, being dead quiet so as not to wake his dad, putting the crap record together. Every now and then one of us suggested that maybe we should drive up to Pennine and beat the shit out of the engineer because there was no doubt about it: he was the one to blame; he knew we were inexperienced. You can get only three or four minutes of great-sounding music on each side of a seven-inch single. That's why, when I'd listened to 'Sebastian' by Cockney Rebel all those years ago, I'd had to turn the record over halfway through the song. I'd always thought it was a bit of a gimmick but suddenly I knew why – and why most hit singles were three minutes long. It's because that's the ideal length for good-sounding audio on a seven-inch single. If you go above that the audio quality gets progressively worse until you end up with a record that sounds like ours did, which had more than six minutes on each side.

Faced with no other choice, we soldiered on and tried to sell it. Debbie was going to chop Ian's bollocks off if we didn't recoup the money so we lugged it from shop to shop trying to offload it as quickly as we could before word spread about the abysmal sound. Knowing that promoters hardly ever played the tapes and records they were given, we used to leave it with them as a calling card, hoping that at least they'd be impressed with the sleeve. Our Nazi sleeve. Knowing that if they ever got round to playing it it would do us no good at all.

In the end we were just giving them away, and weeks after delivery we still had hundreds left over. God knows what became of them – they're worth a mint now, of course. The *An Ideal for Living* EP is probably our most bootlegged item. I get kids coming up to me with a twelve-inch version with the seven-inch sleeve, swearing it's the genuine article.

'No, mate, never came out as a twelve-inch, not with that sleeve,' I tell them. 'Believe me, I wish it had.'

If they still want me to sign it, I write: 'This is a bootleg. Love, Peter Hook.'

One of my favourites of the four of us. The European Tour I think.

Awh bless! My first picture
aged three in Salford.

Postcard to my
Gran from my
mum in 1961.

The good ship
Ascania, a disco
now?

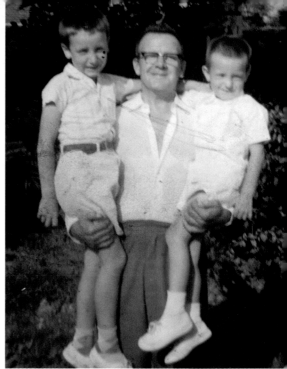

In the garden in Phoenix Avenue with our next door neighbour. I used to look after his chickens and was paid in boiled potatoes with butter.

Me, Chris and Bill in Jamaica, 1962.

School photo. One for the dartboard? I can see Crazy Mike Thomas (soon to be a fireman), Daley (my desk mate), Nidder (mad as ever), Barney and then me!

The lads get ready to go to Butlins. Danny McQueeney is taking the photo. Left to right: his girlfriend, Greg Wood, Gordon Benbow, Pete Houghton(he came to see us off) Deano and me. Outside Chorlton Street Bus Station; amazingly still there!

Boys will be boys. Recognise anyone?

Deano takes the pic this time. Left to right: Me, Danny Mcqueeney, Greg Wood and Benny in the chalet at Butlins. Happy despite it all.

My brother Paul and my beloved scooter – I pushed it for miles! Salford 1973.

In my bedroom in Rothwell Street, just ready for Pips. With Grandad Hook's old double breasted jacket on. Called 'vintage' now!

MR. & MRS. R. WOODRUFF

request the pleasure of the company of

Kelvin + Elayne

at the marriage of their daughter

DEBORAH

with

MR. IAN CURTIS

at St. Thomas's Church, Henbury,

on Saturday, August 23rd, 1975,

at 3-30 p.m.

and afterwards at

The Bulls Head Hotel, Macclesfield.

" Arnwood,"
Heyes Farm Road,
Broken Cross,
Macclesfield.   R.S.V.P.

Courtesy of Kelvin Briggs.
His invite to Ian's wedding.

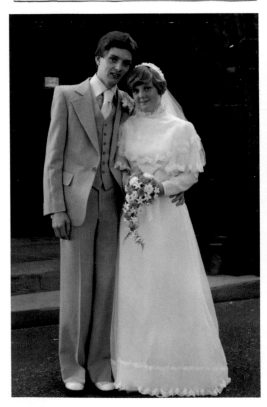

The happy couple. So young – scary!

Kelvin, the best man, and Ian lark about.
Great zoot suits!

The Sex Pistols at The Lesser Free Trade Hall . . . Thanks lads!

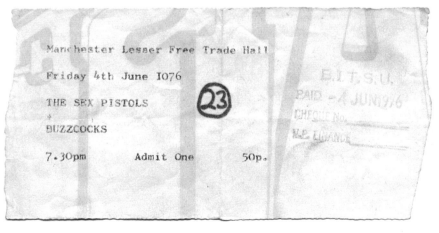

Manchester Lesser Free Trade Hall

Friday 4th June 1076

THE SEX PISTOLS

+

BUZZCOCKS

7.30pm   Admit One   50p.

E.I.T.S.U.

PAID - 4 JUN 1976

CHEQUE No.

M.P. ELOANCE

23

My Sex Pistols ticket.

Bury Town Hall. Twinny gets a kicking.

Twinny after kicking . . . with my best shirt on!

'I told him exactly where he could stick his vibrators'

In between recording the EP and Barney doing the sleeve we decided to change our name.

We were still sharing managerial duties at that time. When it was my turn I used to sit at work with the *NME*, going through the live listings and phoning up trying to get a gig – like, 'Hello, is that the Elephant & Castle? We're a band from Manchester and we're looking for a gig.'

'What's your name?'

'Warsaw.'

'Warsaw Pakt? Oh yeah, I've heard of you ...'

'No, just Warsaw.'

They'd go. 'Oh? Just Warsaw? Not Warsaw Pakt? Oh, right, not interested, mate ...'

The phone would go down and I'd be left wondering, *Who the hell are Warsaw Pakt?* Our group wasn't getting gigs because we weren't Warsaw Pakt. This was very puzzling. Not long after there was a big piece about them in the *NME*, in which it sounded like they were a pretty shit punk band but with a good gimmick: they'd made an album direct to disc. I think they'd recorded it in one take in a cutting plant, the idea being to cut out the tape stage or stick it to the man or something. I don't know. Who cared? All I knew was, they were stopping us getting gigs.

Warsaw Pakt had links with Pink Fairies and Motörhead, and their album, Needle Time, was notable for being recorded direct to acetate at Trident Studios, released within twenty-four hours and then deleted after a week. Despite the publicity, the band split up shortly afterwards – but as far as the Manchester-based Warsaw were concerned the damage had already been done.

Even though we'd been using the name Warsaw for longer, they'd effectively taken it over. During the usual band meeting in the pub we decided to change ours, and so began the long conversations about what we should be instead. Obviously Ian had read *House of Dolls*. He'd already pilfered it for the spoken-word bit on 'No Love Lost', and now he took Joy Division from it too – and thank God he did, because he saved us from the shame of being called Boys of Bondage or Slaves of Venus. Barney went off and started doing interesting typographical things to it. He gave it Germanic lettering for the *An Ideal for Living* EP, and an exclamation mark. And that was it, we were Joy Division.

Now, of course, it's a full-time job trying to safeguard the name. There's even a Joy Division in Germany that does marital aids, vibrators and stuff: 'joy sticks'. Which is pretty weird when you consider the origin of the name. I rang the guy up. I do that when I see people ripping us off: bootleggers, photographers, you name it. Normally they back down, meek as kittens. I get them to make a donation to the NSPCC, send me the receipt along with a T-shirt or whatever, and we part on good terms. But this guy wasn't having it. We ended up having a full-scale row and before I slammed the phone down I told him exactly where he could stick his vibrators. He's still selling them now as far as I know. Wanker.

Quite funny, really: I remember having an argument with Barry White about bootlegging. What he construed as bootlegging was someone copying his LP, selling it and not paying him royalties, whereas I thought bootlegging as somebody recording you live and putting it out as a live LP. So I was arguing from one standpoint saying, 'Well, it's a compliment, and it's good that the fans do it,' and he was going, 'Shut the fuck up, motherfucker, you don't know what you're talking about,' because of course we were talking about totally different things.

I suppose it all goes back to when we were investigated by the taxman because of the Haçienda and foolishly we went to meet them. You don't have to go, but our accountant let us. It wasn't a great meeting. The taxman tore us apart. Rob was shaking. One thing that did come out in the meeting was them saying, 'We've looked through all your accounts and can't see any receipt of monies for Joy Division T-shirts. Why is that?'

We went to great lengths to explain ourselves: how we didn't believe in self-promotion; we didn't believe in ripping off our fans; we didn't do merchandise because we thought it was blatant profiteering, the work of the devil, etc., etc. He listened patiently then said, 'How come wherever I go I see Joy Division T-shirts, then?'

We were stumped, struck dumb, and after what seemed like an eternity he said, 'I don't believe you and I'm fining you accordingly.'

The only band ever to get fined for not doing their own T-shirts. £20,000. Bang!

Anyway, after the name change, of course, the Nazi shit hit the fan. Changing our name to Joy Division, calling the EP *An Ideal for Living* and having a picture of a Hitler Youth banging a drum on the front of it – well, looking at it now, I can see the problem. I mean, *An Ideal for Living*? It even sounds Nazi. Not to mention the way we dressed and Barney shouting out about Rudolf Hess on the *Short Circuit* record. Let's face it, there was quite a lot of evidence against us.

But there was nothing more to it than a bunch of lads – Barney and Ian in particular – who were a bit obsessed with the war. Everybody was back then. We'd grown up with bomb craters behind our houses. It was the time of the big epic war films like *A Bridge Too Far*, and of *Warlord* and *Commando* comics. Little kids played with toy soldiers and big kids read Sven Hassell books. Everybody was fixated on the war and punks, being punks, focused on the most unpalatable, shocking side of it. This started with the Pistols, who often had swastikas on their clothes.

But it was about being shocking, not about ideology. We didn't have a political bone in our bodies – none of us did, not even Ian. Arty stuff was what he liked, not political. Yes, we were naïve and stupid and probably trying too hard to get up the noses of the older generation, but we weren't Nazis. Never have been and never will be.

Rock Against Racism had been formed in August 1976, in the wake of Eric Clapton's drunken comments supporting the National Front and a resurgence of interest in the far-right. The Anti-Nazi League was another organization formed in opposition, and would go on to organize awareness-raising concerts featuring the Buzzcocks among many others. Thus Joy Division's flirtation with Nazi imagery went very much against the political tide, and the band not only found themselves asked about it during many interviews but also began to lose local popularity. The Nazi imagery would turn off Tosh Ryan at Rabid Records, as well as Bob Last at Fast Product, both of whom passed on Joy Division, and in June Sounds *reviewed the* An Ideal for Living *EP with the headline 'Another Fascism for Fun and Profit Mob'.*

It followed us around for years. Me and Steve did an interview on French TV in 2004 and the first question was, 'Why did you glorify Nazism with the name Joy Division?'

We thought, 'Fucking hell, mate, you're talking about twenty-six *years* ago.'

All of that was yet to come, of course, and in the meantime we tried to put the shit-record fiasco behind us and concentrate on rehearsing and writing songs. Steve was so creative on the drums that we were riffing off that, and for the first time it felt like the group was four people matched in ability and vision.

Having said that, Ian, who was by now our driving force, did go through a period of being unhappy with Bernard, and called a group meeting when he was on holiday. According to Ian, Barney wasn't playing enough rhythm guitar – it was all lead stuff – and the group was suffering. Ian wanted that Iggy Pop wall of sound, whereas Barney was into the lightness and separation like the Velvet Underground. Though at the time we all agreed to get another rhythm guitarist in, at some point we must have come to our senses and realized that the band wasn't just about any one instrument, it was about all of us, and if we messed with that formula it was fucked. Thank God we did. Bernard's a brilliant guitarist. He knew exactly what he was doing, and that sparseness and space of his guitar lines was one of things that makes Joy Division special.

Anyway, it was me who ended up providing the rhythm guitar, because it was around then that I started playing high on the bass, all because of a new speaker I'd bought. I already had my Sound City amp (for which my mother, bless her, had taken a loan from A1 on Oxford Road) but I still needed a speaker. Every night I read the 'Articles for Sale: Musical Instruments' column in the *MEN*, and finally came across an advert for 'Bass Speaker £10' with a phone number. So I thought, *Great, it's in Salford*, and phoned up to say I was interested in it. 'What kind of speaker is it, mate?'

He went, 'Oh, it's a Celestion eighteen, two hundred watt.'

I didn't know what he was on about, so I said, 'Sounds good, I'll have it. I'm on my way now.' Drove up there, knocked, and my old art teacher opened the door.

'Oh, all right, sir, Mr Hubbard, sir?' I said.

'Peter, how are you? And you don't have to call me "sir".' And he invited me in.

'I didn't know you were a bass player, sir,' I said. Funny habit that; I still call him "sir" now.

'Oh yeah,' he said, 'I'm the bassist with the Salford Jets.' They were a very well known band in Salford and Manchester – the first band I ever saw live, funnily enough, as Smiffy in their glam-rock phase at the Willows. Mike Sweeney, the lead singer, is a lovely guy. Anyway, I couldn't try it. He said it sounded great with his set-up so I gave him the £10, got home, wired it up to my Sound City amp and it sounded dreadful, absolutely fucking awful. When I played a low note it farted. It made me feel physically ill to hear it. For a while I struggled with it, playing my farty low notes, but it was just awful. I couldn't even hear it above Barney's amp, not unless I played high on the neck of the guitar, and it was Ian who said, 'Oh, Hooky, when you play high, it sounds really good. We should work on that. Barney, you play the bar chords. Hooky, you play high and Steve do some of them jungle drums …'

That was how we got it – the Joy Division sound. We developed it in our new practice room at T. J. Davidson's. TJ's really became *our* place; we were one of the first bands in and nearly every other band in Manchester followed suit. We stayed there right up until the end of the group. It was where a lot of the famous Joy Division photographs were taken. Also where the 'Love Will Tear Us Apart' video was shot. An old, disused mill on Little Peter Street, it was split into many rooms with a band taking each one. Sad Café were in there; the Buzzcocks too. It had a great vibe – just right for our music – because everything had been ripped out then left. There was empty shelving everywhere, exposed pipes; the floorboards were filthy and covered in cigarette butts and there was even an old mattress at one end of our room.

When we first got in there it was great because the boiler was working so it was dead warm and, like all the other bands, we'd come in and gone, 'Oh, this is brilliant. We'll take a room for three weeks – no, a month.' But then the oil in the boiler ran out and was never refilled, and from then on it was absolutely freezing. We had to buy a little heater from a second-hand shop; Ian used to sit on it all the time but it gave him piles because his arse was dead warm but the rest of him was freezing. The rest of us could never get near it, of course, because we were playing, so he hogged it – and paid for his selfishness in piles.

We used a storeroom in TJ's, too, which was decorated with cans of our piss because the toilet was miles away so we used to piss in empty cans then stack them on the shelves, where they were always getting knocked over. Very funny, that was, when some poor unsuspecting bastard knocked over our cans of piss. We shared the storeroom with a band called the Inadequates, Gillian's band – Gillian Gilbert, of course, who later joined New Order and ended up marrying Steve – and we occasionally 'borrowed' their PA, like the night we played at the Oldham Tower Club.

It's a gig that never appears on any listings in books or on websites, but I'll never forget it. Sad Café had played there the month before and sold it out, which sounded encouraging to us. Plus we were getting thirty quid for the gig, which wasn't bad at all. So we borrowed the Inadequates' PA, got it to Oldham, had a good look round the venue, liked it, sound-checked, all the time really looking forward to the gig, thinking it was going to be a great night.

Nobody came. Not a soul. By ten o'clock there was still no one in, not even bar staff, only the manager, an old black guy, who said to us, 'You've got to go on. You've got to go on now. You've got to play.'

'But there's nobody here.'

'Well, tough. If you want the money, you've got to play.'

Whether he was taking the piss or not, I don't know, but after our third song he started sweeping up, and when the next song finished, said, 'Do you guys know any Hendrix?'

Ian said, 'No, mate. Sorry, mate.'

'Oh, shame, man. Shame,' he said, shaking his head.

We played our next song. Finished that.

'Are you sure you don't know any Hendrix?' he said.

'No, mate. Sorry, mate.'

'Oh, shame, man. Shame.'

So, anyway, we got about halfway through the set when these two punk girls came in, quite attractive girls, and we bucked up a bit. Wahey. Couple of fit girls in. Played another tune, finished, and one of the girls went, 'Hey?'

Ian went, 'What?'

'Are you the Frantic Elevators?'

The Frantic Elevators. *Fucking Mick Hucknall's band.*

Ian said, 'No. We are not the Frantic Elevators. We're Joy Division.'

She turned to her mate and said, 'See? I told you we was in the wrong club,' and they both left. That was it. We played the last three songs to an empty room, finished, packed the gear up, got our £30 off the guy and went home.

Because of that, the way I've always been is: if there's anybody there at all, I'll do the gig. I've had none at Oldham Tower club and 125,000 at Glastonbury, and with anything in between I'm happy. I accepted this DJing gig at Reading a while ago, but in the meantime got offered a mini-tour in Greece, which would have paid really well, so I phoned the promoter in Reading and said, 'Look, I've been offered this tour but it clashes. Is there any way of postponing the gig?'

He was like, 'Oh, sorry, Hooky, I can't. It's been advertised and every-thing. There's been loads of interest, lots of people coming.'

Grr.

So I blew out the Greek tour, drove down, got to my hotel, which turned out to be a B&B, and when I tried to talk to the promoter about what time he wanted me at the club, he was being really cagey. First of all, I'd have to play for only half an hour, he said.

'Well that's not very long, mate,' I said. 'I could do with a bit more time. It's already half-eight. What time do you open?'

And then he starts umming and ahhing and swerving the question.

Until in the end I almost lost it with him: 'Look, why don't you tell me what's going on?'

'I've got a confession to make, Hooky.'

'What?'

'There's no one here,' he said, 'but I'll pay you anyway, mate; I'll pay you anyway.'

I said, 'Look, it's only half-eight. Why don't we give it a bit longer and see if anybody turns up?'

So we drove down to the club, and I cooled my heels in the car park while he went in and checked. Then he reappeared looking shame-faced. 'No one in there. Look, I'll give you the money and take you back to the B&B.'

'What?' I said. 'So there's nobody there? No one? Not a soul?'

'Well, no, there's about eight people.'

'Well, fuck it,' I said. 'If there's eight people there, we'll do it. At least the eight people have had the decency to come out. Let's go.'

Lo and behold, we went and did it and I had the eight of them on stage with me, playing the tunes, dancing round. They were all New Order fans and it was brilliant, a really, really, good night.

'Wow,' the promoter said, 'I can't believe it. I wouldn't have thought you would have done it.'

'Listen, mate,' I said, 'I've played for no one before. Anything more than that is a bonus.'

Anyway – back in 1977 and at least things were looking up for our next gig, which was a New Year's Eve party at the Swinging Apple in Liverpool. I took the seats out of my Mark 10 Jag to get the Inadequates' (again, 'borrowed') PA in and take it to Liverpool, where we discovered that the Swinging Apple wasn't really a venue so much as a club; but for some reason they'd decided to put a band on as a special New Year's thing, and we were that band. But it was brilliant, actually. Everybody was dancing all night and we were in a fantastic mood, firstly because gigs had been a bit hard to come by during that period and we were pleased to at least be playing, and secondly because we'd been given a crate of beer. I was driving, as I always was back then, but still. *A crate of beer*. We got paid a lot of money for the gig, too – about sixty quid, if I remember correctly. I even think we played our set twice.

So it was a good end to what had been an eventful year. We'd got the band going, found a drummer and begun to really nail our style. Even so, we were waiting for something to happen. And we felt that something *needed* to happen. Something big.

TIMELINE TWO:
JUNE 1976–DECEMBER 1977

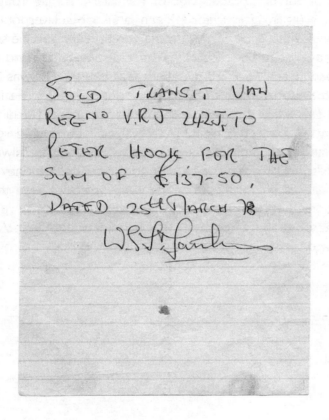

4 June 1976

The Sex Pistols play Lesser Free Trade Hall, Manchester. Peter Hook, Bernard Sumner and Terry Mason decide to form a band.

20 July 1976

The Sex Pistols play their second gig at Lesser Free Trade Hall, Manchester, with support from the Buzzcocks and Slaughter & the Dogs.

4 September 1976

The Sex Pistols make an infamous appearance on Tony Wilson's *So It Goes* for Granada TV. Peter Hook, Bernard Sumner and Terry Mason make contact with Ian Curtis, who joins the band.

> "One of our first practice rooms was above the Swan pub on Eccles New Road in Salford. Much later, around the time the Haçienda was taking off, Twinny started drinking in the Swan so I ended up going back – back to our old rehearsal rooms. It did my head in, really freaked me out. It was exactly the same, apart from the fact that the pictures were missing from the wall and you could see where the wallpaper around them had faded. I was bawling like a baby that night, I'm telling you. It brought everything back. Ian. Joy Division. We never used to talk about it. The years that followed Ian's death were for getting on with New Order and the Haçienda, not for mourning and wallowing, but every now and then something like that would catch you unawares. You'd walk into a room you associated with Ian and suddenly you were poleaxed."

1 December 1976

The Sex Pistols make their notorious appearance on the *Today* programme with Bill Grundy. After this they embarked on their Anarchy tour. Public outrage in the wake of the Bill Grundy interview saw to it to it that that most of the dates were cancelled. However, they did manage to play Manchester twice, at the Electric Circus on Collyhurst Street.

29 January 1977

The Buzzcocks' *Spiral Scratch* EP released. Produced by Martin Hannett, it becomes the third-ever UK punk single (after 'New Rose' by the Damned and 'Anarchy in the UK' by the Sex Pistols).

April 1977

The Electric Circus begins to host regular punk nights on Sundays.

29 May 1977

Billed as Stiff Kittens, Warsaw (later Joy Division) play their first-ever gig, the Electric Circus, Manchester, supporting the Buzzcocks and Penetration. Admission: £1.

> Stiff Kittens aka Warsaw aka whatever-they're-called-next-week rate zero even on my Mary Whitehouse odometer. The guitarist must be some refugee from a public school, the neatest thing about the bassist is his headgear and the singer has no impact whatsoever. By the fifth number or so they can just about put together a coherent riff, but I don't think even the most demented headbanger could get off to this. Someone tells me it's their first gig. So let's pass over the rest. Next, please.
>
> Probably the band's first-ever review: from an unidentified source, reprinted in *Joy Division and New Order – A History in Cuttings 1977–1983*

"Tony Wilson was in the audience. I can never remember anything if I'm nervous, and I must have been shitting myself about that gig because I can't remember a thing!"

31 May 1977

Warsaw play Rafters, Manchester, supporting the Heartbreakers. Admission: £1 at the door or 75p in advance from Fagins' reception.

June 1977

Slaughter & the Dogs' 'Cranked Up Really High' released on Rabid Records. Produced by Hannett and partly financed by Rob Gretton, who produced the Slaughter & the Dogs fanzine.

3 June 1977

Warsaw play the Squat, Manchester. Part of the Stuff the Jubilee festival; the bill also includes the Fall, the Drones, the Worst and the Negatives,

plus a new-wave/punk disco. Warsaw are joined by John the Postman singing 'Louie Louie'. Admission: 50p.

6 June 1977

Warsaw play the Guild Hall, Newcastle, supporting the Adverts, Penetration and Harry Hack & the Big G. Admission: 75p.

> "This was the first appearance of Barney's sleeping bag. Having piles was a feature of being in Joy Division. Ian got them from sitting on the heater at T. J. Davidson's and both Twinny and I got them from the van during the European tour in 1980. Terry Mason's would explode regularly. But you know what? As far as I know, Bernard never had piles, just a sore arse."

16 June 1977

Warsaw play the Squat, Manchester, featuring last on the bill after Harpoon Gags, Bicycle Thieves and Split Beans. The event is billed as 'Time's Up' (in homage to the Buzzcocks bootleg) and held in aid of the 'Windscale Festival', according to the flyers. Admission: 50p.

25 June 1977

Warsaw play the Squat, Manchester.

> "This was Tony Tabac's last gig. We'd been introduced to the Squat by Pete Shelley. He said, 'Oh, there's a place in Manchester where you can just turn up and play,' which sounded great because it was really difficult to get gigs; the normal clubs just weren't into punk gigs at all. At the Squat there would be more people from bands than there was audience. It was very dingy. There were no lights and it was freezing. Everyone who went there remembers it, though."

30 June 1977

Warsaw play Rafters, Manchester.

"This was Steve Brotherdale's first gig. A running-order squabble-fest with Fast Breeder led to us meeting a pre-Factory Alan Erasmus for the first time, as well as speaking to Martin Hannett by telephone."

July 1977

Warsaw enter 'A Talent Contest', the Stocks, Walkden.

"This was run by an agency from Bolton and the Stocks wasn't far from where I lived. The idea was that you just turned up and played and if you were good the agency would sign you up.

Perfect, we thought. *We can't go wrong.*

Things started to go wrong straight away, though, when the proper old-school compere asked us how we'd like to be introduced. Result: blank faces all round.

After struggling to get anything out of four inarticulate punks, he blurted out, 'Do you like Deep Purple?'

And with that he left for his build-up to a coachload of old ladies from the Farnworth Flower Arranging Club, during which he said the immortal lines: 'If you like Deep Purple you'll love these lads! Put your hands together for Warsaw!'

We trudged on and played but were too loud: our volume kept tripping the DB meter on stage, which then cut the power to our amps. Chaos. The old ladies all had their hands over their ears. We struggled through for a couple of numbers until Ian stormed off in disgust. When we went back into the dressing room to commiserate, he was buzzing.

'The female singer before us was changing when I came in,' he said. 'Saw her tits!'

With that we packed up and drove to the Ranch, where Foo Foo let us set up and play. Great gig; went down a storm. Those were the days. The Ranch was our regular haunt for ages, marred only by us getting chased by Teddy Boys occasionally. But it came to an abrupt end when the cloakroom gave Barney's leather jacket away one night – he went ballistic and we were barred."

18 July 1977

The Warsaw demo session, Pennine Sound Studios, Oldham. Tracks recorded: 'Inside the Line', 'Gutz for Garters', 'At a Later Date', 'The Kill' and 'You're No Good for Me'. These are the only recordings to feature Steve Brotherdale on drums.

20 July 1977

Warsaw play Tiffany's, Leicester, supporting Slaughter & the Dogs.

16 August 1977

The Buzzcocks sign to United Artists on the bar of the Electric Circus. Elvis Presley dies.

27 August 1977

Warsaw play Eric's, Liverpool, supporting X-Ray Spex. This is the band's first gig with Steve Morris, comprising two slots at the legendary Liverpool venue: a matinee in the afternoon for children and then an evening show.

> "Roger Eagle was a really nice guy. It struck you straight away, as soon as you met him, that he was different to other people. He was just a really nice bloke who loved music and looked after you."

14 September 1977

Warsaw play the Rock Garden, Middlesbrough. Set list: 'Reaction', 'Inside the Line', 'Leaders of Men', 'Novelty', 'At a Later Date', 'Tension', 'The Kill', 'Lost'.

> "Bob Last, the promoter, came into the dressing room after the gig. 'Anyone want a tape?' he said.
>
> No one but me replied, and this was the start of what was to become a collecting obsession. That tape he gave me is the only recording of us live as Warsaw and was the first time I'd ever been

able to listen to the group. What a great revelation – we were really good. Warsaw 'Live in Middlesboro', it was called: I treasured that tape for thirty years until it was stolen and bootlegged very recently."

24 September 1977

Warsaw play the Electric Circus, Manchester, supporting the Rezillos.

The Rezillos' roadie/manager Bob Last was an early supporter of Warsaw but would eventually baulk at singing them to his influential Fast Product label – legend has it because of the Nazi associations then dogging the band.

2 October 1977

Warsaw play the Electric Circus, Manchester, on the second night of the club's final weekend. The gig is recorded by Virgin for the *Short Circuit* album to be released the following year. The recording includes 'At a Later Date' and the release is later re-labelled 'Featuring Joy Division'.

7 October 1977

Warsaw play Salford College of Technology, supporting Slaughter & the Dogs, the Drones, Fast Breeder and V2.

8 October 1977

Warsaw play Manchester Polytechnic, supporting Slaughter & the Dogs.

13 October 1977

Warsaw play Rafters, Manchester, supporting Yachts.

19 October 1977

Warsaw play Pipers, Manchester, with the Distractions, Snyde and Nervous Breakdown.

November 1977

The Panik's *It Won't Sell* EP released on Rob Gretton's Rainy Days records – the only release for both band and label.

24 November 1977

Warsaw play Rafters, Manchester, supporting the Heat and Accelerator.

14 December 1977

The *An Ideal for Living* EP sessions, Pennine Sound Studios, Oldham. Tracks recorded: 'Warsaw', 'No Love Lost', 'Leaders of Men', 'Failures (of the Modern Man)'.

> "Not long ago I was DJing in Eden in Ibiza with this guy called Dave Booth from Garlands in Liverpool. On the flight home we got talking about places in Manchester and he mentioned that he DJed at Pips.
>
> I went, 'Pips? You're joking! Me and Barney took our first record to Pips for the DJ to play.'
>
> 'Yeah,' he said. 'That was me. I was the one who put it on – cleared the fucking floor, it did.'
>
> Small world . . ."

31 December 1977

Warsaw play the Swingin' Apple, Liverpool. This New Year's Eve gig is the last the band perform using the name Warsaw.

PART THREE

'Transmission'

'It was like *The X Factor* for punks'

We played our first gig as Joy Division at Pips, as I've already said. After that ... Nothing. Not for two long months.

It was my turn to manage the band. I was still working at the Ship Canal, and would phone up, say, Dougie James, who used to run Rafters on Oxford Street, hoping to get a support gig, *desperate* to get a gig. For us back then every minute without a gig felt like a week, like forever. So I was bugging the hell out of promoters, and especially Dougie, who was a nightmare to pin down.

I'd get him on the phone and he'd go, 'I'll speak to you later, mate. Come and see me. Bring me a tape.' Just fobbing me off. Always some excuse for not hearing me out. Twice I bussed it into town to try and catch him and speak to him face-to-face. Couldn't see him. On one occasion I went at dinnertime and had to walk back to work because I didn't have the money for a bus both ways. But I did eventually get to see Dougie, when I followed him into his office and more or less cornered him.

'All right, Dougie? I'm Peter Hook. We spoke on the phone. I was hoping to get a support gig for my band.'

He was sighing like he'd heard it all a thousand times before and, to be fair, he probably had. 'We haven't got any gigs. We've got no gigs. We've got loads of fucking supporting bands. We're all full up.' Blah, blah, blah. It's quite funny, really, because naturally I'm a bit shy but when it came to the band I never was. I was so driven and so desperate for the group to do well that I was always dead pushy, like I was then in Dougie James' office: 'Well, what about that Siouxsie & the Banshees gig you've got coming up? It's not even been advertised yet. You must need a support for that.'

He sighed again. 'Oh. Let me have a look. Let me have a look,' and he flicked through his book, pretending to look. 'Oh sorry, mate,' he said at last, 'I can't give you that one. Someone else is doing that.'

My face fell. 'Who?'

'Joy Division,' he said. 'Group called Joy Division are doing that; bad luck.'

I said, 'That's great because *we're* Joy Division.'

You've never seen anyone back-pedal like it. 'Oh no, no, no. I mean, I mean ... someone else is doing that. Look, fuck it, fucking don't bother me, all right. Get the fuck out.' He threw me out. That was it. I walked back to work feeling very down and demoralized, which is a feeling you have to get used to when you're managing a band, any band, but definitely ours at that time. We were hurting for gigs, and we needed a manager to help us get them.

The Stiff Test/Chiswick Challenge, a touring talent show set up by the two labels, came to Manchester Rafters on 14 April 1978. Local groups affected to scorn the enterprise for its London-centric air, but twelve or thirteen turned up to play anyway, hoping to impress the label heads. They included an impatient Joy Division as well as a 'joke' band, the Negatives, formed by journalist Paul Morley and photographer Kevin Cummins. Meanwhile, Ian Curtis barracked Tony Wilson for failing to feature Joy Division on So It Goes.

The Stiff/Chiswick night was like *The X Factor.* Except it was like *The X Factor* for punks, so a bit of a free-for-all and a very highly charged night indeed. The sight of our roadie, Platty, chasing Kevin Cummins out of Rafters, with him clutching his drum kit and screaming like a baby, is going to stay with me for the rest of my days – I hope.

It was Stiff we wanted to impress. They were *the* cool record label. They had Wreckless Eric and Kilburn & the High Roads – later to become Ian Dury & the Blockheads – and was run by a guy called Jake Riviera, a bit of a legend in the music business, who might sign you if he liked you. Needless to say we were dead keen to get on the bill but the competition was fierce. Like the last night of the Electric Circus, everybody turned up and everybody wanted to play.

Having already been shafted by Fast Breeder, we knew that if we went on too late all the punters would have buggered off, so we were desperately trying to get on as early as we could. Trouble was, so were all the other bands. It was already dog-eat-dog, with everybody thinking that this could be their big chance and arguing about who was going to go on, when Morley turned up with Kevin Cummins and some others in tow, taking the piss with their made-up punk group. They thought it was going to be dead funny to audition as a band who couldn't play. What a hoot. Maybe it would have been funny – I mean, let's not get all no-sense-of-humour about it – maybe we would have seen the funny side if we hadn't been a group who could play, were deadly serious about what we were doing, desperate to get a gig and a contract. We weren't writers or photographers larking about to make some obscure arty point that nobody understood anyway. This was serious for us. Life or death.

Morley started by telling us that they were going on first. And we were saying, 'Oh, fuck off, you're not fucking pissing about and pissing off the judges before we come on; you can fuck off.'

'No, we're fucking going on.'

'Fuck off are you.'

Ian was livid. One thing I remember about that night is that Ian was pissed and angry the *whole* night. Which was why he'd gone up and had a go at Tony Wilson, of course. I wasn't there for any of that, but I know in Debbie's book she says he first wrote Tony a note calling him a twat and all sorts, then went up to him to have a go at him for not putting us on TV. Tony was apparently pretty good about it, but I don't think he knew much about us at that point. He said on the *Joy Division* film that we were next on his list, but I'm not so sure about that. I don't think we were really on his radar then – not until that night, in fact.

Anyway. Our argument with the Negatives escalated. I was threatening Paul Morley, Ian was threatening Paul Morley, Barney was under a piano and Steve was hiding in the corner, and we finished by basically chasing the Negatives out, so they ended up not playing while we went on last, at about twenty past two in the morning, played about four or five songs and played our socks off. Being so angry gave us a bit of an edge – it always did – and it was probably one of our best performances. Well, we thought so. But we never heard from Mr Stiff, or Mr Chiswick, come to that.

Sounds writer Mick Wall called the band 'Iggy imitators', while Paul Morley of the NME, *evidently putting aside the evening's rivalry, wrote that 'with patience they could develop strongly and make some testing, worthwhile music.'*

Even more impressed was Granada TV's Tony Wilson, who later said, 'It took just twenty seconds of Joy Division's set to convince me that this really would be a band worth investing in,' as well as Rafter's resident DJ, Rob

Gretton, who, after his experiences with the Panik, was looking for a new band to manage. That night he decided he'd found one.

'[Joy Division] were blazing madmen,' Gretton later said. 'Best band I've ever seen. They sent a tingle up my spine. I was dancing all over [...] I went up telling them at the end, telling them how brilliant I thought it was [...] I went raving about them all next day.'

There were further developments. For some time Ian Curtis had been a regular face at the northern promotional offices of RCA Records, where he had befriended manager Derek Brandwood and his assistant, Richard Searling, a noted northern-soul DJ in his own right. Curtis had given Brandwood a copy of the An Ideal for Living *EP; though Brandwood had been unimpressed, his teenage son had liked it. Not long afterwards, Brandwood and Searling were asked by the owner of the American Swan Records, Bernie Binnick, if they knew of an English punk band available to do a cover of the northern-soul track by N. F. Porter 'Keep On Keepin' On'...*

I think he'd come into contact with RCA thanks to a part-time job he'd had at Rare Records – which is quite funny, because when I'd worked at the Town Hall I bought records from there, so I'd probably bought some off him. Anyway, he'd started hanging around their offices in Piccadilly Plaza. The guys who worked there used to give him records: Iggy Pop and Lou Reed. Trouble was, the other record they gave him was this N.F. Porter song called 'Keep On Keepin' On' that they wanted us to cover – but in a punk style. God knows why. I think they thought that RCA was missing out on the Manchester punk scene and maybe thought we were their way in. Where the northern soul connection came from I cannot imagine.

We listened to the record and hated it. We tried to learn it, but it changed into something completely different, which later became our song 'Interzone', but we turned up our noses at the idea of doing a cover. Then, at a meeting with the RCA guys and John Anderson, who was going to produce it, Ian and Steve were offered a deal. They started to hear things like, 'advance of £20,000', 'go and record in Paris' and 'American tours', which made them jump around, even making Steve squeal 'Paris' two octaves higher than normal, according to Ian. It all turned out to be a load of rubbish, though, because although we were impressed enough to take the deal we didn't get an advance and the studio wasn't in Paris. It was Arrow Studios in Deansgate, Manchester, and on the day we arrived there was a voiceover guy doing an advert for Littlewoods lotteries that I can still remember now: 'Littlewoods Lotteries. Things go better with Littlewoods ...' The guy kicked off proper when Ian walked in on him, tutting, 'How unprofessional.' We looked at each other – me, Barney, and Steve – and thought, *What have we got ourselves into here?*

But it was too late to back out and we ended up recording an album with John Anderson – and what a turkey it was. Everything he suggested ended up sounding cabaret and we were getting more and more frustrated, especially Ian, of course, who'd been thinking, *RCA: Lou Reed, Velvet Underground, Iggy Pop* ... only to hear it come out like the most awful un-rock-'n'-roll, anti-punk, most conventional sound you can imagine. Nothing like Iggy. Nothing like the Velvets. We'd be doing, say, 'Ice Age', and suggest having some wild feeding-back guitars on it, but John Anderson would scratch his chin and say, 'I was thinking more along the lines of getting some girls in to do backing vocals ...' Which we all know is the kiss of death.

Holy shit. It was awful. We ended up recording eleven or twelve songs with him, all the ones that ended up on the album, which – despite the fact that we were hoping it would never see the light of day, please, God – has since been bootlegged to death. Then we left the studio with our tails between our legs, feeling worse than ever.

We couldn't even get gigs. All the other groups in Manchester were trying to be a bit arty, like the Buzzcocks, but we weren't. We were just dead working class and had no pretentions. Ian, I suppose you'd say, was the most pretentious of us, with his love of Burroughs and Kafka and whatever, but I think when other groups looked at us they saw a bunch of yobs. So we were getting pushed out; we felt like outsiders, and nobody wanted us to play.

Not long after that I remember being manager again. I phoned up the Elephant & Castle one day from work and in my best phone voice said, 'Can I speak to the booker, please?'

And she went. 'All right, darlin', I'll put you through to the booker.' And then she went, 'Hello, booker, Elephant & Castle.'

And I said, 'Oh, hello there. My name's Peter Hook. I play in a band called Joy Division and we're trying to get support gigs in London ...'

She stopped me. 'What was that? What was your name?'

'Joy Division.'

'Listen darlin',' she said, 'you'll never get a gig in London with a name like Joy Division,' and hung up.

I didn't know what she meant but it didn't matter. I stared at the phone thinking, *Typical. Shit album. Shit single. No gigs.* We were at a very low ebb.

All I can say is: thank fuck Rob Gretton came along.

'We need to get rid of this Nazi artwork'

Barney was out from work in one of the phone boxes by Spring Gardens Post Office, talking to Steve, when suddenly this guy yanked open the door. A big bloke with a beard, wearing glasses that he pushed up his nose before he spoke.

'Fucking hell. You're out of Joy Division, aren't you?'

It was Rob.

'I watched you at the Stiff /Chiswick night,' he carried on. 'I want to be your manager.'

Christ, did we need a manager. Barney hung up on Steve, chatted to Rob and invited him down to see us at T. J. Davidson's.

Of course, Barney then promptly forgot and didn't tell any of us, did he? We were standing around playing when Rob came in, perched himself on the edge of a step and sat there, nodding in time to the music.

Me, Steve and Ian were looking at each other, like, *Who's this?* – with Barney off in his own little world, obviously. Then the song finished and there was an awkward silence as gradually we turned our attention to Rob, who looked at us, still nodding, as though he was pleased with what he'd heard. Until at last Barney said, 'Oh, lads, I forget to mention. This is Rob Gretton. He's the DJ at Rafters. He saw us play the Stiff/Chiswick night. He wants to be our manager.'

There was a collective sigh of relief. I wasn't the only who hated managerial duties: Ian couldn't do it; Steve couldn't do it; Barney couldn't do it; Terry certainly couldn't do it, God bless him. But without one we were fucked, so this was like offering a straw to a drowning man. Plus, of course, we liked Rob straight away; he seemed to know what he was talking about, probably because he'd already managed the Panik and had a lot of band experience working with Rabid and Slaughter & the Dogs. And, even though we hated Slaughter & the Dogs, and Rob had had precisely zero success with the Panik and in truth had the same managerial experience we all had, he seemed to say the right things.

The first being: 'This record's shit.' (Straight-talking would become his forte.)

He held up a copy of our *An Ideal for Living* EP.

'Yeah,' we mumbled.

He pushed his glasses up his nose. 'What we need to do is get it re-mastered. We need to make it into a twelve-inch.'

He was already referring to us as 'we', which I liked. This was some-one who was on our side.

Next he pointed at the picture of the Hitler Youth drummer. 'We need to get rid of this Nazi artwork, too.'

Music to our ears and to Ian's especially; he was desperate to recoup the money that he'd borrowed from the bank for his non-existent fur-niture – to get Debbie off his back as much anything.

So one of the first things Rob did was recover the masters and repress *An Ideal for Living* as a twelve-inch with a different cover, a pic-ture of some scaffolding on King Street, solving both the sound and Nazi problems. Next he persuaded Tosh Ryan of Rabid Records, which was Slaughter & the Dogs' label, to buy and distribute the rest of the seven-inches along with the twelve-inches. Paying us up front. The seven-inch ended up having an official release in June, the twelve-inch in October, and in one fell swoop Ian was paid off.

Now *that* is how you start off managing a group. We'd told him all about the Arrow Studios debacle and he cut a deal with John Anderson, offering him a grand for the master tapes. From then on any gig money we earned went into a pot managed by Rob, until we had enough to pay John Anderson and retrieve the tapes. (How, if we bought back the masters, did the record later appear as a bootleg, you might ask? That's a very good question, but one I can't answer here, because I've already given enough money to lawyers and have no desire to give them any more, thank you very much.)

By this time I'd sold the Jag and saved enough cash to buy an old petrol-blue Transit van. I was over the moon about that because I was sick of squeezing the gear in my car, or having to hire a van when we needed to take our own PA, which was a total ball-ache. I'd crashed a hired Bedford van when we did Pips. Only a little bit. It had a side hinge that jutted out from the door and I'd hit another car, taking the paint off and bending it a little bit. For that the rental place swiped my £20 deposit, but the rest of the group said it was my fault and refused to chip in. So having my own van was a massive relief. From then on, I drove it and all the gear, Terry and Twinny came with me, while all the rest of the group went in Steve's car. Having it made us more self-sufficient and meant that as long as Rob could get us gigs we could earn money. And he was good at getting us gigs.

In fact, from the moment he stepped on board things changed for us: because we couldn't organize shit and he could. You watch *Control* and the character comes into our lives like a whirlwind, with a big personality right from the start, but in real life it wasn't really like that. At first, he was calm, rational, quietly spoken and very logical, always scribbling away in his notebooks. Later he got more like his character in *Control*, when he became a very domineering, almost intimidating personality – he was a big guy and he used it. He could cut you dead and often did. He had a biting tongue. But in him we knew we had someone who shared our vision and had the same ideals, who wasn't going to suggest we hired backing singers or recorded northern soul covers. He was like us, but a larger-than-life version of us, a more forthright us.

Things started to happen right off the bat. I mean, apart from what I've already mentioned, just look at the way we started to develop when he became our manager: the relationship with Tony Wilson began, and we all know where that led; he got us involved with the Musicians' Collective, so we started playing gigs regularly; and we began getting known among the promoters. All of that gave us confidence to grow, leave Rob to go off and to do the shit we didn't like to do and concentrate on doing things we did. (Writing songs.)

We got better and better – we could tell, because a song like 'Transmission' suddenly was stopping traffic. I remember the first time. It was at the Mayflower club, Belle Vue on 20 May 1978, a gig we did with Emergency and the Risk. The Mayflower was a horrible hole with a pond of rainwater in front of the stage where the roof had gone and let all the water in like a moat. Normally we wouldn't have gone within a mile of the place but we did it as a favour to Emergency, who we knew very well. It was a bit of a you-scratch-my-back-and-we'll-scratch-yours set-up: we used to borrow their PA for out-of-town gigs and in return would help them out when we could. At this particular gig at the Mayflower they were promoting themselves as headliners, so they wanted decent support; they asked us if we'd do it, knowing we'd bring a few people along.

Rob was there with us that night – his first gig in charge – and it was also when we first met Oz McCormick and Ed, from Oz PA, who did the gig on the night and ended up being our sound guys for years. Right through Joy Division and New Order, out-front and fold-back respectively.

Not only that but we got plenty of time for a sound-check, during which we played 'Transmission'. We'd recorded it for the awful Arrow album but we hated that version and we'd worked on it a lot since – so this was the first time anybody outside of our circle had heard it as we wanted it to be heard. The funny thing about writing a song – any song – is that you never know how good it is when you write it. The last one always seems the best. We were lucky in Joy Division that we wrote several songs that are regarded as absolute classics: 'Digital', 'Disorder', 'Transmission', 'Love Will Tear Us Apart', 'Atmosphere', 'Shadowplay', 'She's Lost Control'. But we never thought, *This is a classic.* That isn't your place. We knew they were all right, mind you. But the best we hoped for was that they matched up to the calibre of the other stuff, the stuff we knew people liked. It was only when we played them live and gauged the reaction that we started to get an idea of how good they really were.

Playing 'Transmission' there was probably the first time that we had a real stop-the-press moment. I distinctly remember playing it at that sound-check and the crew turning around, the guys in Emergency and the other support band, the Risk, coming front of stage to watch us; the PA guys, too, were watching us instead of getting on with stuff.

We were looking at each other, like, *What the fuck's going on here?* because we'd never experienced that kind of reaction before. Looking at each other we were thinking that, maybe, just maybe, we might be able to make a go of this, a living out of it. We might just be able to pull this off. It was a big moment for the band. A big confidence-booster.

The gig itself, well, it went off all right, apart from the Risk's bassist getting a hiding from some of the crowd. Poor bloke was wearing a T-shirt that said, 'My fists are my side-arms' and I can distinctly remember standing there during sound-check, seeing this T-shirt and thinking, *That's a bold statement.* You've got to be fairly confident to carry off a T-shirt like that.

His band were a bit of a nuisance, to be honest: they spent the whole night arguing with us and Emergency. So I've got to say – and

God strike me down for it – I wasn't that bothered when a section of the crowd took exception to his T-shirt, dragged him off the stage and leathered him. Funnily enough, his fists weren't his side-arms.

Otherwise it was a great gig and as a band we were breathing one long, giant sigh of relief because Rob had parachuted in to take a whole load of pressure off us. Before, with managers – well, Terry, then each other – we'd always be looking over the shoulder of whoever was doing it, to make sure everything was being done properly, and then moaning accordingly. It was strange: when someone else was doing it you knew you could do it better, but when you did it everything went wrong. With Rob we didn't do that. He'd have told us to fuck off and kicked us if we'd dared.

Another of Gretton's managerial duties involved corresponding with Tony Wilson about his new protégés. On 19 April 1978 Wilson replied to his letter saying the band were the best thing he had heard in Manchester 'for about six months'. Nevertheless, Ian's desire for Joy Division to appear on So It Goes *was not to be. Wilson's music programme had ended, and as a result he was looking for new ways to stay involved in the music business. At the same time his friend Alan Erasmus ended his association with Fast Breeder and the two cast about for ideas, taking on management of the fledgling Durutti Column. They looked into venues in the hope of featuring the band and settled on the Russell Club, which they booked for four Fridays over two months. Located on Royce Road in Hulme and run by colourful local character Don Tonay, the Russell Club had been used by drivers for the bus company SELNEC and was well placed to appeal to the nearby student population. Erasmus saw a sign saying 'Factory Clearance' and suggested 'Factory' as a name for the club. To design a poster Wilson hired the services of graphic designer Peter Saville, who had introduced himself to Wilson at a Patti Smith concert. Saville earned £20 for the design, which used the colour scheme of the UK's National Car Parks and included a 'warning' sign from his college workshop; he also misspelt the club's name as 'Russel' (this error was repeated – perhaps intentionally – for the next two Factory club posters). Famously Saville delivered his poster – which was later given the catalogue number FAC 1 – two weeks into the four-week run.*

In the meantime, Tony Wilson had written to Gretton a second time, on 9 May, reiterating how much he liked the An Ideal for Living *EP and inviting Joy Division to play at the new club. They did, on the fourth night of the initial run, 9 June 1978, supporting the Tiller Boys.*

The Tiller Boys were very wacky. They stood chairs up in front of them on stage so you couldn't see what they were doing and played tape loops, probably inspired by the Pop Group and Throbbing Gristle. Cabaret Voltaire without the songs, really, which is saying something. That's about all I remember about that gig, funnily enough, despite the fact that it was the first Factory event to involve us and that it marked the beginning of a period during which we started to play a lot more regularly, really honing our sound and getting the message out there.

Rob had got us to join the Manchester Musicians' Collective, which used to meet in a room above the Sawyers Arms pub in the city centre. Dick Witts from the Passage was chairman and the idea was that all Manchester's musicians would get together and support each other, to stop some of the backbiting and treachery that generally went on between local bands. If truth be told, we revelled in the backbiting and treachery (would we have been as good at the Stiff/Chiswick night if the Negatives hadn't pissed us off? Probably not) but we wanted to get gigs. So despite that, and the fact that we secretly thought the whole thing was a bit poncey, we went along and listened. We'd heard they were going to put on a gig a month at the Band on the Wall, and we desperately wanted to play.

The collective was on to them. In the sleeve notes to the album Messthetics #106: The Manchester Musicians' Collective 1977–1982, *Kevin Eden of the Elite says, 'Joy Division joined and there was initially some grumbling that they were trying to grab gigs, but they allowed MMC to use their gear when possible.'*

So on the one hand we got to play more but this did mean that every now and then we had to meet to discuss music, which I thought was a monumental drag because they were so earnest and arty about it all and frankly it was like being back at school – like in a society or something. Steve didn't go, as far as I can remember, but me, Ian and Barney had to. Ian thought it was all right, mind you. He liked anything arty.

Meanwhile, the *An Ideal for Living* twelve-inch EP came out, and at last we had a record we could be proud of. Then the *Short Circuit* album came out, and suddenly we looked like part of a movement. As well as playing loads of gigs around that time we had a go at promoting; one such instance was at Band on the Wall, where we got a bit more 'Insight' into Rob's character.

What he'd done was spend all our money on a big PA because he believed we should sound the best we could and present ourselves in the best possible way. Not a bad philosophy, of course – no one's going to argue with that. Got a gig, all sold out, lots of profit? Let's put it all into a bigger PA and more lights. Nobody I've ever never met was as talented at spending money as Rob Gretton: he was the proverbial Big Spender – and that gig at the Band on the Wall saw the seeds of his philosophy being sown.

Only one of us noticed at the time, though: Ian. Before Rob came on board he was the one with the ideas. Musically he'd introduced us to loads of new stuff – Kraftwerk, Throbbing Gristle, Velvet Underground, the Doors, Can and Faust – and when it came to the direction of the band he was always the most forthright. He had the plan and the rest of us were his tools to carry it out, if you like. Having someone new arrive with plans of his own – notebooks full of them, in fact – well, there were bound to be problems. The rest of us were going, 'Yeah, yeah, do whatever you want, Rob.' Might as well have had rings through our noses, we were that easily led. But not Ian. It didn't take long for the pair of them to bang heads, the two dominant personalities of the group fighting for control.

The other thing Ian had to deal with was Debbie being pregnant. Not that Ian ever announced it as such; the news just gradually leaked out, but there it was – soon he'd have another mouth to feed. So there was even more reason why Rob's grand gesture didn't go down too well. Ian was probably thinking, *My slice of that PA would have bought a pram.*

Tell you what, though: it was a good PA and we did sound amazing. So Rob was right, I suppose – particularly because it turned out to be one of those gigs that did wonders for our profile. We got two good reviews from that gig, one in *Sounds* and one in *NME*, from Paul Morley, our former mortal enemy, who was comparing us to Magazine and the Fall, the two big post-punk groups. Then – at last – we got on the telly.

Joy Division's first TV appearance was on Granada Reports What's On, which was then in the habit of pre-recording local bands to broadcast when news slots suddenly became vacant. So it was that on 20 September 1978 presenter Bob Greaves, speaking live, introduced Joy Division by saying, 'We hope that we're launching them on a real "joy ride" as we have so many other others, haven't we, Tony?' Then there was a cut to a pre-recorded Tony Wilson, who said, 'Seeing as how this is the programme which previously brought you first television appearances from everything from the Beatles to the Buzzcocks, we do like to keep our hand in and keep you informed of the most interesting new sounds in the North West. This, Joy Division, is the most interesting sound we've come across in the last six months. They're a Manchester band (with the exception of the guitarist, who comes from Salford – very important difference). They're called Joy Division and this number is "'Shadowplay'".'

Fucking tosser – 'the guitarist who comes from Salford'? Two of us came from Salford. I was really annoyed. I was proud of my roots, whereas Bernard always played them down.

It was a momentous day, though. Rob again decided that we needed to invest in ourselves and took us to town shopping. We all got new shirts to wear on *Granada Reports*. Two pounds fifty each, they were, and we felt dead spoilt, like dogs with our bellies tickled: fantastic. But also another example of Rob's – what would you say? – 'unique' managerial style, because he'd never just give you the money to go and get a shirt for yourself; oh no, he'd have to buy it for you. Me, Barney and Steve: fine about that. We all lived with our parents; we were used to being mothered (it turned out Steve's mum bought all his clothes anyway) and were over the moon with our new shirts. Ian: not so fine. Whether it was Debbie bending his ear or what, I don't know, but he always took exception to things like that.

Later on, in New Order, Rob would behave the same, except the stakes were higher then, so it would be, 'Look, here's two grand, give yourself a holiday.' Or, 'Here's money for a car.' But it all started off with that blue shirt that I'm wearing to play 'Shadowplay' on *Granada Reports*.

The other thing about that performance is that I had blond hair. The reason for that is that after we'd changed our name to Joy Division we thought we needed a gimmick; and, during a group meeting in a pub in

Piccadilly, it was decided that we were all going to bleach our hair. The next day I bought a hair kit called 'Born Blonde'. It cost £1.25, dead expensive. Got home, put the plastic cap on, bleached my hair, got a clip round the ear from my mum for it. She hated it – hated anything like that, God rest her soul. She kicked the shit out of me when I got my first tattoo, then didn't speak to me for three weeks. I was thirty-two!

Anyway, I'd dyed my hair, and next time I went to rehearsal was dead excited about seeing everyone else with their blond hair. Except when I got there it turned out that I was the only one who'd done it – and them lot were laughing their arses off at me.

Those fuckers.

I went, 'I thought we were all bleaching our hair blond!' And they just laughed. They'd stitched me up, the bastards.

Apart from that, it was a good performance, and I remember enjoying the day, being overwhelmed to be in Granada studios. Me, the big *Corrie* fan. Then recording it, and being really pleased with how it came out, because it was a good showcase for what we were about, really. I mean, you see Ian's dancing. Not nearly as full-on as it was when we played live but it's there; Bernard with his guitar high, picking out those dead-brittle guitar lines; Steve, like a machine; me with my bass starting to get low.

The low bass was an idea I got when I saw the Clash at Belle Vue and was fixated by Paul Simonon, who looked the dog's bollocks – one of the coolest men ever. Staring, I thought, *How come he looks so good compared to other bass players?* Then I realized it was the strap. He was playing the bass dead low. There and then I decided it was a long strap for me from then on.

Ah, but what I discovered when I got home was that that my playing style is nothing like Paul Simonon's, which is easy to play with a long strap. My kind of bass? Really hard to play with a long strap.

Didn't stop me, though. Fuck it: I dropped my strap by about six inches and – typical of me, always taking everything to obsessive levels – carried on dropping it until I was physically bent double. All of which meant that I ended up playing the bass high, which is my sound, but with the lowest strap, because what happens is that the lower you play, the more you have to bend your hand over, to play the notes, and that's the hard bit, that bend. Which is also why I make so many bum notes. I'm renowned for them.

Sound-wise I was most influenced by Jean-Jacques Burnel of the Stranglers. I used to listen to his bass on 'Peaches' and '5 Minutes' and think, *That's how I want to sound.* When I went to see them at the Bingley Hall in Stafford I wrote down his equipment, a Vox 2×15 cab and a Hi-Watt head, then went out and bought the lot, and it was magnificent, sounded wonderful. So, I got my sound from Jean-Jacques and my strap from Paul Simonon. I'm so pleased I never got into Level 42.

It was around about that time that we played a gig where one person turned up. The Coach House in Huddersfield on 28 September 1978. We'd borrowed the PA that night, either from the Inadequates or Emergency — one of the two, or both — and lugged it all the way up these really steep, winding stairs, only to get one person in the audience. A bloke who stood there for half the gig then left. I mentioned it in a newspaper interview and all the fans online were going, 'What's Hooky talking about? What gig in Huddersfield?' It wasn't well advertised, which was the reason it had slipped through the net. Then not long after that piece was in the paper a guy came up to me somewhere and said, 'Hello. Do you remember me?'

'No, sorry,' I said.

He said, 'I'm the guy who came to see you in Huddersfield. It's me.'

'No way!' said I.

Joy Division's relationship with Roger Eagle of Eric's in Liverpool was partly responsible for Eagle suggesting to Tony Wilson that they join forces and release a compilation album. Names suggested for the Manchester-Liverpool union included Joy Division, the Durutti Column and Pink Military, but the project faltered at the negotiating stage when Eagle preferred a conventional twelve-inch format while Wilson, having dropped acid, had conjured an image of a double-seven-inch pack. He had the money: a £5,000 inheritance from his mother, who had died in 1975; the idea was greeted favourably by Saville, Erasmus and Hannett; and so the A Factory Sample EP was conceived, with the release to feature contributions from Joy Division, the Durutti Column, John Dowie and Cabaret Voltaire. Graduating from club night, Factory became Manchester's fourth independent label after Rabid, New Hormones and Object (the label started by Steve Solamar, the Electric Circus DJ) and at the vanguard of independent labels in the UK.

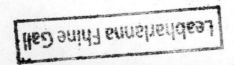

We weren't signed and didn't have a publishing deal, so when Rob told us that Tony Wilson wanted to meet us, and maybe put one of our songs on his EP, we were like, 'Wow, yeah, sounds great.'

Well, when I say that, what I mean is that me, Barney and Steve sat there scratching our heads while Rob and Ian discussed it – and how it was an EP of bands that Tony Wilson, *Mister Granada,* liked, the bands he'd picked up on and was championing, so it was also an establishment of loyalty between us and Factory as much as anything else.

Money never came into it, of course. That was one thing we never really talked about in the early days. 'How much are we getting for doing it?' 'What's the deal on the record?' 'What's the split, man?' There was none of that, which was wonderful because it was just about going forward, working with people you liked and trusting that the rewards would come. Now, having had more experience, I know that we should have done a deal. Or certainly Tony should have done a deal. The songs on the Factory sampler belonged to us, even though he'd paid for them to be recorded. No way would that happen now, and it happened then only because both parties were young and naïve and a bit too idealistic. I mean, looking back, we had 'Digital' on the sampler, one of our best early songs and a possible hit in its own right. Yet we put it on the Factory sample, limited to 5,000 copies. We were giving away the chance to have a hit single: not the cleverest move in the world, surely.

But we were all in the same boat and Tony was as naïve and idealistic as we were. We first met him in a pub, the Sawyer's Arms again, I think it was, and were bowled over by his enthusiasm. For whatever reason we hadn't had a lot to do with him when we did the *Granada Reports* recording, so this was our first opportunity to get the measure of him. We felt like we were in exalted company. He dressed much older than we did. He was still wearing all that tail-end-of-glam gear: velvet jackets, big collars, big kipper ties. He always wore a suit because of his job, whereas we were all punk, but I liked him straight away. He made us feel very welcome and comfortable. He wasn't at all intimidating or threatening; even though intellectually he could run rings around us all day he never made us feel like that. He wasn't one of those people you got to know well – he was never a close mate – but he was a colleague and he certainly had an aura and presence, and we were in awe of him right from the word go. I mean, he was on TV and you can't overestimate that. I was watching him every night at six o'clock so to suddenly be sat next to him was wild. It felt like an amazing aspect to what we were doing, that we got to meet people like Tony Wilson. *The* Tony Wilson. Who liked our band, liked what we were doing, wanted to make a record and put us on it.

He and Ian hit it off most, of course, probably because Ian was more on his intellectual level as well as being a lot more worldly about music. The thing about Ian was that he was into the bands we all grew to love; he was into them first. Not only that but he could also talk in depth about them in a way that appealed to Tony. You could tell that he was pleased to have this equally knowledgeable guy around, and you could tell that Tony felt the same way. I doubt there were many people who worked at Granada who knew about Throbbing Gristle.

So that was it: it was decided that we'd do the EP with Tony; go into Cargo Studios in Rochdale and record it with Martin Hannett.

Which brings me to Martin. I think we'd heard of Cargo Studios – it was the most famous punk studio in the North. I think the Gang of Four had done their record there, which was a great record, and John Brierley was renowned as an excellent engineer/producer. [*This was the 'Damaged Goods'/'Love Like Anthrax'/'Armalite Rifle' single, recorded at Cargo for Fast Product with John Brierley as the engineer.*]

I've also since found out that John was a proposed original member of Factory. So when it first started out it was Tony, Alan Erasmus, Peter Saville, Martin Hannett and John Brierley, with John putting the studio into the partnership. The idea was that Martin was going to produce the bands, Saville would do the sleeves, Tony would be the talking head and Alan Erasmus would be the enforcer. Saying that, I don't think that from that day to this anyone has ever figured out exactly what Alan Erasmus did in Factory – he was just incredibly important in some way no one can seem to figure out. He always was, and remains, a complete mystery, a true enigma. The funny thing about Alan is that he always moans about his lack of presence in the Factory legacy but just you try coaxing him out of the woodwork to get involved. He was moaning to me about the Grant Gee Joy Division documentary, saying, 'How come I'm not in it? Cheeky bastards never asked me.'

So I said to him, 'Look, I'm making a Factory documentary; why don't you come and meet me and you can be on it?' He said yes and came down. I stuck the microphone in his face and asked the first question. All of a sudden he spluttered, turned puce, then remembered a prior engagement and ran away. Literally ran away. So he's his own worst enemy without a shadow of a doubt. Big heart, though.

Anyway. Back to John Brierley. John sussed out pretty quick that the Factory lot were a bunch of amateur, disorganized lunatics, so he bailed. Pretty smart move. He just said, 'Pay me as usual for the studio,' and went to being the engineer for the Factory sampler, with Martin as the producer. We went in with our two songs, which were 'Digital' and 'Glass', which I think were the two newest songs that we liked the best – as I said, it's always your most recent material that you rate the most highly. So in we went and met Martin Hannett for the first time. I'd seen him before; I saw him play bass in Greasy Bear once, in a clothes shop in Manchester. But this was the first proper meeting.

Prior to opening Cargo, John Brierley had worked at Granada. He'd built his own mobile recording truck in an ex-ambulance that had been used for recording bands on Tony Wilson's So It Goes, *and at the end of 1977 left Granada to open Cargo on Kenion Street in Rochdale, running it from 1978 until 1984. Gang of Four's arrival in 1977 paved the way for the post-punk bands who liked it for its 'live' sound, while its most famous client was Martin Hannett, who recorded, among others, Joy Division, Orchestral Manoeuvres in the Dark, Durutti Column, Crispy Ambulance, A Certain Ratio and Section 25 there. Hannett liked the sound of Cargo, while the reasonable rates of hire gave him the freedom to experiment.*

'Whenever he was in for a session he would bring all this extra gear in,' writes Brierley on cargostudios.co.uk, 'his AMS Digital Delays, AMS Digital Reverbs, several synths and that along with all my Rebis delays and noise gates, Compressors, MXR delays, MXR harmonizers and echo plates, Roland chorus units, various analogue delays and effects [meant] he had a phenomenal amount of choices. Because he had so many choices it was inevitable that he would come up with some interesting effects, and many of his good sounds came about by accident. I was always impressed by his use of very fast delay on the snare drum, it did sound good and very punchy. His mixes were a combination of very obvious effects and a lot of very subtle effects, just a hint of delay here or a touch of reverb there. The result was often stunning.'

Hannett, meanwhile, was counting his blessings. He loved the 'space' in Joy Division's sound and was especially impressed with Steve Morris's drumming – not to mention the fact that the band never argued with him. 'They were a gift to a producer,' he said, 'because they didn't have a clue.'

Cargo was great. It was a converted warehouse that from the outside looked like a factory unit but inside was stuffed with gear. It had dry-stone and brick walls and thick hanging drapes everywhere, and we arrived to find Martin already ensconced in a vast black leather chair behind the desk, John Brierley running around and virtually no room for anyone else.

I think we all thought Martin was a bit bonkers, because he was a weird, larger-than-life character, no doubt about it, even at that stage before the drugs got hold of him. Thinking back my first impression of him was his big curly hair and the trampy, hippy look he had going on. That and the non-stop smoking – dope and cigarettes – so that the atmosphere in the control room was like that of a wizard surrounded by smoke and in charge of his strange machines – a lunatic wizard who never used one word when he could use twenty-one, nineteen of which you couldn't understand.

John Brierley, on the other hand, was the opposite: a straightforward, very business-like, quite formal bloke. Bit brusque, you might almost say, but I got on well with him.

We didn't realize it then, of course, being so green, but Martin and John, they were two of the best, certainly in the region, probably in the country, and Cargo, despite its size, was a great studio. For a start we were recording on a sixteen-track, which was for us – when you bear in mind that our demos were done on a four-track and the *An Ideal for Living* EP on an eight-track – a big step up. Cargo had a Cadey sixteen-track machine using two-inch tape. It was a valve recorder, making it really warm- and fat-sounding and frankly the best recording medium that you can ever use. Sounds immense. We were delighted about that. All of which made it an easy session. Tony and Alan were floating about that day, so the Factory lot were very much in attendance, and the atmosphere was good. The whole thing, in fact, was very, very straightforward, none of the fooling about with Martin that would come later. He put some sound effects on. You can hear them in 'Digital' and 'Glass', which both sound amazing – *easily* our best record-ing up to that point – but I don't remember him doing it while we were there. My main feeling was just, *yes*, because my parts sounded good. It's only when your work starts disappearing that you get fed up. So if you listen back you'll hear a happy me, because the bass on 'Digital' is kicking it. As a musician your ego and self-confidence really grow if your part is getting used, whereas they can take a huge blow if your part is downplayed, which is what happened to me on 'Atmosphere' later on. On that record Martin mixed the bass down, but when we played it live it was loud in the mix. During the session I was like, 'No, no, make it louder,' but Martin just grinned and told me I was outvoted. Now I listen to 'Atmosphere' and I think it's ... okay. But he must have been going off me because on *Closer* he mixed the bass right down. The guitar too, actually. Both Barney and I fell out with him on *Closer*.

Anyway, all that was still to come. During this particular session I was feeling pretty good about my contribution, but other than that I just kept myself to myself. You've got to remember that we were in the presence of some pretty big characters: Rob, Tony, Alan, Martin, so us lot just sat in the corner quaking.

After the session we did the sleeves. It was a double-seven-inch and we got paid to put them together. I think we went to Alan's flat at Palatine Road. I seem to remember that it was in was the scruffy hippy kitchen that we did it. Tony didn't have to pay us really, but me, Ian and Barney got 50p for every 100 that we folded and put in the sleeves, 5,000 altogether. Not for the last time, either. Later on, Factory released the Durutti Column's debut, *The Return of the Durutti Column*, which came in a sandpaper sleeve, and I got paid for sticking bits of sandpaper on to 2,000 Durutti Column albums.

Inspired partly by Far Eastern record packaging and partly by the arty designs of Fast Product releases, Tony Wilson suggested a heat-sealed gatefold format for the A Factory Sample *package. Peter Saville's design echoed his poster for FAC 1, and the EP included a set of stickers, one to represent each band, with Joy Division being a sailor's marionette. Its intricacies, however, made it more difficult to assemble than anticipated and a Christmas Eve release had to be postponed. Tony had scheduled* A Factory Sample *for release in December 1978 but Peter Saville missed the deadline for completing the artwork, pushing the release date back to January 1979. Wilson, however, was determined to give copies of the EP as Christmas presents to all the musicians who had played on it. So on Christmas Eve he photocopied Peter Saville's design and made his own sleeves with careful use of paper and glue, putting in the already pressed discs and delivering them himself, like a punk Santa Claus, to the homes of the twenty musicians, including Ian Curtis, Stephen Morris, Bernard Albrecht and Peter Hook. A Factory Sample eventually appeared in two batches in January and February.*

In the meantime we resumed playing live, still in the North West and mainly in Manchester but elsewhere too. On 24 October we played the Fan Club at Brannigan's in Leeds, a really nice club in a very dodgy area, the red-light district. It was a good gig; I didn't think too much of it until not long after, when I answered a knock at the door one night and there stood two plain-clothes police officers on the doorstep, faces of stone.

'Yeah?' I said.

'Can we speak to the owner of a blue transit, VRJ 242J,' said one of them.

(And that again, by the way, is the *actual* registration number of the van. How I can still remember it after all these years is beyond me, but I do. When I told Anton that detail for *Control* he laughed; he thought I was mad.)

'Oh, yeah, that's me,' I said. 'I'm the owner.' Thinking, *Aw, no, what's this all about? Tax? Insurance? Speeding?*

A lot worse than that, it would turn out.

'Right, we need to talk to you.'

They came in. Still I thought it was motoring: I had a bent MOT on the van. I'd bought it for a tenner, couldn't afford to fix it ...

'Right,' he said, when we were all sat down. 'We've had reports that your van has been seen in the red-light districts of Bradford, Huddersfield, Leeds, Moss Side ...' He looked at me. 'Want to tell me why that is, son?'

For a moment my mind went blank. All I could think was: *Yorkshire Ripper.* This was during the time they were searching for him. He preyed on prostitutes in Leeds, Bradford, Manchester ...

'Oh, hang on a minute,' I said, 'I'm in a group. I play bass in a group. Where you're saying, they're gigs we've played.'

They looked at each other, all doubtful like. 'What's your group called?'

'Joy Division.'

'Never heard of them.'

Probably Level 42 fans.

'Really,' I insisted. 'I play bass and all the gigs that we play are in the red-light districts.'

'Why's that then?'

'Well, we're sort of a punk group and they're the kind of places punk groups play.'

'Can you prove that, then?' he said.

'What, that we're a punk group?'

'No, that your group has played in those places.'

'Oh, yeah, yeah, of course,' I said. 'Our manager's got all the dates written down. And proving it's no problem. We've had punters – I mean, audience – watching, you know. And we've been reviewed and stuff.'

They seemed satisfied. 'Well, in that case, we won't ask you to come to the station or anything, but you must bear in mind that you're appearing in all these areas where there have been Ripper killings, so you can consider yourself under investigation.'

I was nodding like a bastard, pleased to be off the hook, as it were. 'Yeah, yeah. I'll give you any help I can, anything you want.'

And he went, 'Right, okay, we'll leave it at that for now.'

Off they went. And, though I breathed a sigh of relief, I chuckled a bit about it, too.

The next day I got a call from Steve.

'All right, Hooky. Have you had the police round?' he said, voice trembling.

'Yeah,' I said. 'They came and asked me about the red-light district and all that. Did they come to you?'

'Yeah,' he said. 'They came round and I panicked and they arrested me.'

Oh dear. He was so nervous they'd thought they had their man, dragged him off to the police station, cuffed him, locked him up and interviewed him. His mum had to come down and rescue him.

Oh, did we laugh. Not that it was particularly surprising. Poor old Steve. We used to call him Shakin' Steve, he was that nervous all the time. The police must have taken one look at him and thought, *Got him. We're looking promotion in the face.*

119

'The biggest rain of spit I've ever seen in my life'

In November we joined a tour with the Rezillos and the Undertones. A bit of an ill-fated tour, that one, because the Rezillos fell out following the first gig, after which it was just a matter of time before they split.

What's more, the Undertones were all very young, about fourteen and fifteen, and this was the first time they'd been away from home so they were really, really homesick. Us, though, Joy Division? We were okay. I mean, I thought it was a bit of an odd billing because they were a pair of power-pop bands and we were ... what we were. But we were pleased to play, to get the gigs, to do the travelling. Plus we got to stay in hotels and B&Bs for the first time, which was pretty exciting. First time we'd stayed away from home for a gig.

But then of course the Rezillos had this big bust-up. We played Brunel the next night and I remember that well for two reasons. Firstly because the Rezillos singer, Faye, got changed in front of us and our eyes were on stalks as we tried desperately not to look. She probably didn't have much choice, it being a shared dressing room and all, and being in a band I'm sure she was quite used to decking off in front of the other guys, but even so we were shocked. The second reason was that the crowd wouldn't stop spitting. There was a gap between the stage and the crowd, like a no-man's land, and every now and then some twat would run into the space and gob at Ian as we were playing. So I started twatting them with my bass. It had this hook on top of the headstock, the Hondo, and every time one of these little fuckers darted through the crowd to gob at Ian I swiped him in the ear with the top of the bass. I got about ten of them that way, little bastards. There was a speaker stack in the way so they couldn't see me when they came running in. Got a nice surprise.

Even so, there were too many, and we called it a day after seven numbers and fucked off. It's horrible, spitting. I remember one awful night where the Buzzcocks were getting spat at at the Electric Circus and it was happening so much that Pete Shelley ended a song early.

'Stop the gig, stop the gig, stop the gig,' he squealed. 'Listen, right, if you lot don't stop spitting, we're not going to play.' The crowd stopped. It lasted for about three seconds before he was showered in the biggest rain of spit I've ever seen in my life. Everybody just spat at him all at once – and he shrugged and played on. Should have walked off. That was how Joe Strummer got hepatitis, from swallowing someone's spit. Disgusting.

Anyway, a couple of the gigs were cancelled because the Rezillos had walked off the tour. Then when we turned up to the Locarno in Bristol to play we were told that *we* were off the tour. We'd done the sound-check only to be suddenly told that they'd brought Chelsea in instead, and John Otway. Fuck me, we had a massive row with them. Gene October, Chelsea's singer, was such a twat and was being so fucking arrogant that Ian wanted to kill him, to bottle him. Rob was freaking, too. It went the way all fights between gobby Cockneys and gobby Mancs go:

'You fucking Manc bastards, I'll have you.'

'You bunch of Cockney twats. We'll fucking do you.'

Ian started throwing punches, and the Chelsea guys were hitting back. We were just so fucked off because we really wanted to play. I mean, I still don't know why the Rezillos leaving the tour meant that we had to leave the tour, too; why didn't they just put us and the Undertones on? But in the end we were actually physically ejected, chased out of the building.

It was not long after that they we had our first gig in London, at the Hope & Anchor. Bernard's sleeping bag made another appearance. That night we discovered that there was something wrong with Ian. Something really wrong.

First off, it was a really big thing for us to play London. We were dead excited and nervous about doing it, as though the whole of London would be there to look at us. In reality the gig was in the base-ment of the pub. The Hope & Anchor is a legendary venue, don't get me wrong, but still: it was hardly the Marquee. It was a nightmare jour-ney into London to get there. The others hadn't turned up, so it was left to me and Twinny to unload and set up the gear. We had to load it down the beer chute into the basement, which was cold and damp, pretty horrible, if I'm honest. Meanwhile, the rest of them – Steve, Ian, Bernard, Rob and I think Gillian was there, too – had been lost because Steve was a rotten driver, a terrible driver. He collects tanks these days, of course, and all I can say is that I hope he never takes them for a spin because he is the world's worst. He held some kind of Macclesfield record for having the most driving lessons and tests. Something like 400 driving lessons and twenty-five tests. He was so nervous. Insisted on driving with a cigarette in his hand so he'd only ever have one hand on the wheel.

'Put both hands on the wheel!' they'd scream. Whenever he followed the van in the Cortina he'd always drive way too close. So close that I'd have to stop and say to him, 'Steve, listen, you're driving too close, mate; you've got to back off, 'cause if I have to brake you're going to kill us all!'

Also, we had this sort of flimsy 'no girlfriend' rule, one of Rob's ideas: it was okay to bring your girlfriend along to a gig in Manchester but not to away gigs. There wasn't any sleazy reason for it; it was just logistics, really. You've got your band, your crew, your gear. There isn't really the room for girlfriends; it made sense. But not to Steve – Steve would always bring his girlfriend along. First it was Stephanie, and because there was no room for her she'd have to sit on someone's knee all the way to Sheffield or Aberdeen or wherever. Then, of course, when he started going out with Gillian he began taking her along to every gig too.

I can't say for sure whether she was with him that night. What I do remember is them all turning up expecting to get warm, then coming into the basement of the Hope & Anchor and their faces falling when they discovered that it was freezing down there. This was especially bad news for Bernard, of course, who had the flu. We had to literally drag him from his sick bed just so he could make our first big London gig, only to find that it was in this cold basement – no heaters or radiators. Probably didn't have a toilet either. Honestly, kids in bands these days, they don't know they're born. (And yes: I know I sound like an old fart but fuck it, it's my book.) They don't. With their sound-men and stage managers, and over-proud parents, poncing in and expecting everything laid out for them. You go to a gig now, like at the Academy or some-thing, and it's got toilets with paper in them, and central heating and everyone gets a rider and coffee and clean towels and all that. Not in 1978, you didn't. Most gigs were like that one: complete chaos: 'There's the stage; set up and shut up.'

Most times you managed to muddle on through and a mixture of good luck, better songs and the love of it all magically creating a great gig. But we didn't have luck on our side that night; we were fresh out of the love of it all and even the songs sounded diabolical and there was no fucker there. I tell a lie: there were twenty people there. Got us our first bad review, too: 'Joy Division were grim but I grinned.' Cheeky bastard. Afterwards I did the sums: it had cost us £28.50 in petrol to do the gig and we'd earned £27.50 from the door, so we'd lost a quid doing it. When it was all over we packed up our stuff and drove home.

We were driving down the motorway together, me checking in my rear-view mirror occasionally. Obviously I'd warned Steve to back off because he was scaring the shit out of me; and I was pleased to see that he was taking notice at last when all of a sudden they disappeared. My heart sinking, I pulled over on the hard shoulder and we waited – and waited.

Don't forget that in those days there was no traffic. You could be stopped on the hard shoulder of the M1 for an hour and not see another car. So we sat there in the freezing cold. We couldn't keep the heater running, of course, because it was a waste of petrol, so we just shivered in the cab of the van, rubbing our hands together to keep warm, moaning about them. Like, maybe they'd broken down. Maybe they'd stopped for something to eat. It would be just like them to stop off for a fry-up. But then again, no. Bernard, the last I saw of him, had looked like something out of *Night of the Living Dead*, he was that full of the flu. They were potless anyway, plus I hadn't seen any services open along the way. No, they couldn't have stopped.

So maybe they'd broken down. Well, if they'd broken down they'd be all right because Steve was in the AA. I wasn't even sure I had enough petrol left to go back for them *and* get home anyway. We had no room in the van anyway. So in the end we made a decision: we'd go home. Which is what we did, and it was only the next day in work that I phoned somebody and they told me what had happened. I just remember thinking, *Oh shit. There's something wrong with Ian.*

During the return journey from the gig there had been a minor altercation in the car. Disconsolate about the evening's performance, Ian had been talking about leaving the band and then pulled flu-ridden Bernard's sleeping bag from him. Having wrapped it around his head, he began lashing out at the doors and windows: he was fitting. The others pulled the car over on the motorway and laid Ian down to restrain him on the hard shoulder. This event culminated with a shaken Steve Morris taking the cigarettes out of Ian's pocket, as immortalized in 24 Hour Party People. Then they drove him to the nearest hospital, Luton and Dunstable, where he was given tablets and referred to his doctor. Ian was dropped home to a worried Debbie by Steve and Gillian, and was given an appointment to see a specialist. In the meantime he began having more fits – three or four a week – until on 23 January 1979 at Macclesfield District and General Hospital he was officially diagnosed with epilepsy and prescribed more tablets.

VIRGIN RECORDS LIMITED

A R T I S T R O Y A L T Y S T A T E M E N T   ARTIST   Joy Division

Period 1st January 1979 to 30th June 1979

Balance at 31st December 1978   £ ....74.86..........DR/CR

Add Advances to date   £

28.2.79   De Cross-Collateralisation
             of Publishing Royalties   136.19

                                    £   .....136.19...........

Less Royalties for period

28.2.79   Publishing Royalties for
             period ended 31.12.78   36.19
30.6.79   Recording Royalties   17.44
30.6.79   Publishing Royalties   28.50

                                    £   82.13
                          BALANCE DUE/DUE

                                    £ _____20.80_____

24 January 1978

Tony Wilson and Alan Erasmus devise their 'management project', the Movement of the 24th January (or M24J for short) formed to oversee the career of the Durutti Column. They later launch the Factory club to provide the band with a live outlet and go on to start Factory records.

25 January 1978

Joy Division play Pips Discotheque, Manchester. This is the band's first gig under the new name.

14 April 1978

The Stiff Test/Chiswick Challenge Battle of the Bands, Rafters, Manchester.

Having been confronted by Ian Curtis earlier in the evening, Tony Wilson was impressed by Joy Division when they went on at 2.15am, following an argument with the Negatives, and delivered a suitably fired-up perform-ance. Rob Gretton also saw the light that evening; and soon he and Wilson, who were already friends from Rafters, were comparing notes.

May 1978

Rob Gretton visits the band, who accept his offer to become their manager.

3–4 May 1978

The unreleased-album sessions, Arrow Studios, Manchester. Tracks recorded: 'The Drawback (All of This for You)', 'Leaders of Men', 'They Walked in Line', 'Failures', 'Novelty', 'No Love Lost', 'Transmission', 'Ice Age', 'Interzone', 'Warsaw', 'Shadowplay'.

20 May 1978

Joy Division play the Mayflower Club, Manchester, with Emergency and the Risk.

3 June 1978

An Ideal for Living seven-inch EP officially released as part of a distribution deal with Rabid. (Enigma PSS 139.) Photography by Gareth Davy. Cover design by Bernard Albrecht. Track list: 'Warsaw', 'No Love Lost', 'Leaders of Men', 'Failures'.

9 June 1978

The *Short Circuit – Live at the Electric Circus* ten-inch LP (Virgin Records VCL 5003) is released, featuring 'At a Later Date', credited to Joy Division (though the band were called Warsaw when it was recorded on 2 October 1977). Other bands featured are the Fall, Steel Pulse, the Drones, John Cooper Clarke and the Buzzcocks. Produced by Mike Howlett. Design/artwork & typography by Russell Mills.

9 June 1978

Joy Division play the Factory, Russell Club, Manchester, supporting the Tiller Boys as part of the Factory club's opening concerts. Admission: £1.

12 July 1978

Joy Division play Band on the Wall, Manchester, a Manchester Musicians' Collective gig.

15 July 1978

Joy Division play Eric's, Liverpool (matinee and evening shows), supporting the Rich Kids.

"They wouldn't talk to us, and wouldn't even let us in the dressing room. The only one of them who was nice was Midge Ure. He actually spoke to us."

27 July 1978

Joy Division play Roots Club, Leeds, supporting the Durutti Column.

"We went for a meal before the gig and that was where I first noticed how sickly and delicate Vini Reilly was. You know when you look at someone and think, 'Fucking hell, it's going to be tough on you, mate'? We went to an Indian restaurant in Leeds for something to eat before the gig; I remember Vini asked for Heinz tomato soup. In an Indian restaurant in Leeds. Because of his constitution he couldn't eat anything else.

Also, I can't say for sure but I think the third support was the Fairbrass brothers, who later became Right Said Fred. Years later I was at a Skin Two fetish party in London that ended with an unrepeatable story involving them, lots of naughties and Cleo Rocos. Earlier that night one of them had said to me, 'We supported you in Leeds in 1978 as Joy Division,' and gave me a big cuddle. The next time I saw him was through the roof of one of those huge stretch limos, and he was ... Well, let's just leave it there."

28 July 1978

Joy Division play the Factory, Russell Club, Manchester, supporting Suicide with the Actors. Admission: 'A quid at the door'.

"Ian and Steve were really thrilled about this gig because Suicide were a pretty avant-garde group and those two, being the most musically forward-thinking of us all, loved them. I got into a lot of music through Ian and Suicide were one of the bands he introduced me to. I love how all their songs sound like intros."

29 August 1978

Joy Division play Band on the Wall, Manchester, with Stage 2 and the Elite.

4 September 1978

Joy Division play Band on the Wall, Manchester. The gig is promoted by Rob Gretton, who also designed the poster.

9 September 1978

Joy Division play Eric's, Liverpool, supporting Tanz Der Youth. (Andy Colquhoun of Warsaw Pakt was a member of Tanz Der Youth for a time.) Admission: 60p members; 90p guests.

10 September 1978

Joy Division play the Royal Standard, Bradford, supported by Emergency 'and disco'. Admission: 80p in advance; £1 on the door.

> "It was full of National Front skinheads. That was a terrifying evening. We had to pretend to be Nazis to get out alive. How ironic."

20 September 1978

Joy Division appear on *Granada Reports*, introduced by Tony Wilson; they play 'Shadowplay', overlaid with negative offcuts from *World in Action*.

> "They put those cars on it because they thought we were boring to look at, but that was what Tony liked about us – that we were reserved. Maybe Ian took it to heart, I don't know, but it was around then that he started doing his dancing more often, which became his trademark."

22 September 1978

Joy Division play the Coach House, Huddersfield.

> "One person turned up. It was diabolical."

26 September 1978

Joy Division play Band on the Wall, Manchester, with Dust and A Certain Ratio.

> "ACR had a guitarist whose hair was like a chunk of cheese. So we used to call him Cheesehead."

2 October 1978

Joy Division play the Institute of Technology, Bolton, supported by the Curbs.

> "I remember going to that gig, because I remember parking outside (which is always handy). I don't remember anything else about it, though."

10 October 1978

The *An Ideal for Living* twelve-inch EP (Anonymous ANON1) is released. This is a twelve-inch reissue, 2,000 copies only. Recorded at Pennine Sound Studios, December 1977. Cover design by Steve McGarry. Photography by D. B. Glen. Track list: 'Warsaw', 'No Love Lost', 'Leaders of Men', 'Failures'.

11 October 1978

The *A Factory Sample* session, Cargo Studios, Rochdale. Produced by Martin Hannett. Engineered by John Brierley. Tracks recorded: 'Digital', 'Glass'.

12 October 1978

Joy Division play Kelly's, Manchester, with the Risk, for Rock Against Racism. Admission: £1 on the door.

> "This was in aid of a great cause. We were proud to support it."

20 October 1978

Joy Division play the Factory, Manchester, supporting Cabaret Voltaire and the Tiller Boys. Admission: £1.

> The intensity, the passion of this music completely eclipsed any-thing the audience had seen in a long, long time.
> Mick Middlehurst, writing in the *Face*, 1980

The poster for the event was given the catalogue number FAC 3 (FAC 1 was Peter Saville's Factory-club poster and FAC 2 was the A Factory Sample EP, not yet released).

> **"The first time we played at the Factory there were, like, fifteen or twenty people there but by this stage we had two or three hundred turning up. It was great to play with Cabaret Voltaire, too. Mal and Richard, lovely lads. And it was a great poster. I still have a lot of the posters, but people borrow them for exhibitions and what-ever and never give me them back. I've lost loads."**

24 October 1978

Joy Division play the Fan Club, Brannigan's, Leeds, supporting Cabaret Voltaire.

> **"Come to think of it I don't think any of the Cabs were under investigation for being the Yorkshire Ripper. Hm ..."**

26 October 1978

Joy Division play Band on the Wall, Manchester (possibly a Manchester Musicians' Collective gig).

4 November 1978

Joy Division play Eric's, Liverpool (matinee and evening shows), sup-porting Ded Byrds and John Cooper Clarke.

"Ded Byrds had a female saxophonist, and Terry and Ian did something to the reed on her saxophone that I can't possibly repeat here. I'm sorry, but I'm just going to have to leave it to your imagination – but judging by her face it tasted vile! Meanwhile, Barney and Twinny were also up to something unrepeatable round the back of the car park. An action-packed gig, that one, on stage and off."

14 November 1978

Joy Division play the Odeon, Canterbury, as part of their tour with the Rezillos and the Undertones.

"The Undertones – they were so young. They'd bought an air pistol and were having target practice backstage, shooting cans off the stairs. Then someone brought in letters from home because they'd been away touring for a while, and next thing they were all crying in the dressing room reading letters off their mums. Me and Ian were looking at each other like, *Aw, isn't that sweet?*"

15 November 1978

Joy Division play Brunel University, Uxbridge.

Unfortunately the set was cut very short; there can't have been any more than four or five numbers. The reason being that a part of the audience was still into the spitting thing and took a big dislike to Ian. They covered the poor man from head to foot. At the end of 'Digital', Ian had clearly had enough and said quite politely to the audience, "I see you are not educated down south," and promptly walked off. He was quickly followed by Sumner and Hook. Steve Morris realized it was over and scrambled from his drums, unfortunately he had to walk past the front of them to exit the stage and he tripped on a speaker cable, the crowed jeered and heckled him, he picked himself up, hurled some obscenities and walked off.

Martin (fan), on *joydiv.org*

19 November 1978

Joy Division sound-check but don't play Locarno, Bristol.

> The last time I saw Joy Division was at the Locarno in Bristol. They'd travelled down from Manchester to be told that The Rezillos had split up and instead John Otway and Chelsea were to headline that night, with us on stage first. No room on the bill for Joy Division. That's showbusiness, that is.
>
> Mickey Bradley, bassist, the Undertones

20 November 1978

Joy Division play the Check Inn, Altrincham, supported by Surgical Supports and Bidet Boys. Admission: £1.

> Joy Division were okay and could well prove to be to next year what The Fall have been to Manchester this year and what Buzzcocks were to last year.
>
> *Record Mirror*

"We'd been told all the posh girls lived in Altrincham and Hale, and we thought, *Wow: yes! for* that reason. Otherwise we had the feeling that the Check Inn wasn't going to be very wild and (lo and behold) when we played it, it wasn't. It was a dreadful gig and a dreadful audience, no girls at all. The only redeeming factor was that we didn't have far to go home."

26 November 1978

Joy Division play the New Electric Circus, Manchester, supported by the Passage.

"This was an Alan Wise promotion, I think, but I don't remember the gig. It's nice to say that we'd eclipsed the Passage by then, though."

1 December 1978

Joy Division play the Salford College of Technology; they are second on the bill, with Ed Banger (Ed Garrity) headlining and Fast Cars (with Steve Brotherdale on drums). Admission: £1.

22 December 1978

Joy Division play the Revolution Club, York, supported by Cabaret Voltaire.

27 December 1978

Joy Division play the Hope & Anchor, London. Admission: 60p.

> **"This was, I suppose, the first time that we thought, *It's not all perfect*."**

Nick Tester's Sounds *review of the Hope & Anchor gig was scathing:*

Joy Division try to be a grim group, but I just grinned. This retracted grimness is alienating, but not for intended provocative or creative reasons. I found Joy Division's "tedium" a blunt, hollow medium, comical in its superfluous angst [...] They may have gathered a tight following in home town Manchester but they failed to ignite a similar impression in front of a new (though not necessarily more objective) audience. An off-night maybe, but Joy Division's lack of an enlivening approach could be improved by an all-round sharper articulate stance and musical method. Joy Division could be a good band if they placed more emphasis on poise than pose.

PART FOUR

'Love Will Tear Us Apart'

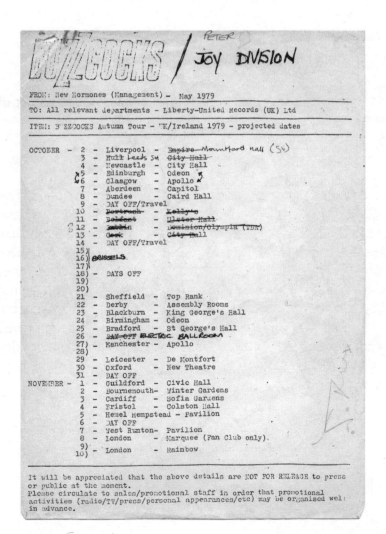

BUZZCOCKS / PETER JOY DIVISION

FROM: New Hormones (Management) - May 1979

TO: All relevant departments - Liberty-United Records (UK) Ltd

ITEM: BUZZCOCKS Autumn Tour - UK/Ireland 1979 - projected dates

```
OCTOBER  -  2  -  Liverpool  -  Empire Mountford Hall (SU)
            3  -  Hull Leeds SU  City Hall
            4  -  Newcastle   -  City Hall
            5  -  Edinburgh   -  Odeon
            6  -  Glasgow     -  Apollo
            7  -  Aberdeen    -  Capitol
            8  -  Dundee      -  Caird Hall
            9  -  DAY OFF/Travel
           10  -  Portrush    -  Kelly's
           11  -  Belfast     -  Ulster Hall
           12  -  Dublin      -  Dominion/Olympia (TBA)
           13  -  Cork        -  City Hall
           14  -  DAY OFF/Travel
           15 )
           16 ) BRUSSELS
           17 )
           18  -  DAYS OFF
           19 )
           20 )
           21  -  Sheffield   -  Top Rank
           22  -  Derby       -  Assembly Rooms
           23  -  Blackburn   -  King George's Hall
           24  -  Birmingham  -  Odeon
           25  -  Bradford    -  St George's Hall
           26  -  DAY OFF ELECTRIC BALLROOM
           27 ) Manchester    -  Apollo
           28 )
           29  -  Leicester   -  De Montfort
           30  -  Oxford      -  New Theatre
           31  -  DAY OFF
NOVEMBER -  1  -  Guildford   -  Civic Hall
            2  -  Bournemouth-  Winter Gardens
            3  -  Cardiff     -  Sofia Gardens
            4  -  Bristol     -  Colston Hall
            5  -  Hemel Hempstead - Pavilion
            6  -  DAY OFF
            7  -  West Runton-  Pavilion
            8  -  London      -  Marquee (Fan Club only)
            9 )
           10 ) - London      -  Rainbow
```

It will be appreciated that the above details are NOT FOR RELEASE to press
or public at the moment.
Please circulate to sales/promotional staff in order that promotional
activities (radio/TV/press/personal appearances/etc) may be organised well
in advance.

'Peter's fell off his chair again'

I hated being the one who drove the van. Apart from making me a suspected serial killer, it meant I had to load and unload the gear all the time. And what do most bands do after gigs? They get pissed and chase girls. Not me. When a gig finished and everybody ran off to the bar I was left to pack the bloody gear. Twinny and Terry might lend a hand if I could collar them before they got a pint in their hands, but they weren't getting paid so it wasn't like I could insist. As for the rest of the band, well, Steve would occasionally lend a hand, bless him, but Barney and Ian were always too busy chasing skirt/meeting the fans. I used to have to literally drag them away. Oh God, it used to wind me up so much. Drove me mental! I was always saying to them, 'Let's just get the gear done and *then* go to the bar,' but it always fell on deaf ears.

As a group you've got to have responsibility for your gear: let's face it, without it you're useless. But that fact was lost on those two. Even Ian still had a PA to shift. I'm sure they thought it got in the van by magic.

'Well, that's what we've got roadies for, isn't it?' Bernard would sneer.

'Listen, they're my mates. They don't get fucking paid to shift your shit. They don't get fucking paid at all. Do your own fucking shifting or get your own fucking friends to move it.'

The fact was that Terry and Twinny would do the carrying in the afternoon, no problem. Set it up, sort the sound-check, look after it till the doors opened, no problem. But that was because there were no distractions in the afternoon. At night? Forget it. No one wants to do the gear at the end of the night. The only one doing it was the daft bastard driving the van, yours truly.

Some mornings I'd come home from a gig, change into my suit then drive straight to work. There was a pelican crossing outside the docks, right opposite work, where I always used to fall asleep. There was something about reaching that point, eight o'clock in the morning, feeling knackered but nice and warm in the van, and just … feeling … sleepy … My snoozing hotspot, that was.

My workmates would bang on the window to wake me up, laughing.

I'd get to work and try to keep going, but after a really late night I'd have to go hide in the file room and fall asleep on the floor. Either that or risk it at my desk, but I'd just black out and go …

Thump.

'Oh look, Peter's fell off his chair again.'

So I was tired. Exhausted, actually.

And I didn't have epilepsy.

There's a lot been written about the effect it had on Ian. How he felt embarrassed about the condition, and how the drugs affected him. We saw bits of that: his mood changed a bit; he was quieter, less ready to laugh and more introverted than before, which was understandable. Otherwise he just soldiered on. So instead of taking time off for Ian to rest, and instead of getting together and working out how to adapt to our lead singer's epilepsy, we buried our heads in the sand, all of us, Ian included, and – and you'll be hearing this a lot throughout the rest of the book – we just carried on.

Meanwhile, far from slowing, the pace began to pick up.

Rob had jacked in his job at Eagle Star Insurance on Princess Street. His base was his attic flat in Chorlton and with plenty of time to devote to management work he'd come to us with gig offers all the time. We never said no. Wherever it was, whatever it was, we'd agree.

Christ, it must have been exhausting for Ian. (After we found out I eased off getting on at him about not moving his amp, so at least that was one advantage of being epileptic – every cloud and all that.)

But seriously. I mean: if I was that knackered I was nodding off at the pelican and sliding off my chair at work, how did he feel? But, because Ian was Ian, and didn't want to let us down, he allowed us to keep on going like nothing had happened, and nobody – not us, Tony, Rob, Debbie, his parents, doctors or specialists – stepped in to say he should do anything different. All of which suited us fine, I hate to admit, because the discovery of Ian's epilepsy coincided with a period when the band was really beginning to take off.

Having the *An Ideal for Living* EP out as twelve-inch had made promotion so much easier. We didn't have to apologize for it the way we'd had to with the seven-inch. With the twelve-inch out, both Rob and the band had something great to work with – something that represented us really well.

God knows how much time Rob spent in phone boxes. He must have used them like an office, phoning round for gigs and reactions on the records then phoning us. We were easily reachable, so Rob would just grab a load of coins, go to the phone box and ring us up. I'd pick up the phone at work, probably exhausted from a gig the night before.

'All right, Hooky. It's Rob.'

'All right, Rob.'

'John Peel likes the record. He wants us in for a session.'

I'd put down the phone and I wouldn't think, *Aw, that's going to be stressful for poor old Ian*; I'd think, *Fucking hell, we're going to do a session for John Peel!* and go for a run.

We were totally in awe of John Peel and his programme, and he'd already played tracks off the EP. Somewhere I've still got the tape with the places marked in biro where John introduces our tracks, can still remember listening to it in the car, freezing, taping off the car radio on one of those portable cassette players. Doing the session was mind-blowing. For a start, when you work for the BBC you get paid personally: the money comes to you, not to the group. (Later, in New Order, I used to love doing *Top of the Pops* because I got a cheque for £280 when I was getting nothing off the group.) But it was also mind-blowing because John Peel was a hero, a true musical hero. His was the only show on radio for people like us to listen to, so to be offered a session, well, that was like getting a chart placing back then, only better. We didn't give a shit about chart placings. Right then success for us was about playing the music we wanted to play: that was that. For us, in Joy Division and New Order, it was always about playing without compromising your music. Doing that was the only success.

When you did a Peel session there was no messing about. It started at two, finished at four and there was no overrun. Hours overdubbing? Forget it. 'Hey, why don't we try some synth here?' None of that. You were in and out.

Which suited me down to the ground. A great way to do things, if you ask me. Nowadays you're so spoilt by technology you can spend hours and days and months on the computer perfecting every tiny detail. Of course there's some great music being made that way. But is it greater than the music being made back then? No.

'Fuck. Martin's got a boot full of stolen car radios'

We were still at T. J. Davidson's, where we were being very productive. From two rehearsals – one on a weeknight, for an hour or an hour-and-a-half, cost us £1.50, then three hours on Sundays, which was £3 – we'd get an idea a week and write two to three songs a month; and I'd say that from the time we wrote 'Transmission' onwards they just flowed like rain. I mean, writing songs is easy when you're just starting out. It gets a lot harder and takes longer when you've written two or three hundred. You get overdrawn at the riff bank. But back then we couldn't stop writing them.

All four of us had ideas. One of us would have been listening to Kraftwerk and suggest using that sound as the basis for a song. We'd all chip in and by the time the song was finished, even though the seed of the song had been Kraftwerk, it wouldn't sound like Kraftwerk at all. That was the art. It sounded like Joy Division. In this particular case it sounded like 'Digital', in fact.

'Shadowplay' happened in a similar way: Bernard had been listening to 'Ocean' by Velvet Underground and wanted to write a track like that, with the surf sound, a rolling feeling in it. So we started jamming and that's how we came up with 'Shadowplay'. You wouldn't say it sounded anything like Velvet Underground, but once you know you can hear the root.

That was the thing about Joy Division: writing the songs was dead easy because the group was really balanced; we had a great guitarist, a great drummer, a great bass player, a great singer. As soon as Ian died it became difficult. He had an ear for us, a great ear, and all bands need one of those. You could tell he would have been a great guitar player too. His guitars of choice were the Vox Peardrop and the Vox Teardrop, very idiosyncratic; the Teardrop had some wild built-in effects that he loved. He'd picked the guitar up late, starting around the time we were writing the songs that would become *Closer*. Maybe Barney's playing was still bugging him, but a more likely explanation was that we were featuring more keyboards and Barney was switching between the

140

two. Maybe Ian thought he'd fill in. He played on the video for 'Love Will Tear Us Apart' and was obviously quite a rudimentary player, but you could tell he would have got so much better because he had that ear – he thought like a musician. The way it worked was that he'd listen to us jamming, and then direct the song until it was ... a song. He stood there like a conductor and picked out the best bits.

Which was why, when we lost him, it made everything so difficult. It was like driving a great car that had only three wheels. The loss of Ian had opened up a hole in us and we had to learn to write in a different way. It was hard, that period, just starting New Order, and we suddenly found it very difficult to adjust. We felt like we'd been cheated. It had been so easy, so good when it was the four of us. We were so tight, as a group, we didn't even use a tape recorder half the time. Didn't need one. We had the odd one, of course, but they never lasted or the quality was so poor as to make them virtually useless. But it didn't matter because we could do most things from memory. Everything up to and including *Unknown Pleasures* really existed only when the four of us were in a room together playing it. Not written down, not recorded, just from memory.

Peter Saville has a wonderful theory that musicians stop writing great music when they learn about the formal process of making music. Why? Because then they won't take any chances. When you're young, you go, 'G, B. Oh yeah, man, that fucking takes your head off that! Weird but sounds great!'

Then, when you get older and you know a lot more about how music is *supposed* to sound, you go, 'Oh, that G, B, that jars a little doesn't it? Oh no, try E flat. That's better,' and the edge is gone. I agree with him. The more proficient you become at writing music the less chances you take because you become aware of all the rules and theories that may well be the proper way to do things but end up constricting you, throttling all the creativity out of what you've got. No more risk-taking. Back then we didn't know rules or theory. We had our ear, Ian, who listened and picked out the melodies. Then at some point his lyrics would appear. He always had his scraps of paper that he'd written things down on and he'd go through his plastic bag. 'Oh, I've got something that might suit that.' And the next thing you knew he'd be standing there with a piece of paper in one hand, wrapped around the microphone stand, with his head down, making the melodies work.

We'd never hear what he was singing about in rehearsal because the equipment was so shit. In his case it didn't matter because as he delivered the vocal with such a huge amount of passion and aggression, like he really fucking meant it. It was great. Who cared what he was saying as long as he said it like that. When we were mixing Rob Gretton always use to say, 'Make it go WOOOMPH!' and Ian always did.

Later, of course, I'd listen to the lyrics and try to pick them apart, but for two years in the rehearsal room all I really heard was a scream and that was what important to me. I just thought, 'The guy means it.' It doesn't matter what you're playing really, as long as you mean it.

It was only after we recorded *Unknown Pleasures* that I could hear and begin to take notice of the words and it was quite startling then to see how they changed between that album, where they were still quite detached and aggressive, to *Closer*, which is even darker and not detached at all but really introspective and quite frightening – especially of course when you listen to it in light of what later happened.

Still, we hadn't yet even made an album, but because we were being so productive talk turned to making one. There was a feeling that we had enough material – enough *good* material – to do it, and to be perfectly frank with you we weren't that fussy about who we made it with. As far as we were concerned there were a lot of record companies out there and they all did pretty much the same thing, which was get records out.

Despite the fact that none of us had a fondness for London – as a place or for the record labels – we all assumed we'd end up following that well-worn path and going there. Which seemed perfectly natural to us – desirable really – because we were in a band. Nobody starts a band so they can stay in their hometown. You yearn for London and Paris and America and all that – all the freedom that comes with it. We weren't really loyal to any Manchester scene. We'd always been a bit outside it anyway.

Out of all of us it was Rob, of course, who was much more pro-Manchester. Everywhere was important, not just London, he said: 'Fuck London' – that was one of his favourite catchphrases. We'll do what we do here, build up a following in Manchester. We were resistant at first but he worked his magic on us (i.e. he browbeat us until we would have said anything just to make him stop) but the idea did grow on us. Lucky it did, because in retrospect he was right – absolutely right.

So Rob went into talks with Tony about doing our record with him. The deal was a 50-50 split with the label to pay for recording and man-ufacture. (This deal was a mistake for Tony and Factory. He had inadvertently offered to pay the Mechanicals from their 50 per cent, so 8 per cent of the cost of the record went straight to the BPI for Mechanical royalties – and was then paid straight back to us. As Tony protested for years after, it meant that the deal was 58 per cent to 42 per cent in our favour: a bone of contention between them till the end and also sowed the seeds for when Factory couldn't pay us all that they owed.) The deal was great on the one hand, but had a drawback: there would be no advance, so we couldn't give up our jobs. Rob didn't have a job, of course, but he knew that us giving up our jobs would be best for the band, giving us the freedom and time to con-centrate on making music. So with the Factory offer on the table he started fishing around, making enquiries. One of the bites he had was from Genetic, a part of Radar Records, which in turn was a part of Stiff Records. They had a good reputation. They offered us a multi-album deal and £70,000 advance. That was so much money it was hard to comprehend.

We were like, 'Woah, woah, woah, yes!'

Okay: me, Bernard and Steve were like, 'Woah, yes!' Rob, being noth-ing if not a man of many contradictions, had a sudden change of heart and decided he didn't like the idea of an advance. They were like loans, he said. Fuck loans.

'If you take this advance, you'll be signed to them for five albums and if you don't like them and they don't work, it's going to be a problem for your next four, isn't it?'

Which was absolutely true, and the £70,000 would have included recording costs as well; split between the five of us it maybe wasn't such a great deal after all. He convinced us of this, probably in his normal intimidating way, and he did it every time we came to do our publishing deals, too, insisting: no advance. Ian would be screaming at him, and me and Barney would be screaming at him, and Steve would probably whisper something as well, but he'd never budge. He'd push his glasses up his nose and go, 'We're better off getting a bigger deal at the back end.'

Of course he hated London. From the day he was born to the day he died, he hated London. So naturally it really appealed to him to stay in Manchester and have control, because Tony was offering more or less complete freedom musically. We could do what we wanted.

So poor old Rob at this point – it must have done his head in: Genetic were in London offering an advance, and he hated London and distrusted the advance, *but* ... His band could give up their jobs. Factory were in Manchester and were offering the split, and he loved Manchester and thought the split was best in the long-term, *but* ... His band would have to stay working.

His band, don't forget, with the lead singer who suffered from epilepsy, who really needed as much rest as possible.

So there was plenty of um-ing and ah-ing. In the meantime Martin Rushent invited us down to the studio to record some demos, just to see if we were going to gel. He'd produced the Buzzcocks and the Stranglers by this point so we were very excited by the prospect and went down there.

Rushent was based in offices above the Blitz club in Great Queen Street, where he'd been monitoring the early appearances of the major players in the burgeoning New Romantic scene. His assistant, Anne Roseberry, had seen Joy Division in Manchester and told Rushent about it; Rushent in turn saw them and said, 'My jaw hit the floor.' Keen to try them out for his own label, Genetic, he invited them to his Berkshire studio, Eden.

When we got there we saw that Martin Rushent had a brand-new Jaguar XJS – and as it happened I'd been reading this article about how nine out of ten Jag owners don't lock the boot of their car.

So I thought, *I wonder if that's true?* – tried his boot and, lo and behold, it was unlocked. When I looked inside it was full of stolen car radios; you could tell they were stolen by the way the wires were dangling off from where they'd been ripped out.

Me and Terry were looking at each other, thinking, *Fuck. Martin's got a boot full of stolen car radios.* And then, *Wonder if he'd miss a couple ...*

All day, actually, whenever there was a break in the recording, we'd be daring each other to go back in his boot and nick one each for our cars – because they were proper high-end stereos – but I was going, 'Oh no, we can't, because he might be our record company. We can't nick fucking cassette players off our record company.'

So we didn't take any. Christ knows what he was doing with them, though. We never asked him, and anyway he was too busy moaning about the boil on his bum. It was giving him real gyp and he was in agony with it. So much that he couldn't sleep in his bed and had to sleep in his car instead – couldn't get comfortable otherwise.

He went on about that a lot, his boil, and it meant he kept having to get up to walk around and ease the pain, but otherwise the session was great. It was a really nice studio and he worked well with Ian on the vocals, did a few overdubs and stuff, nothing wild, very low key. The tracks were 'Glass', 'Transmission', 'Ice Age', 'Insight' and 'Digital'. He was a nice guy; we got on well. He was a lot better than Martin Hannett in one respect: he spoke English and you could understand what he said. But he was nowhere near as exciting or unpredictable and, to be honest, once I'd heard the results I much preferred Hannett's production to his.

I got offered the tape of that session back, recently. Eden Studios was taken over by a firm of solicitors and left in a storeroom, hidden in the bowels of it, were the Joy Division master tapes. One of the staff found them. He got in touch with me through a third party to offer me the tape. He wanted £50,000 for it and I just thought, *Oh, fuck off.* This was in 2006 or something. Even then there was no way on earth you could make a record and hope to recoup fifty grand. I offered him a finder's fee, two grand, but he said no and I've never heard from him since; it's never appeared, so I don't know what's happened to that one. They used monitor mixes for the Eden versions on the *Heart and Soul* box set but I was offered the twenty-four-track master tapes, so it could have been remixed. Shame, because as far as I know the only Joy Division multi-track that still exists is for 'Love Will Tear Us Apart'.

Ah well. It's a funny thing, people trying to sell you back bits of your own past, but I'm getting used to it, to be honest. We have the same problem even with studio staff. When Strawberry Studios closed someone spirited a load of master tapes straight from the skip to their parents' loft. I caught them hawking the tapes round a few Joy Division collectors. They wanted £20,000. I patiently explained how you can't make any money these days, what with illegal downloading, etc., and offered the usual £2,000 finder's fee. They sneered, 'I'd rather deal with Steve and Gillian!' I instigated legal proceedings on that one. But lo and behold, one day, as we were negotiating, their car got broken into and all the tapes and digital copies got stolen. They even had the police-report number. Ah well, the ones that got away. Although in this day and age I challenge any thief to even recognize thirty-year-old recording tapes, let alone know what to do with them. They are huge. Strangely enough they were hawking the same tapes around again a few months later. The thief must have returned them.

'It sounds like a fucking helicopter'

Pleased with the demos he'd recorded with Joy Division, Rushent brought them to the attention of Genetic's owner, Warner, who were less impressed, reportedly telling him to forget about Joy Division and the New Romantic groups and concentrate instead on finding the new Angelic Upstarts. History was to prove Rushent correct, not only in the case of Joy Division but also with Visage, Ultravox and Spandau Ballet, while he would go on to produce the Human League's masterpiece, Dare. Either way, Joy Division had decided not to join Genetic, wanting the greater artistic freedom of their relationship with Factory as well as preferring the financial terms offered. During Joy Division's gig at Band on the Wall on 13 March, Gretton and Wilson agreed that Joy Division would record their debut album with Factory, with all concerned assuming that the band would make just one album with the label before moving on to a major.

So what actually happened was that we were presented with two very different scenarios: London plus advance and small profit split or Manchester with no advance but great profit split. We all plumped for the latter. We thought that as long as we were able to stay at home and play the songs we were writing, that was enough. Everything else would be a bonus. In the end it was an easy decision to make. We met with Tony and told him our decision. He was delighted and must have thought, *Fuck this is a great band, we need to get them on a record and get it out right away.* He was absolutely right.

Even so, it was a bit of a wrench because we still had in our minds the idea that if we had a contract with an advance, and could give up our day jobs, everything would be fine and dandy. Follow the Yellow Brick Road. But what Rob and Tony were suggesting was *not* giving up our jobs, taking an independent-label deal, which meant that you had to put a lot more work in and there was no safety net and all the things that you normally do in a group full-time you had to do at the same time as you were working. You'd still be doing the gigs, coming home sometimes at six in the morning and then having to go to work at seven. Which was, like I say, exhausting.

But Rob convinced us it was the best thing to do. The deal was great – probably the best deal a band had ever had, actually. For us to make any money, though, we had to make a great record that sold well. So the pressure was on. We prepared for the sessions with two storming gigs. The first was at Bowdon Vale Youth Club, where we were being filmed by Malcolm Whitehead as part of his short film about Joy Division. It was a cracking gig and one I really remember because I felt at the time that we were very nearly the finished article. For a start we looked like a great group. If you see the film, I'm getting the swagger on and Bernard's more into himself, doing his not-moving-type thing, which made a nice contrast. We sounded good too. Personally speaking I was really pleased with the bass sound pretty much from then on. I'm sure Ian wouldn't mind me saying that a lot of the vocal lines were guided by the bass and I was coming up with some good riffs. I mean, going down the set list for the Bowdon Vale gig, just look at the bass lines: 'Exercise One', 'She's Lost Control', 'Shadowplay', 'Insight', 'Disorder', 'Glass', 'Digital', 'Transmission', 'I Remember Nothing'. You stand and fall on your riffs and I was just amazingly, sickeningly lucky in that I was coming up with them. To write something like 'She's Lost Control' and have the whole song based around it. That's one of our most famous songs, really personal to Ian, and for him to base those lyrics around my riff was so fucking cool. As a player I was being featured very highly, was an integral part of the sound of the band, which was great for me, a wonderful platform. To be a part of something like that when I was a) tone deaf and b) self-taught was amazing.

It wasn't all roses, though. I still had to drive the fucking van. That kept my feet firmly on the ground as well as causing me no end of problems, not least of which was paying for the maintenance. Because you might think that if something went wrong with the van then paying for it would come out of the group purse. You might think that. You'd be wrong. Anything like the clutch going, a puncture, a flat tyre, and I had to pay for it. I'd go to Rob and say, 'Listen, I've had to pay for this tyre.'

And he'd go, 'Well? What's that fucking got to do with me? I'm not paying for your fucking van; you fucking pay for it.'

On our way to our next gig, in Walthamstow, we were driving down the motorway when the van's top hose split and water blew on the distributor cap. It backfired and peeled the exhaust like a banana.

We pulled over.

'What are we going to do?'

'We've got to fucking go,' said Rob. 'We've got a fucking gig.'

I said, 'Fuck off. I can't drive through London like that, with no exhaust. It sounds like a fucking helicopter.'

He was going, 'No, no, it's fine, fine – we'll fix it when we get to Dave Pils' house.'

They all piled back in the Cortina and we had to drive all the way down the motorway, which wasn't too bad, actually, apart from the fact that me, Terry and Twinny were completely deaf by the time we got there. We drove through North London to Walthamstow, parked up, and I said to Dave, 'Listen, we're going to have to get it fixed.'

'Kwik Fit round the corner,' he said.

I didn't have any money, of course, and looked at Rob, who said, 'Well I'll lend you the money to fix the van.'

'*Lend* us the money? I can't afford to pay for the fucking thing myself.'

So he gave me the cash and I went to Kwik Fit and got it sorted – £13 for a new exhaust – and while I was out they'd had a group meeting at Dave Pils' house. Waited till I was out, the rotten bastards, and had a group vote.

'We've decided that we're not paying for it,' said Rob when I got back. 'We'll lend it to you but you've got to give us the money back.'

I said, 'Right, from now on you can hire a van because I'm not fucking paying to drive you twats about when you're keeping the gig money and I have to fork out. Fuck off, the lot of you.'

I stormed out, didn't I. Went for a walk round the block, calmed down and when I got back to Dave Pils' house they were all sat in the living room.

Rob said, 'It's all right, Hooky, we're going to pay for it.' So it was sorted. I didn't have to pay back the money. I was still pissed off, and would pretty much stay pissed off until 13 August, when ... Well, we'll come to that.

In the meantime, we had an album to record. Sheesh!

'He was looking for that spark'

Strawberry Studios in Stockport is offices now, but for years it was the major studio in the North West. If you go to where it is in Waterloo Road they have one of those blue plaques up with a list of all the legendary artists who recorded there: Paul McCartney, Neil Sedaka, Stone Roses and the Syd Lawrence Orchestra.

No mention of us, the bastards. Even though that was there we went in April 1979 to record our debut album (and, later, to record 'Transmission' and 'Love Will Tear Us Apart', among others). Tony Wilson always gave massive credit to 10CC for putting Strawberry in Stockport. The way he saw it, they'd reinvested the money they made from their music back into Manchester. He was right. Thanks to them we had one of the country's best studios on our doorstep, and we were pretty excited about it: our first foray into twenty-four-track recording, with the ability to overdub, in four-star luxury. We were once again being produced by Martin, who was using all sorts of great gear. The AMS, of course, as well as the Marshall Time Modulators (Marshall Time Wasters, the engineers called them), which he used a lot on the guitar, especially on some of Bernard's more … *economical* playing, shall we say. So to be honest it felt like such a thrill. Like taking the next big step up. We were all raring to go and happy and had enthusiasm to burn.

If only I'd known then what I know now I'd have savoured making our first album – because by the time we got to the second one there were already divisions beginning to form and we were very worried about Ian. Martin was having a hard time with the drugs so it got very fraught and very stressful. Then, on *Movement*, the first New Order album – well, we were fucked from that album on as far as I'm concerned. Whatever record we were making from that point on, there was always some elephant in the room. Whether it was Ian's death, or business matters, personal disputes, the Haçienda sucking the life out of us or Factory going to the wall, there was always something. Always an elephant. Should have given it a catalogue number.

There was no elephant on *Unknown Pleasures*, though. It turned out to be the only album we made where we were focused, and relaxed, and enjoyed the wonderfulness of being young and in a band and going in to record your debut album on your new label with a producer who had mad hair and looked like a wizard and spoke in riddles.

He told us we needed forty minutes' worth of music for the album so we presented him with a batch of songs. Of those we recorded sixteen, ten of which were used on the album, all recorded at the weekend. We all had jobs in the week. No advance, remember. And it was cheaper at weekends. Even cheaper if we worked at night, which suited Martin down to the ground, of course, because he liked to work at night. So the band would arrive at the studio straight after work on Friday, record until seven in the morning, then return later in the evening on the Saturday and work until seven in the morning. We'd be going home at seven on Monday morning, trying to escape before the cleaner arrived and started Hoovering. Even now the sound of a Hoover goes right through me. We recorded for the first two weekends and Martin mixed the third weekend. So that was two days to record *Unknown Pleasures*. *Closer* took three weeks. *Movement* took about two months and *Waiting for the Siren's Call*, New Order's last, took three years.

Usually when a band went into the studio, back in the late seventies anyway, you'd have one eye on the clock and be concentrating on not messing around. The accepted way of doing this was to get the band in the studio and get them sounding as live as possible. There was no such thing as click tracks or backing tracks in those days. It was all recorded live. So for the most part what we used to do was go in and run through all of the tracks in one go, with Ian in the room – he'd do the vocal in isolation later, when we had the take. Now, normally when you record a band you have a microphone on each of the instruments, and each records to a track on the master tape, but you get a bit of leakage from one microphone to another, so you'll get a bit of the bass down the guitar mic and so on. If you want to feature, say, the guitar more prominently, then you turn up the guitar track, but because of the sound spill the other instruments come up, too. Martin hated that.

Martin being Martin wanted the live feel of the band playing but without sacrificing the clarity of the instruments. So he set us up to get maximum separation, and the way he did that was to record us separately, especially the drums. Martin wanted them isolated so he could work on the drum sound, which of course he ended up doing a lot, creating that very clean, precise-sounding, almost clinical drum sound that became his trademark.

Of course, it was only much later, when we heard the finished product, that we knew what he was going on about. What we heard at the time was Martin and Chris Nagle, his engineer, constantly going on and on about keeping everything clean and separate, right from the start, the very opposite of what we wanted. The first song we played him was 'She's Lost Control'. He loved the drums on it, he said; then said it would be great if they were separate. Next thing we knew he was getting Steve to take his kit apart. Off came the snare and the toms. Martin wanted zero spill from the mics so he had to record each drum individually. Of course that meant that Steve was rarely playing his whole kit. He was allowed to play only one drum at a time and ghosted the others. So what happened was that we ran through 'She'd Lost Control' live, then Martin recorded the drum track, we took the kit apart and Steve played his parts again – one drum at a time. It made everything very laborious and really hard for Steve, because he didn't have a click track to keep time to, so he kept speeding up and slowing down. Steve had to learn how to play the kit, but play it like a drum machine. He once said that his ambition wasn't to be a drum machine but Martin demanded the separation. It even got to the point where Martin was taking the drums themselves apart, taking the tightening springs out, because he said they squeaked. Only he could hear it.

Of course it had to be done in a matter of hours. If you went into the studio now and wanted to recreate the sound of Unknown Pleasures it would probably take you years. But we were young and Martin was pushing us, and it had to be done double-quick, so it was a constant battle between Martin's desire to experiment and the time we had left in the studio. We worked very quickly. None of that farting about – all that happened later. For Unknown Pleasures we'd go in with our list of songs. We'd set up the instruments, sound-check, 'Right, "'Disorder'"'.

We'd play 'Disorder'.

'Is that all right, Martin?'

'No, didn't like it. Try it slower but faster. Meaner but kinder.'

We'd look at each other like, *Oh, do fuck off.*

We'd play 'Disorder' again.

'How was that, Martin?'

'That was better, yeah, a bit on the buttery side but fine; we'll go with that one.'

So then we had our master. Ten backing tracks, ready for editing, manipulating and adding to. Next Martin would record the drums, and often he'd get Barney to put some heavier guitar on top, too; he was a big fan of layering the recordings. He'd do the vocals last, right at the end, so they were clean without any spill from the instruments. When it came to the vocals Tony suddenly became very vocal, suggesting strongly that Ian listen to Frank Sinatra's *Greatest Hits* so he could incorporate a bit of Frank's crooner style into the vocal lines. This made us all laugh and, while I didn't hear a direct influence on Ian's vocal style, I was quite surprised to see a few lyrical references of Frank's in the lyrics. Notably 'I Remember Nothing' with its 'We were strangers' refrain. Strangers in the night, anyone?

The band had its first studio row, actually, the first of many over the years, because Barney insisted on using infrared headphones and adjusting the levels to fit them, even though it fucked up the levels for the rest of us, plus we fell out a couple of times over songs that he didn't like and was reluctant to play. Martin had encouraged us to write a couple more in the studio so we had a better choice for the LP. Me and Steve jammed out 'From Safety to Where' and 'Candidate'. Ian then worked on vocals. Barney didn't like that song either and his reluctance to play on it was marked. Martin had to turn the tape over so the songs were backward. He liked them then and played. Martin span it over so the tracks had backward guitars and a few fed-up-sounding EEEKS! Apart from that, it was a pretty peaceful atmosphere, which was mainly down to Martin, of course, because he wasn't yet the tyrant he later became.

Back then he smoked a bit of dope but he wasn't into heroin, as far as I know. To be honest, I don't think he had the money for it. His drug problem really only became a problem for us when it came to *Movement*, when he refused to start the session until we brought him a gram of coke. 'Where the fuck are we going to get a gram of coke from?' We'd never even seen cocaine. (At that point, I mean. We'd certainly put that right later.)

'I'm not fucking starting until you bring me a gram of Columbia's finest,' he insisted, and then sat there for hours with his arms folded while the rest of us tried to persuade him to begin the session. After phoning God knows how many people, Rob laid his hands on some and brought it into the studio.

'Right,' said Martin, handing it over to Chris Nagle, 'You sort that out, Christopher, and I'll get started.'

What a twat, we thought. All that fucking time wasted. Never is the saying 'time is money' truer than when you're in the studio. The average cost then was £1 per recording track per hour (so, for example, twenty-four-track: £24 per hour). Fair enough, I suppose; he was struggling. It's a well-known fact that he took Ian's death hard. I mean, recording 'Ceremony' and 'In a Lonely Place' was easier because Ian had left the lyrics and the vocal lines for those two, so it was only our vocal efforts that amused and frustrated him. But doing *Movement* he found the album tough going from the start, and he let us know it. It was like that great car with the wonky wheel again. Martin was constantly having to fix New Order and he wasn't in good enough physical or mental shape to do it. He was off his peak. We all were.

He hated that we used to bug the shit out of him, me and Bernard especially. One on either side. Always on his case. Questioning everything. 'Why are you doing that?' 'Isn't it too quiet?' 'Isn't it too loud?' 'More bass!' 'More guitar!' 'More everything.' Ian was much more easy-going, and perhaps that's why he was Martin's favourite. But maybe Ian was more easy-going because there was only so much Martin could to the vocals, whereas he could do a lot to the instruments. And he did a lot to the instruments. Which was, after all, what he was there to do. As a sound-manipulator Martin was in a class of his own, and the atmosphere, clarity and depth he gave to the songs is still astonishing.

He was lucky, though. Like I know myself, when you're producing a band and they come in with great songs you rub your hands with glee, because you can have such fun with a great song. But when someone brings you a poor or average song you have to start changing it and you're thinking, *Can we write a better middle eight? Can we improve the chorus?* That's not as much fun. It can be really hard work.

Martin had fun with Joy Division because the songs were so fantastic. He didn't have as much fun with *Movement* because, while the music was fantastic, we were lacking confidence on the lyrics and vocals. Struggling to do them to his satisfaction. We were feeling our way in the dark. He knew that and it pissed him off. And, along with fires and infestations of rats, the one thing you don't want in a studio is a pissed-off Martin Hannett because he was ruthless, a right dictator at times. Derek Brandwood, who ended up managing him towards the end of his career, once said that you could put him in a studio with a band with who'd been the best of friends for forty years and within five minutes Martin would have them at each other's throats. So true.

His bag was winding people up. I remember he made Bernard sing 'Cries & Whispers' by New Order forty-three times. He wanted a complete take and if there was one error, or what Martin *thought* was an error, he made Bernard do it again. Barney was totally pissed off with it all, and quite rightly so, but Martin fed off that. You could see the look in his eyes, like, *This'll get him.* He was looking for that spark, something intangible. But to him always a catalytic spark.

Did he get it? Well, it would be great if this particular anecdote ended with Bernard doing the performance of his life and 'Cries & Whispers' becoming one of our greatest songs, but it doesn't because we told Martin to fuck off and stormed out. So no, he didn't get it. What he got was band and producer at each other's throats, which was all part of his divide-and-conquer ethic. And if you were looking for any support from Chris Nagle you might as well forget it: Martin's big thing was that the group should do their bit and then piss off, and Chris was very much his right-hand man on that. Even though he was our age he always took Martin's side against the group and the pair of them would visibly gang up on you, sniggering together like schoolgirls if you suggested anything.

I'd go, 'Can we turn up the high-hat, Martin, please?' and the pair of them would look at each other and dissolve into giggles.

I'd be like, 'What's so fucking funny about that? What's so fucking funny about turning up the high-hat?' But the pair of them would sit there sniggering like bastards. Infuriating.

If that failed they would try to freeze us out. They sat at the desk in the middle of the room, where it was warm, while we had to sit at the back under the air-conditioning that they'd jammed on full to get rid of us. Barney had to produce the sleeping bag yet again. It wouldn't have been so bad if 10CC had kept the heating on at night, the tight bastards. But you literally had icicles hanging off your nose.

When we'd finished recording we had to decide what songs were going on the album and in what order. Looking back now at the tracks we recorded, I'd say that 'Exercise One', 'Only Mistake', 'They Walked in Line' and 'The Kill' were a bit punkier than the tracks we ended up picking, and maybe didn't fit in with the album so well. 'Exercise One' is the best one. 'Only Mistake' is a good song as well. 'They Walked in Line' and 'The Kill' are a bit too punky, a bit throwaway.

Once we'd decided what was going to make the cut, Martin tuned it so that each song was in a sympathetic key, so it didn't jar but instead sounds like a smooth, ear-pleasing progression rather than a harsh transition, like harmonic mixing – so 'Disorder' into 'Day of the Lords' was in tune and so on and so on. Martin introduced us to all that. Very, very clever.

Then we could hear it, of course.

I can't remember if we were there for the mixing. Maybe not. As I said, Martin hated us hanging around when we weren't playing, getting on his nerves. 'Get these fucking musicians out of here,' he'd scream.

He used to say 'musicians' like it was a swear word. What difference it would have made to the finished article if we'd been sitting on his shoulder while he mixed it I couldn't say. Back then we didn't know enough about the process to have much of an opinion. All we saw was him pressing buttons. He could have been releasing squadrons of bats for all we knew. So whether we were there or not, Martin mixed *Unknown Pleasures* his way.

Ian and Steve loved it. Me and Barney hated it. We thought it was too weak. We wanted it to be miles heavier. We wanted it to go *RARRGH!* And instead it went *ptish.* All the things I now love about the album – the spacey, echoey ambient sound of it – were all the things I hated about it when I first heard it.

I was properly upset about it, too. The kind of upset you get when you're in the minority – because when Tony and Rob heard it they loved it as well, so it was fait accompli, mate. That was the end of it.

For me it was almost like the *An Ideal for Living* moment, when I got the record home and put it on only to hear that it was absolutely shit. *Unknown Pleasures* sort of had the same effect. To make us sound so … weedy. It made me feel sick. *Oh my God, he's taken all the guts out of it. All the balls. How could he do that?*

Now, of course, I can see the error of my ways. Now I can see that what Martin gave us, which was the greatest gift any producer can give any band. He gave us timelessness. Because *Unknown Pleasures* is just one of those things: it's a truly ageless album. Think of the millions of albums influenced by *Unknown Pleasures* that *have* aged, while *Unknown Pleasures* hasn't. That was his gift to us. We gave him the brilliant songs and he put them in little capsules so they'd stay brilliant forever.

Bernard had of course done a great job on the *An Ideal for Living* cover. And I'm not being sarcastic: I really think he did. He was always on the lookout for images to put on our stuff; and looking through a book, *The Cambridge Encyclopaedia of Astronomy*, he saw a diagram of a pulsar, showed it to Peter Saville and that was it. Bernard doesn't get nearly enough credit for that, because he couldn't have made a better choice: that image is now forever associated with Joy Division and *Unknown Pleasures* the record. Talking of which, I can't remember who came up with the title. Ian again? Either way Peter went off, applied his magic and turned it into *Unknown Pleasures,* putting all his great little touches on it: the textured paper, the text on the reverse and the light and shade of having the outer sleeve black and the inner sleeve white. To be honest, I wasn't that interested in the art. I was just pleased that they didn't intend to feature the band. We'd seen too many punk bands standing there scowling in black and white, their name sprayed on the wall behind them. We were all behind playing down the personality. Our image was a kind of anti-image, about anonymity and being chilly and grey and buttoned-up against the cold. In lots of our pictures we're hunched up or have our backs turned, which was a mixture of being cold and not giving a fuck about the whole business of image, really. We didn't want it to be about us. We certainly didn't want it to be about our looks, 'cause we were such a bunch of ugly bastards. We wanted it all to be about the music.

It was the same with journalists. Right from the early days Rob had been dead against us giving interviews – especially me and Bernard, because we just used to sit there and say stupid things. Taking the piss.

Rob's response was, 'Right, you two. You don't speak. At all. Just sit there and look menacing.' He didn't do it to create a mystique around the band but because he thought we were a couple of cretins. The result was that it created a mystique around the band. Absolute genius.

Anyway, we finished the album in April and, despite me and Barney protesting that we wanted to sound like the Sex Pistols, the master went off to the pressing plant and they pressed 10,000 of them.

One night Rob phoned me up and said, 'Come on, we've got to go and pick the record up.'

'Fucking hell,' I said, 'Ten thousand of them. Isn't anybody else coming?'

'No, just me and you.'

I hired a van from Salford Van Hire and had to tell them I was moving house (they had a sign on the wall refusing to hire to 'musicians, hawkers and gypsies'). Then we drove down to London to pick up the records from the plant. Loading the van took an age then we drove them back up to Manchester, thinking the axle was going to snap any second, taking it slow so we didn't fuck up the van. At Manchester we went straight to Palatine Road and started handballing them up the three flights of stairs to Alan's flat. Margox was there. That's Margi Clarke, the actress out of *Letter To Brezhnev* and *Corrie*, of course, but back then she was called Margox and she did bits of singing and TV presenting and she was there at 86a with Alan's flatmate.

This was about 7pm and she said, 'Oh, what you got there, love? Is this your record, like? Can I have one?' We ignored her and they disappeared off into the bedroom. Sure enough, as we loaded the records in we did it to a background noise of them having very noisy orgasms, thinking, *Fucking hell, could this be any fucking worse?*

She came floating out much later, when me and Rob were sitting there dripping in sweat from having carried 10,000 copies of *Unknown Pleasures* up the stairs.

'Can I have a record?' she said.

Seems a bit mean now, but it was just the culmination of a bad day; I'm ashamed to say that Rob told her to fuck right off again.

Quite funny, really, because at our very next gig, at Eric's in May, who should be there as our support? Only Margox again. She did this act where she sang over other people's records – Kraftwerk, Sex Pistols and stuff – just shrieking over the top of them. Absolutely awful, it was, and I'm sure she'd be the first to agree. Still, we loved her. How can you not love Margi Clarke? That really earthy, rude character you see on screen is like a toned-down version of the real one. What you see is what you get there, let me tell you. She is wonderful. So when we were in the dressing room before the show, and Twinny winked at us before saying to her, 'Show us your tits, love,' I don't know why we were surprised when she went, 'Here y'go, la,' lifted up her top and showed us them in all their glory.

We went bright red and stayed bright red when she didn't put them away. Just waited until we were at maximum discomfort, our faces burning so hot you could fry eggs on them and silently plotting revenge on Twinny and his big mouth, until at last she put us out of our misery, saying, 'That taught you a lesson, lads?'

'Yes,' we mumbled like naughty school boys.

Top down, she left the room pissing herself laughing. She'd played us at our own game and won hands down. She was wild – a great girl – and I was chuffed when she started on *Coronation Street* years later. Like I say, it's one of those programmes that I always feel is inextricably linked with my life, right from listening to the theme tune at the top of the stairs with our Chris, to Margi Clarke, and then to Tony Wilson telling us how he'd started its most famous siren, Pat Phoenix, on drugs. He'd got her into dope, or so he said, and once she was into it she wouldn't leave him alone. She became a proper spliff-head.

'Where's that Tony Wilson with my drugs?' she used to scream in the office. 'Come on, where is he? Tony! Where's my fucking drugs?' Tony would be hiding under the desk to try to get away from her. He'd created a monster. It's funny because I remember, just before I started the group, being in Kendal's department store in town and I looked up and she was there, Elsie Tanner, and I went, 'Oh, Hiya,' and she glared at me like looks could kill and went, 'Oh, fuck off, will you?' and stormed past. My first brush with celebrity.

One of Manchester's most famous sirens telling me to fuck right off. Two years later Margi Clarke telling me to fuck off too – the Peter Hook curse of *Coronation Street*.

'Not that I'd change anything'

Unknown Pleasures was released to great critical acclaim, with the NME hailing at as an 'English rock masterwork' and Melody Maker as one of the year's best debuts. Though initial sales failed to match the acclaim, word began to spread and Factory soon sold around 15,000, earning the label between £40,000 and £50,000 profit inside six months.

Our next job was a session for Piccadilly Radio, where we recorded our first version of 'Atmosphere', called 'Chance' at that point, along with 'Atrocity Exhibition', which went on to become the opening track on the next album, *Closer*, except in a Hannett slowed-down stripped-down, effect-heavy version.

To be honest, I always preferred it sounding like the version we did first – or better still when we did it live. 'Chance', on the other hand, improved a lot when we re-recorded it. The version we recorded during the session had an organ on it, an old one that Barney had borrowed from his gran. She'd bought it from Woolworths in the 1950s and it was made of old, hard plastic that had gone brittle by the time we got our hands on it. Had a wild sound, though. We liked it straight away, thought it sounded immense and would be great on 'Chance'. Pleased with the way it sounded, we decided to play the song at our next gig, at the F Club in Leeds with the Durutti Column, and took the organ along. There was no case for it but we stowed it on top of the gear, until Vini came along, put his guitar on top of the stack and knocked the Woolies organ off. All that brittle plastic just shattered when it hit the floor. Gutted. We loved that organ.

Ah well, onward and upward. *Unknown Pleasures* came out in June and got fantastic reviews. The distribution wasn't great, of course – that's what you get for being independent – but our stock was rising; we were in demand. We became like a touring machine.

Me, Bernard and Steve found it exhausting juggling the late nights with work, and we weren't married. For us, home was a sanctuary. For Ian, once he got out of Steve's Cortina at night, he was stepping straight into another world of problems: a wife who was uncertain about how she fitted into her husband's new life, and who felt excluded from it, a victim of Rob's no-girlfriends policy. An unhappy wife, in other words. And, of course, a new baby ...

Natalie had been born while we were recording *Unknown Pleasures*, and the fact that I can remember so little about it says less for my memory and more for the fact that Ian hardly mentioned it. There was no big announcement. No session down the pub to wet the baby's head. I don't think he would have said anything at all apart from the fact that he'd fainted at the sight of Debbie giving birth, falling, splitting his head open and leaving Debbie to give birth alone while the nurses looked after him. We asked him more about the cut. In *Touching from a Distance* Debbie says that Ian had had a fit and cut his head, so what the truth of the matter is I'm not completely sure. All I know is that's how we found out Ian had become a dad.

Why didn't he announce it? I don't know. A mixture of things, I suppose. A desire to keep band and family separate, which was always Rob's philosophy, and a sign of the times, when men didn't go dotty about their kids like we do now. All wrong, of course, and it must have made things more difficult for him having to keep wife, kid, *and* the group all happy. Trying to follow his dreams at the same time. With the benefit of hindsight you can see how damaging it would have been and I'm pleased to say that I've learned from it: since New Order's split in 1993 I've always gone out of my way to make sure that family and friends of all the band members aren't excluded but very much *included*.

Great thing, isn't it, hindsight?

In July we went to Central Sound Studios in Manchester for the first of the 'Transmission' sessions. The tunes were pouring out thick and fast. 'Atmosphere', 'Dead Souls' and 'Atrocity Exhibition' all came during this period. I think if it hadn't been for the great reception at the Mayflower we wouldn't have bothered with 'Transmission' as a single, to be honest. But the Mayflower had been the first of a series of occasions where 'Transmission' had blown people away live. We'd begun to think maybe we had something a bit special on our hands – so special we should leave it off the album and release it as a single.

It's one of our songs that should have been a hit – and probably would have been if we'd been on a major, or even if Factory had done things differently. If we'd done things the way normal groups do them, in other words, and released 'Digital' as a single, which would have been big. Then 'Disorder' should have been a single and that would have been bigger. By then we'd have had the kind of foundations we needed to make 'Transmission' a monster, and by the time we got to 'Love Will Tear Us Apart' we'd have been ready to take over the world.

But we didn't do it the normal way, of course. We did it the Factory way.

Not that I'd change anything, mind you. I'd stop Ian hanging himself, obviously. But otherwise I really wouldn't change anything. I wouldn't change the fact that we downplayed the singles or that we left singles off the albums that we didn't promote. Because in many ways it's made us who we are. Besides, the way we did it seemed better than doing what a lot of bands had done. Siouxsie & the Banshees, for instance, had signed to a major and had to sell something like fifty times as many albums to make the same money we did, plus had less freedom and control and had to play the game, the awful game, which is all about selling albums. For us, the punk ethic that had brought us into it moulded the whole way we behaved, and we had a manager who fervently believed in the same ideals, who let us grow and develop at our own pace, without A&R men breathing down our necks, without having to do loads of press we didn't want to do. We would have had to if we'd been on the dreaded major.

So the first session for the 'Transmission' single was at Central Sound Studios, right next to the Odeon in the centre of Manchester and right next to the best kebab shop in town. We got the shock of our lives when we realized where the studio was. We'd been going to that kebab shop for years, never knowing that there was a recording studio next door. What a bonus. The kebab shop, I mean.

It was a cheaper studio, not like Strawberry, but was good for demoing the songs before we went to record them properly. We did 'Transmission', obviously, and it was a good run-through. Plus 'Novelty', despite the fact that it was one of our really early, raw ones, one that I'd written, actually, that Ian had been generous enough to take and mould and make into a song. But for whatever reason Rob really liked it, so we just agreed and recorded it. Badgered into it, probably, because comparing it to the others it sounds very young – a young song from a young band learning their craft. 'Something Must Break' was left off the single because there was no room and Rob didn't want to compromise the sound quality of 'Novelty' because he loved it so much. It was an interesting song for us, though, being the first time the band had used a synthesizer. Martin had used them, of course, but the thing about us in Joy Division – especially me, Bernard and Steve – was that we were sponges constantly learning off Martin. So you'd have this situation where on *Unknown Pleasures* me and Barney were moaning about Martin using a synth, then a couple of sessions down the line we were using it ourselves. Bernard would embrace all that more than me, and on 'Something Must Break' he used a synthesizer instead of the guitar; there's no guitar on it. It's the same technique we used to write 'Love Will Tear Us Apart', actually. There was no guitar on that when we first wrote it, just Bernard playing the synth, me on bass, Steve on drums and Ian's vocals. Even live when we used to play it there was no guitar on it, which gave it a different, unusual sound. It was still a fantastic song and the melody was a great one. Later, when Ian mastered the guitar a little, he played on both.

With *Unknown Pleasures* out and 'Transmission' in the can, it really felt like we were taking off: drawing ahead of the competition a bit. That meant we had to do more interviews, of course, which was a downside. But, again, the fact that we were on an independent meant that we could be awkward bastards if we wanted to be. In fact Tony and Rob encouraged us to be – and, believe me, we did want to be awkward bastards. I mean, we'd all been reading the *NME* and *Melody Maker* for years but, being the kind of contrary types that we were, rather than embrace the music press we kicked against it. The way we saw it, looking at most band interviews, was that if you took the name of the band off they were all exactly the same. Amazing that the *NME* and *Melody Maker* got away with it week after week, because most people said the same thing. Then there was the fact that people kept bringing up the Nazi thing. Once we'd answered that but kept being asked about it, and once it had been made plain that the band didn't have Nazi sympathies but people still went on about it, well, it was bound to piss us off. So we insulated ourselves against it by being awkward bastards right from the beginning of any interview.

'Tell us about your new album.'

'No.'

I used to love that. I once did an interview with John Peel's producer, John Waters. It was for the first Peel session and he said, 'So, tell us how the session's going?'

'It's all right.'

And he went, 'Oh right. Would you like to tell us about your plans?'

'No.'

'Oh, right.'

Afterwards he said it was the most difficult interview he'd ever done, which of course I thought was hilarious. But it wasn't really a plan. Being bloody-minded just amused me – and when it became part of our persona and one of those things that got us remembered, that suited us fine. We were lucky. We had the luxury of being awkward because we were coming out with great music. We didn't really care if we pissed off any journalist. The way we looked at them was, *Where were you when we were playing to an empty room?* It's one of the eternal frustrations of being in a group. One minute you're playing to a handful of people yawning their heads off then six months or eight months later you're playing the exact same material to a packed audience all going bonkers and you think, *Where the fuck were you when we played at Oldham Tower Club?*

What was good about our rise was that we were well managed by Rob, who kept our feet on the ground, kept us level-headed and focused on the music; because, even when we had *Unknown Pleasures* out and the *NME* was saying it was brilliant, and we had 'Transmission' coming out and a buzz around us, gigs coming out of our ears, he kept our feet firmly on the ground. The beauty of Joy Division is that we never made much money while the band existed so there was nothing to sully it – no piles of drugs or cases of booze in the dressing room. We went everywhere in a convoy of knackered van and Steve's Cortina and stayed with friends – no hotels for us, just the odd B&B. Even when we went to London to record *Closer* we stayed in a quite scruffy pair of flats with £1.50 per diem: you could spend how you wished, dinner or a couple of pints but not both. We didn't yet have any money from the record. (Publishing, as in who wrote what in the songs, brings nearly all bands down. I remember the immortal quote from the Mondays: 'Why is the one playing the maracas getting as much as me who writes the songs?' Ironically Bez is now as important as all the songwriters, if not more. How the world turns.)

There was one memorable occasion with Ian putting a drum case on his head and marching round TJ's, screaming at Rob about money, so maybe we had the odd fall-out, but nothing major. The gigs we were doing weren't big payers anyway. We just kept on doing our thing, which was playing, recording, winding up journalists, and in late July appearing on Granada TV's *What's On*.

Now that was excellent and we were very excited to do it – even more so when we went to the subsidized canteen and found it full of Roman soldiers. Rob was following me and Twinny going, 'Don't you nick anything. Don't you fucking nick anything, you pair of bastards.'

In those days Granada was very unionized. It was a very old-fashioned union; you had to be a member to work there. It was very powerful. You had to adhere to very strict rules. When we came to set up there was a light that somebody had taken down from the ceiling and put in the middle of the stage, and we said to the sound guys, 'Do you mind if we move this light, mate?'

They all shook their heads. 'Oh, don't touch that; that's Lighting. We're Sound. They're Camera. That's Lighting. You can't touch that.'

'Okay, but we need to move it, mate, to play.'

'You can't touch it.'

We were like, 'You what? What are you talking about? We've got to have a sound-check.'

They were going, 'No, don't touch it.'

They stuck tape around it to mark it out of bounds.

Our mouths were hanging open. 'We can't sound-check.'

'You'll just have to wait.'

Rob wasn't having that. He went to grab at the light and one of the guys started shouting at him, 'Oh no, don't touch that. Touch that and we're going out on strike, the lot of us. That light belongs to the Lighting Union.'

Rob was in his face. 'You fucking what, mate?' but they weren't budging. Someone called Lighting, who said they'd send someone over, and we all looked at each other in disbelief then sat around to wait, Rob with steam coming out of his ears. Finally, an hour-and-a-half later, this Lighting guy ambled into the studio and picked up the light – 'Sorry about that; must have left it there when I did *Granada Reports*' – and buggered off again.

Brilliant. We leapt up ready to sound-check – *at last* – only to watch gobsmacked as the lot of them turned on their heels and marched out. Not on strike, thank fuck for small mercies, but to have dinner. By the time they returned it was to tap their watches and say, 'Right, you've got half an hour to film it. Better get a move on, lads ...'

They were rewarded with a slightly nervy and shell-shocked performance of 'She's Lost Control' that was broadcast over the end credits of *What's On*. Best thing was that I was wearing the blue shirt that I'd worn on Tony's programme. Very, very fond of that shirt, I was, right up until it got ripped when we were playing with Dexy's Midnight Runners.

'Stop fucking moaning, Hooky'

Talking of Mick Hucknall (which we weren't) his band the Frantic Elevators used to practise in T. J. Davidson's. They also put music out on his label, T. J. M. Records. Come to think of it, he was the butt of a few of our japes, too, as were a lot of the bands in there. I think we reached our peak with the stinky toilet we found loose somewhere, tied a rope to and lowered gently from our window on the top floor, swinging it to and fro until it crashed right through into V2's rehearsal room. When the Buzzcocks' tour came along, Rob treated us to brand-new flight cases courtesy of Bulldog Cases in London, and we terrorized the whole place, locking people in the cases — usually one of a young bunch of fans from Chorley, led by our soon-to-be-roadie Rex Sargeant, who used to hang round watching us practise. We'd push them down the stairs, over and over again. It was a good testing ground. Sometimes Ian would have a ride but only with Barney's crash helmet and gloves on because he was allergic to foam. We used to take him for a spin round the car park too.

We liked Tony Davidson, actually. We asked him to be our manager before Rob came on the scene and he turned us down. He already managed the Distractions, V2, the Frantic Elevators — nearly all of the people who used his rehearsal rooms — but he passed on Joy Division; I don't think he got the music. He was absolutely devastated about it later. As soon as we started making it Tony was like, 'Come back, I'll manage you now!' But Rob saw him off. Little tug-of-love between managers there. But again it was one of those funny things that start happening when you see a bit of success, like the press suddenly becoming interested. A manager who turned you down suddenly knocking on your door.

That's what happens. We were still the same band, still doing the same things we'd always been doing: Ian had been doing his dance virtually since the beginning; the music was always there. Maybe we had a bit more swagger about us now — speaking for myself: yeah, definitely, of course — but otherwise the look hadn't changed. What we had was confidence and belief. Staying in Manchester and staying with Factory meant that we were staying with people who'd believed in us right from the beginning – who didn't like us just because we'd had some success, who would have liked us if we'd been successful or not – and that made us different and them special. After our next gig, which was at the YMCA Tottenham Court Road, the guy from the *NME* wrote that we were 'un-cramped by commercial pressure' and he hit the nail on the head. Thanks to Tony and Rob there was no pressure: no pressure to promote, to sell, to kiss the right arse. The only condition was to keep on writing great songs. We were more than happy to oblige. Had we gone down a different route there definitely would have been that pressure. Like I say, the Banshees had it; the Psychedelic Furs, the Cure, they all had it. We didn't.

That gig, though, at Tottenham Court Road, when we played with Echo & the Bunnymen and Teardrop Explodes ... I remember I drove down in the van, as usual (and yes, it's another poor-old-me-in-the-van story coming up, but it's my book), and we parked in central London.

'Right you wait here in case the promoter comes,' said Rob to me. 'We'll go get something to eat.' 'We' meaning him, Bernard, Ian, Steve, Dave, Terry and Twinny, leaving me all alone with the van.

I said, 'Well what about me having something to eat, you bunch of bastards?'

They were like, 'Stop fucking moaning, Hooky,' then buggered off, and I sat there behind the wheel of the parked van, seething, thinking, *What a bunch of rotten bastards. Why do I drive the van? Why do I always get left behind?* The usual. Then I looked across and saw another van parked opposite me, transit with a guy in the driving seat, sitting muttering away to himself. A bloke in a group, you could tell.

I crossed the road to him and went, 'All right, mate?'

He went, 'All right, la.'

'Who are you with, then?'

'Oh,' he said, 'I'm Les. I'm the bass player from Echo & the Bunnymen.' I said, 'You what? You drive the van as well?'

'Yeah.'

'Have they all fucked off and left you here to do the loading?'

'Yeah.'

We became great mates after that, me and Les, both of us the bass player and van driver for our bands. But I was jealous because he had a double-wheel transit: bigger load capacity and a more powerful engine, you see. On the other hand, my single-wheel was cheaper to run, and the band were saving quite a lot of money in travel and van-hire costs because of it. I still hated it, though, because it was me who had to drive and maintain the bloody thing – and even pay for it, remember. There were times I wished we'd never had it.

Well, they do say that you should be careful what you wish for …

'I just went for a piss'

London was still a big and sexy place to us, so it was always a bit of thrill to play there, and to get a gig at the Nashville Rooms was extra special. After all, that was where the Pistols had their famous concert that got them in the *NME* that I saw in the car park at Newquay, which inspired me to go to see them, etc., etc.

It turned out to be one of those brilliant gigs, because this this was the first time I remember seeing the audience mouthing along with the words – and that is a really *Whoah* moment when you're in a band. Quite an odd sensation, really, when you think of where the song has come from – the four of you freezing your arses off in T. J. Davidson's – to see that it's travelled all that way. It's sort of thrilling and embarrassing at the same time.

So it was a storming gig, apart from the fact that halfway through a guy climbed out of the audience – a punk who got up on stage. We thought, *This guy's come up to have a dance or whatever*, and kept on playing, but he sauntered right past us and went back to where the dressing room was.

We were looking at each other, like, *What the fuck's he playing at?* but still playing, when a couple of minutes later he reappeared and went to climb down off the stage back into the crowd. I stopped him. Still playing, I said, 'Where the fuck have you been?'

'Oh, I just went for a piss,' he said.

I said, 'In our fucking dressing room? You cheeky get,' and kicked him right off stage.

Fast forward to about twenty years later, and this guy comes up to me, can't remember where it was, and says, 'Hello.'

'All right, mate,'

He said, 'I saw you when you were Joy Division, at the Nashville Rooms in London. I was with my friend, who got up on stage and went for a piss in the dressing room, and you kicked him off stage.'

'Yeah, I remember him,' I said. 'The cheeky bastard.'

He said, 'Yeah, well, he ended up hanging himself.'

I went, 'Oh. Fuck. He didn't hang himself because of that, did he?'

'Oh, no, not because of that. It was a few years after that.'

I said, 'Well thank fuck for that!' Which I realize wasn't the most sensitive response but I just had this image, you know?

Anyway, back to the gig. What used to happen when we packed the van after a gig was that Twinny would arrange all the gear so he could lie on the bass cab in a sleeping bag (not Barney's) and sleep all the way home. He wasn't there for that particular gig, though, which he was absolutely gutted about because it was one of the first gigs he'd ever missed. But we managed without him and, after the gig, packed the van and set off, me ahead of Steve, who had strict instructions to stay behind me because I was worried about the van not making the journey.

Knackered, it was, the van. We'd lost the petrol cap and someone – not me – had replaced it with a rag to stop the petrol evaporating. Trouble was, the rag was merrily disintegrating and every so often would block the filter on the carburettor and stop it working. I could always tell when it was going to happen because the van started to slow down gradually, which it had been doing on the way to London that day. There was no power in it at all. And I knew that when I got home I'd have to take the air filter off, take the carburettor off, take it apart, renew all the gaskets, clean the main jet, put it back together again, put fucking everything back on and then it would work fine for a while. What a job.

But first I needed to get home, and I was seriously doubting the van would make the trip. It was going really slowly, about thirty miles an hour top speed. We were pottering home. Next to me Terry fell asleep. I looked in my mirror and could see Steve but he'd dropped quite far behind; there was just me and him on the motorway, as it often was in those days, especially in the early hours of the morning.

We'd just joined the M5 when I started to feel sleepy. Terry was snoring away beside me and I couldn't see Steve in the mirror any more. The next thing I knew there was this huge bang and the van suddenly shot forward so hard that my head hit the divider and for a second I was seeing stars, just barely aware of thinking that the carb must have suddenly cleared because our speed suddenly increased, at the same time feeling the van spin around and the pain. That and a massive squealing of tyres.

I must have been dazed. Because when I got my vision back we were sitting on the hard shoulder, facing the right way, and I thought I was dreaming because a forty-foot lorry was sliding down the motorway past me, sideways on, its tyres screeching as it drew to a stop right across the motorway, blocking all three lanes. The next thing I saw was Ian Curtis running down the motorway chasing a drum that was rolling away – a drum that should have been in the back of my van.

My head was still clearing when Ian arrived at the window carrying the tom.

'Are you all right, Hooky? Are you all right?'

'What's happened?' I said, completely befuddled by the whole thing.

Terry was the same, looking around him in a complete daze. Turned out the forty-footer had hit us at about seventy miles an hour, shunting us and sending us spinning in two complete 360s; it had taken out the back of the van, snapping the back axle and flattening the rear doors. My bass cab had come shooting out the back like a comedy coffin, straight under the wheels of the forty-footer.

Thank God Twinny hadn't been sleeping on it.

I spent the rest of the night being held back from punching the lorry driver, who was from Manchester but wouldn't give us a lift back there. We cleared up our gear from the motorway, worrying that the coppers would find out about my bent MOT. I watched as it was towed away. It wasn't really until the next morning – well, it was the afternoon by the time I woke up – that the reality of it all hit me: the van was history. It was an ex-van. It had ceased to be. No more driving the van for me. From then on either Terry, Twinny or Dave Pils drove a hired van, and every night after a gig I lived it up with the rest of the band in the bar, boozing and trying to pull girls.

On the one hand, it was absolutely magnificent. On the other hand, I ended up an alcoholic.

'You shouldn't trust a word I say'

It was at the Nashville Rooms gig that Annik Honoré came into Joy Division's orbit. She and her friend Isabelle, having travelled from Belgium to see the band, approached the sound engineer at the venue then spoke to Rob Gretton, who agreed to an interview for Belgian fanzine En Attendant *(Waiting) on 22 August, after the band's gig at Walthamstow Youth Club.*

I don't remember Annik at the Nashville Rooms, and only very vaguely recall the interview on the 22nd. But, looking at the dates and knowing the way that things played out and the relationship she and Ian started, well, it must have been a slow-burning thing. There was the small matter of the distance between them, for a start. Not to mention the fact that he was married and probably didn't want the complications of falling in love again. After all, he had enough on his plate.

I liked Annik, though, and still do. Years later we talked about that interview she did at Dave Pils' flat. It was featured in *Control* and my character's sitting there saying dopey things about the name 'Buzzcocks', which I hated when I saw it. Made me look a right twat. I told Annik I would never have said anything so daft and she said to me, 'Ah, but I have the tape, 'Ooky, and zat is exactly what you said.'

So there you go. You shouldn't trust a word I say. Both Bernard and I had a go at bagging Annik, actually, but she got the measure of us straight away and we were both a bit pissed off when Ian got her. Not that they were ever lovers. I suppose he couldn't because of all the pills he was on, or maybe didn't want to... How romantic. It was just another one of those things – something else that maybe used to gnaw at him.

Even so, he still used to cop off. He got caught with a girl in one of the riggers' caravans at the Futurama festival in Leeds (I've read that Annik was also there that day, which suggests that they hadn't quite got it together by then). But he'd always be complaining that he couldn't get a hard-on. It was hardly surprising he couldn't get it up, really; he was on that many pills it's a wonder he didn't rattle. We used to take the piss:

'How come you're still copping off when you can't even get a hard-on? Stealing them off us?' But I think he did it just because he could. I mean, there you are, you're the front man of a band and girls always go for the front man. For ages nobody gave a fuck and no girls wanted to sleep with us. But suddenly they did give a fuck and did want to sleep with us. This sort of thing doesn't get talked about a lot, because it's a bit unsavoury and it's not a part of Ian's character that anybody wants to dwell on, but he was no angel in that regard. No shrinking violet. He was poetic and romantic and soulful – of course he was – but he was still a guy in a band and he liked to do what guys in bands do. Which is to cop off with girls and have a laugh. I do think that's why God gave us bands – so ugly blokes can cop off.

What gets me sometimes about the deification of Ian is that it suggests a real division between Ian and the rest of the band that in reality wasn't there. I've no doubt he was different with us than he was with Debbie and Annik, because that was the people-pleaser in him. The Ian who was with Debbie is the one she talks about in her book; he's the one in *Control,* and you see the Annik-Ian there, too. But what you don't see – and what's never really come out – is the Ian we saw in the band. That's because it doesn't fit neatly into the myth, which prefers the idea that Ian existed on another plane to the rest of us. But he didn't. He loved the lifestyle and would have indulged way, way more if it hadn't been for his epilepsy. He loved the music, and he loved the group. He was our mate. When Terry discovered this unusual-looking turd that somebody had left in the toilets at the Leigh Open Air Festival, and made us all look at it because it was so massive – like a pile of Swiss rolls, the most unbelievable turd I've ever seen in my life – Ian didn't go scurrying off to bury his head in a Dostoyevsky, much as he'd have liked Annik or Debbie to think that's how he'd have reacted. No, he was laughing just as hard and was just as grossed-out as all of us. Just like one of the lads.

I think in that sense we definitely had the best of him and you have to spare a thought for Debbie. We'd deliver Ian home and he'd be fucked. That's what you do as a group: you pick them up, take them away, drop them back off and let someone else pick up the pieces. With Ian being married, an epileptic and a new father, that wasn't easy. They argued. Ian and Debbie argued like cat and dog, actually. They had a car, a Morris Traveller, the one with wood on the sides; it was only ever Debbie who drove it and to be honest we always avoided getting in it with them because they'd always be shouting at each other. Following them in Steve's Cortina we'd see them ripping into each other, all the hand movements that go with it, car swerving all over the road: both screaming, both as bad as each other. You've got to look at it from both sides. It must have been hard for them. For him, the eternal people-pleaser, trying to juggle his two lives. For her, always having to pick up the pieces and probably having nothing to show for it. After all, it wasn't like he was bringing home much money as a sweetener.

He hid a lot of the bad stuff from us. The domestic problems, the fits – he fitted much more at home than he did with the band, apparently, which would have been something else to contend with. I really do feel sorry for Debbie, having to put up with all of that. Especially when we got the nice bloke, the good-lad Ian, who was coming on in leaps and bounds, his confidence growing all the time, the adulation building, and she got the exhausted, coming-down Ian, who probably wanted nothing to do with nappies and bills and all of that. Who just wanted to be back on the road with his group, playing music and soaking up all the worship.

You could see how much we were coming along when you see the *Something Else* footage. We were feeling very confident by this point, and even had a backdrop. Rob had paid 100 quid for it, wanting us to look good for our first ever national TV spot. The Jam were on that day, too, and I remember waiting to go on and Paul Weller coming up to me and saying, 'Are you the support band?'

I thought, 'You cheeky bastard.'

I once told that story at an awards ceremony, funnily enough, and it went down like a lead balloon, but it was true: that's exactly what he did – just assumed that every band appearing with the Jam was 'the support'. Wrong, mate, we're Joy Division.

They did a short interview with Tony and Steve. Me and Barney wanted to appear but Rob wouldn't let us. The words 'two thick bastards' were used. Then we played 'She's Lost Control' and 'Transmission' and you can see how much stronger we were by then. Ian seems to be channelling the music. I can only begin to imagine what it must have been like for television viewers to switch on and see this dancing dervish on their screens. The impression he must have made.

Barney had this mate called Doctor Silk, who I think he worked with, or knew through work or something. Strange boy. He was a magician. When you spoke to him he'd be doing things with his hands and would suddenly do a trick. It was all very impressive the first few times he did it, but became tiring really quickly; by the fourth or fifth time you just wanted him to disappear. He had a very strange haircut and he didn't drink, which for some reason annoyed me and Twinny. Maybe I annoy people now that I don't drink. I don't know. Maybe he just had an annoying way of not drinking.

But anyway, because he was always doing stupid tricks and had this irritating not-drinking thing going on, me and Twinny made it our mission to get him pissed. We were doing this gig at the Factory, so after we'd sound-checked in the afternoon we took Doctor Silk down the pub and started plying him with booze.

'Come on, mate, have another tomato juice! Have another!' By now we were putting double vodkas in his Bloody Mary but none in our own, thinking, *Ha, this'll get him.*

When he didn't seem to be getting at all pissed we started putting triple and quadruple vodkas in his drinks. Until, after a while, we realized that we were both pissed as farts and Doctor Silk as sober as a magician who had seen right through us, knew exactly what we were up to, and had been swapping the drinks round all night – giving us the spiked ones and supping the alcohol-free ones himself – which was exactly what we deserved.

Oh dear. By the time we staggered back to the Factory for the gig we were polatic. I found out later that Ian had had a fit in the dressing room, before the gig, but if I was told about it on the night then it didn't register – sorry, Ian – because I was so drunk. The rest of the band were giving me the evil eye, like, *Look at you, you're so pissed,* and I was giving it all that, like, *Pissed? I've never felt better. Bring it on, man, bring it on.*

So we were playing. Me arseholed, the other three sober as judges. We did the gig, the place going absolutely wild, and mid-song I was saying to Steve, 'Faster, mate, faster.'

Steve just looked at me from under his fringe, going, 'Fuck off, Hooky. I can't go any faster.' But I was forcing him to keep up with me, really pushing the songs forward so that each one was flying past and we were whipping the audience into a frenzy. A huge, messy mosh pit had developed at the front, a right melee, even more brutal than usual. And there was this one kid – a real fan, you could tell, because he was by himself and he was mouthing the words to the songs and had lots of badges on his jacket – when suddenly, *Bok*.

Some guy had nutted him on the back of the head. For no reason at all that I could see. No provocation. This guy had just stepped forward, grabbed the fan by the hair and struck. Really vicious, it was, and the fan dropped like all the air had been let out of him.

Straight away I saw red, pulled my guitar off, held it by the neck and swung it at the boot boy, all in one movement. Trouble was, I was pissed. I don't think I even connected. Instead what happened was the weight of the bass pulled me off stage and into the audience where the same kid and his mates descended on me. Swarmed all over, like those little dinosaurs in *Jurassic Park*, and held me down. Then the kicks started landing.

I thought, *This is it. I'm going to die.*

Did the band stop? Did, Barney, Steve and Ian wade in to help their mate getting battered by the boot boys? No they didn't. They played on. It was Twinny who leapt from the stage, twatted one of the kids, grabbed me, pulled me up, punched another and then took the original thug by the scruff of the neck and together we dragged him all the way back to the mixing desk and started leathering him.

Suddenly the kid was going, 'I'm a fan. I'm a fan!' We looked down and he was covered in Joy Division badges: this was just some other poor kid we'd picked up on the way and we'd been beating up the wrong guy. By this time people were dragging us off and I'd hardly had time to apologize before he was gone. Still the band were playing and I was throwing insults at them. I'd climbed back up on the stage and was calling them miserable twats for not helping me – 'I was getting my head kicked in, y'bastards!' – calling them all the names as they played 'Atrocity Exhibition' like nothing had happened. Like I hadn't just almost been ripped apart in the audience. Then I stormed off into the dressing room, picked up a bottle and threw it at the wall – just as Ian came in.

It just missed him, luckily. 'You're such a yobbo,' he said.

'You're such a fucking poof!' I screamed back at him. Bernard, Steve and Rob then arrived. 'I only decked off to help one of our fans. I didn't see any of you bastards wading in.'

177

(Of course, I didn't mention that we had accidentally beaten up a fan. You don't want to let a little thing like that get in the way of your righteous indignation, do you?)

'I tell you what,' I was still shouting, 'you fucking wait until you're getting the shit kicked out of you. I'm fucking leaving you there.'

Twinny resigned on the spot, calling them all the names under the sun, and stormed off, only to be grabbed outside by Mike Nolan, the Buzzcocks' tour manager, who was very impressed by his on-stage actions and asked if he would do stage security for them, for extra money, on the upcoming tour. Twinny came straight back in the dressing room and withdrew his resignation.

The next day we had a band meeting. Of course I'd sobered up by then.

'Why did do you do that, Hooky?'

'You really upset Ian.'

'Sorry, Ian.'

'You almost hit Ian with a bottle.'

'Oh God, sorry, Ian.'

'He'd had a fit earlier.'

'Oh, fuck, I'm so sorry, Ian.'

'Look, come on, it won't happen again.'

It was lucky for me that the bass was integral to so many of the songs: otherwise they would have kicked me out for sure. In the end they settled for Rob giving me a telling-off, although he must secretly have been pleased because we got a lot of publicity out of it. As far as I was concerned it was the beginning of a reputation that I've been trying to live down ever since. Everyone started gunning for me from then on: 'Let's get that fucking twat Hooky because he'll kick off.'

And for a long time, of course, I was only too happy to oblige.

'Bring it on'

Next, Joy Division embarked on a British tour supporting the Buzzcocks, who were promoting their third album, A Different Kind of Tension, *and by all accounts struggling to maintain their edge. Quite apart from the prestige of the tour – and the fact that an on-form Joy Division are widely believed to have overshadowed the Buzzcocks almost every night – this meant the band members leaving their jobs to finally go professional.*

Now this was a bit more like it. We were a proper band now. On £12 a week – £15 for Ian, with a week in hand because he had a family to feed and Debbie had kicked off proper. Rob kept a tally so he could pay back the extra later. Only on £1.50 per diem still, but it didn't matter. We were professional musicians. The first thing we did when we arrived for the opening date in Liverpool was to look up our old friends the Buzzcocks, who we hadn't seen for about a year.

Our dressing room was the kind of dressing room you'd expect for a band on the bones of their arses: some plastic chairs and a couple of wire coat hangers. But the Buzzcocks' dressing room was a completely different proposition. They had the luxury version and, looking at the activity there, we were rubbing our hands together with glee. All kinds of crates and trolleys were being loaded in: beer, sweets, sarnies, piles of clean towels, the works. Earlier one of their crew had been flashing a bagful of interesting-looking pills, one colour to get you up, another colour to get you down, just like in *Quadrophenia*, not to mention a huge block of dope, as if to say, *This, lads, is the rock-'n'-roll lifestyle. Get ready to party . . .*

We were as ready as we'd ever be. Bring it on. They even had a huge tattooed guy with thick chains around his neck standing guard on their dressing-room door to keep out all the undesirables. Perfect.

'Where are you going, dickhead?' he said as we rolled up ready to become reacquainted with the Buzzocks and partake of their beer, sweets and sarnies.

'We come to see our mates the Buzzcocks,' I replied. 'We started with them in 1976. Very good friends with them, we are.'

'Fuck off,' he said, and stepped in front of the door with his arms folded across his chest.

'Oi, you can't do that!' I said.

He could and did. This was Sarge, and he went on to become one of my best mates – he still is. And if Sarge says you're not going in a dressing room, then you're not going in it.

So we skulked off, denied entry. Always guarded by Sarge, the dressing room became a source of fascination for us, the door a portal to another world, a Narnia filled with clean towels, crisps and groupies. If the Buzzcocks were on stage and Sarge went for a piss we'd be straight in there, helping ourselves to beer and biscuits. Or we'd loiter around until the end of the night when they'd all buggered off, move in and hoover up the dregs.

Otherwise they'd be in it, and the only times we saw much of them during the tour was on the night of the gigs, when one of them – Pete Shelley, usually – would tell us what a wonderful time they were having at whichever five-star hotel they were staying at.

'I've had lobster thermidor,' he said to us one night, like Little Lord Fauntleroy. Back in our dressing room with its torn-up seats and wire coat hangers we called them a bunch of bastards who'd forgotten their roots. We were like, 'Lobster thermidor? What the fuck is lobster thermidor?' I thought they were a local band.

I think the Buzzcocks thought of us as their rough cousins, to whom they couldn't say no in case they caused trouble, which we were a bit, I suppose. It might seem strange now, but at the time they were the middle-class arty types and we were the working-class yobbos. I mean, they had a new bass player, Steve Garvey, who used to change his strings every night. *Every night?* I changed mine when I broke one, and in between times I boiled them in vinegar to get the finger fat off. That's how different we were then.

Thing is, they had too much of the good life. They were trying to do something new with the album they were touring, A *Different Kind of Tension*, which had a more adult-orientated rock sound, and they'd got fat and bloated – musically and physically. Meanwhile we were at the top of our game, playing a tight half-hour or so of great music every night, and every night, apart from in Manchester, where they had a very loyal audience, we blew them off stage. A lesson there: never have a support band who are at the top of their game. As New Order we had OutKast supporting us once. Big mistake that was.

So that was good, anyway; it was satisfying to feel like we were at the top of our game, even eclipsing the mighty Buzzcocks. Plus it was luxury for us to not have to get up for work in the morning. I was living with Iris and she'd get upset because I'd still be in bed when she left for work. She hated it so much she used to deliberately miss the bus so I'd have to get out of bed and drive her into the Co-Op in town. I'd have got in at three in the morning, something daft, but she'd insist I drove her in. I found out years later she never really missed the bus, just let it go past. Women. Still beat going in to work, though. All I'd do was hang around until the afternoon, wait for Steve to come and get me, then go on to the next venue, wherever it was, meet Twinny, Terry and Dave Pils and listen to them regaling me with tales of whatever they'd got up to the night before.

The reason? Our crew were travelling with their crew on the tour bus, staying in the same hotels as the band. It was always going to be good. Jammy bastards. They had to be there to set up our gear for the early sound-checks.

'All right, lads, what did you do last night?'

'Fucking great night, mate. We were up till half five boozing with the band, all doing blueys and smoking dope and chatting up these girls. It was fucking excellent, mate.'

They rubbed it in. God, did they rub it in. We were the band and we were snuggled up in bed at night while our crew were living the rock-'n'-roll lifestyle. What a swizz. Me, Steve and Bernard were dead jealous.

But not Ian, of course. Outwardly Ian was the same as he'd always been. One of the lads. But with the benefit of hindsight you can begin to appreciate some of the pressure he was under: his attraction to Annik and the side-effects of the tablets; the responsibility he felt to both band and home. This was the period during which Debbie was most on his case about money (understandably, mind: they had a new baby); we knew that Debbie was on Ian's case because she was also on Rob's case. Debbie was the one who took against Rob's 'no partners' rule the most and she'd be coming in to rehearsal wanting to have it out with him, mostly over money. There's no doubt she was a force to be reckoned with and you'd have to say that if she was like that with us then she was possibly twice as forceful at home. Maybe because of that pressure, or perhaps just a general worsening of his condition, or the fact that he was spending more time with the band and was less able to hide it, Ian began having more seizures, often during the gigs themselves. Rob used to have mega fights with lighting men at the venues, telling them not to flash the lights; the flashing would always set Ian off. But the lighting men must have either thought, *Fuck off, y'Manc bastard, telling me what to do,* or got carried away, or forgot, because they'd start a light going off on the snare, then on the sides. We'd notice but too late: by then Ian would have stopped singing and gone into a trance, and then he'd either fall over into the drum kit or go apeshit on stage. We started using these washes of lights, which became our trademark – yet another of those things that unintentionally ended up defining us – and which we carried through into New Order. But sometimes he'd just go anyway. Ian had excellent microphone craft – you only have to look at the pictures to see how natural he was on the microphone – and of course he had the dance as well. Mesmerizing. Trouble was, it would set him off. He'd work himself up into a frenzy and go. It was like he couldn't help himself, and we'd end up having to carry him off the stage.

There was a bad one on the second date of the tour, at Leeds, when I had to hold him down backstage. Holding his tongue, I thought he wasn't going to come out of it – that he was going to die. After that he should have rested, of course. (And why didn't we insist? Because he said he was all right, that's why. And because it suited us to take his word for it.) But the next night he was playing Newcastle and the night after that we were in Scotland, where we were staying away from home and behaving like pigs at a trough.

Now there's a story. It all started at the Hilton in Glasgow, the first time we got to stay out with the Buzzcocks. The bands and our crew were all in this hotel, drinking in the bar. Drinking like mad things, charging the drinks to other people's rooms, getting absolutely arseholed. Us lot were crowded round Sarge, who was of great interest to us because he'd been in the Hell's Angels – a former sergeant-at-arms, which accounted for his nickname. The sergeant-at-arms is the guy who does all the enforcing. He polices the Angels, and one of Sarge's jobs was to preside over the initiations, which he was telling us about, one of them being that the new guys have to drink a pint of piss.

We were like, 'How fucking disgusting is that?' and Sarge just shrugged.

So Ian said, 'Go on then, you drink a pint of piss.'

'All right,' said Sarge, 'You get a pint of piss and I'll drink it. But it's going to cost you a fiver.'

That was it. Us lot were running around scabbing money off people to pay him to drink the piss, and once we'd got enough we set about filling the pint pot – Terry mainly, whose piss was like treacle it was that thick and brown.

We handed our warm pint pot of thick, treacle piss to Sarge and put it on the table, watching as he looked at it then dipped his hand in it then put it in his mouth.

He went, 'It's warm. I want a tenner.'

We raised more, gave it to him then watched as he downed the pint in one, banged the glass down and said, 'Right, shit sandwich for twenty quid.'

Shit sandwich. We needed some bread for a shit sandwich.

Disaster – we couldn't find any bread. Next thing you know the whole lot of us were tearing around the hotel trying to find bread. Me and Dave Pils ran down a corridor and came across this breakfast trolley that had all the stuff in it you could wish for, so we started rooting around in it and then, for no good reason – apart from that I was pissed and it seemed like a good idea at the time – I turned the trolley over on Dave and pinned him to the floor. Lying there covered in knives and forks, and little pots of marmalade and sachets of brown sauce, he was laughing, calling me a bastard, then he shoved off the trolley and came at me, grabbed a huge plant out of a pot and began swinging it at me.

One messy plant-pot fight later and we got back to the bar, only to find it had been closed because we were getting so rowdy. We weren't having that. They're supposed to leave it open all night if you want. So, even though it was four o'clock in the morning and we were as pissed as bastards – or more likely *because* it was four o'clock in the morning and we were as pissed as bastards – one of the Buzzcocks' lighting crew ripped the shutters off the bar and we all dived in. Midway through that session somebody shouted that the cops were on their way – they weren't; it was just somebody being a bastard – and we all scarpered. Never has a bar emptied of people so quickly. Then we all passed out in our beds.

I woke up the next morning to discover two things: first, that I'd slept with my arm out of the bed; and second, that the police really were on their way. The theft/vandalism/whatever you want to call it in the bar had been discovered and Joy Division were being blamed. For about half an hour we ran about like headless chickens, Rob grabbing our clothes for us and shoving them into bags, desperately trying to get us out of the hotel before the police arrived. The Buzzcocks' management could sort it out later. We just needed to concentrate on not being taken into custody and risk missing that night's gig in Edinburgh.

We made it. Just. Left behind our wreckage and travelled on to Edinburgh, all of us except Steve nursing terrible hangovers and me wondering about my arm sticking out of the bed like that – and this is the funny thing, because ever since that night I've always had to sleep with one arm hanging out of the bed.

We kept our noses clean until we got to Dundee, where we decided that Twinny was getting too big for his boots, because he was always sniding off with the Buzzcocks, so we decided to jape his room.

First order of business was to get all his clothes and tie them to a flagpole outside the hotel. Then we took the bed out of his room and replaced it with a baby's cot we found in the corridor and then, because Twinny's dead superstitious, we took out all the light bulbs, tied a bit string around the coat hangers in his room and fed it through the connecting door, where we waited, giggling.

And waited. Five o'clock in the morning, when Twinny finally got back to his room, pissed as a fart, and we'd long since stopped giggling. But still, we felt extra justified now that he'd spent all night living it up with the Buzzcocks again! So when he got into the room and we heard him flicking the light switch to no avail, we started rattling the coat hangers. He freaked. Shouted something about the room being haunted and tried to escape. But because he was pissed and the room was pitch black he fell over, right into the cot, which smashed to pieces.

He passed out and the next morning was furious, demanding we give him his clothes. We just pointed him in the direction of the flagpole and told him it served him right.

'Turned out to be horse meat'

We had a break from the Buzzcocks tour to do our next gig, which was at Plan K in Brussels, a big arty happening with a William Burroughs reading, screenings of films, Joy Division and Cabaret Voltaire. We were almost late getting there because Terry was driving the van. The thing was, Terry, Twinny and Dave Pils got on really badly sometimes, always bickering, and it was only me that kept them from battering each other. But now that we were a proper professional band with paid road crew (i.e., them) I didn't drive the van any more so I didn't travel with the crew; I went in Steve's Cortina. Luxury. But it did mean that the Three Stooges didn't have anyone to keep them apart; and on the day we left for Brussels they must have had some massive fall-out, because Terry was in a bad mood, and because he was in a bad mood he was driving at Miss Daisy speeds down the motorway and kept pulling over. Never the most competent of drivers, he was telling me that he couldn't get the van to go over thirty miles an hour and I ended up replacing him in the driving seat and flooring it down the motorway rather than risk missing the ferry. I got it up to eighty, though, and we made it to Brussels, which was dead exciting – the first time we'd travelled outside the UK.

Somehow we found Michel Duval, the organizer, who took us to the hotel and we were buzzing – even more so at the thought of the luxurious Brussels hotel he was bound to have chosen for us.

Except when we got there it wasn't a hotel. It wasn't even a B&B. It was a youth hostel. Instead of having rooms with two sharing, which is what we were used to, we had to sleep in this huge dormitory. We grabbed the best beds. Steve, being too slow, got one with a big lump in it where the springs had broken and when he lay on it he was all bent over; Barney was already complaining that he wouldn't be able to get any kip, being such a light sleeper, even though it had never seemed to bother him before; while Ian took one look at the set-up and went off to try to wangle a bed elsewhere – which he did, with Cabaret Voltaire in their normal, nice room, before returning to rub our noses in it.

With our sleeping arrangements sorted we went to the gig, which was at this huge, amazing 'art' space, I suppose you'd have to say. We did our bit and it was really good gig, and afterwards me, Ian and Barney went along to see William Burroughs then stood around as he sat at a table signing books.

Ian was a bit awestruck, but poor, so he couldn't afford to buy one of the books William Burroughs was signing. 'I'm going over to ask him if I can have a book,' he said, after standing there for ages looking over at the table like a kid eyeing up a plate of warm pies or something.

Me and Barney thought this was hilarious. I mean, looking at William Burroughs, how grizzled and world-weary he looked, he didn't seem like the kind of guy who was in the habit of handing out freebies to oiks from Macclesfield. Still, Ian had sunk a couple of Duvels and was feeling brave and we were winding him up something rotten. So when there was a lull in visitors to William Burroughs' table over he strolled over, ignoring us two, who went and hid behind a pillar nearby, sniggering.

'Oh hello, Mr Burroughs,' he said, 'I'm a big fan of yours, and ...'

William Burroughs looked at him and growled. 'Yeah, kid, yeah. Whatever.'

He'd probably been hearing that all night – from people who were at least buying his books.

'Well, I'm in the band Joy Division who played tonight ...'

'Yeah, kid, yeah. Whatever,' growled William Burroughs.

'Well, I was wondering if I could have a book?'

'*Have* a book?' snapped William Burroughs.

'Yeah.'

He looked at Ian. 'Fuck off, kid,' he said and Ian slunk away, tail between his legs, as we wet ourselves laughing. We then spent the rest of the night growling, 'Fuck off, kid,' at Ian – whose response was to get really, really pissed.

He wasn't the only one. Twinny: also absolutely pissed. I found him outside and instead of loading our gear into the back of the van he'd raided the bar and had stacked the van full of stolen beer. We made him put it all back so we could get the gear in, so we could return to the youth hostel. When we got there it was absolute carnage. Back in the dorm, Twinny discovered this Belgian guy asleep in his bed.

'Oi, you, fuck off!' he was shouting, just hollering at the bloke, who in return looked terrified, like a rabbit in the headlights. Twinny was advancing on him and would probably have grabbed the guy if I hadn't stepped between them.

'Twinny,' I said, 'he can't understand you, y'daft bastard. He's a Belgian. You'll have to speak French to him.'

Twinny looked at me, nodded, and went to the guy, 'Oi, You. *Fucky offy.*'

Poor bloke just got out of bed and legged it, by which time the lot of us were in absolute hysterics and there was no stopping us. Ian was laughing because he was going off for a good night's kip in Cabaret Voltaire's room and it was obvious that things in our dorm were only going to get more out of control. Barney was moaning about something then started having a fight with Twinny, but Twinny got carried away and upended Barney's bed, with him on it, so Barney came flying off and hit his head on a radiator. That completely enraged him so he picked up a bottle of orange squash, smashed the end off on the radiator and poured it all over Twinny's bed. Twinny's response was to smash open two bottles of Duvel and pour them on Barney's bed, by which point we were telling them both to calm the fuck down before someone got hurt. Just then Ian got his knob out and started pissing in our ashtray – one of those tall freestanding ashtrays, it was – thinking it was hilarious, looking back over his shoulder going, 'Ha, you wankers, I'm pissing in your room! Ha ha, pissing in your room!' It was one of those pisses that just seemed to go on and on forever, like a donkey's, and we were calling him a dirty bastard when a caretaker walked into the room flanked by two security goons.

The guy went berserk. Ian wasn't smiling any more. He was trying to stuff his cock back into his trousers and at the same time pacify the caretaker, who was turning all shades of purple, calling Ian in French what we'd just been calling him in English, except that now Ian didn't think it was at all funny.

'I don't understand French,' he was saying. 'I'm sorry. I don't understand French. Just tell me what you want me to do and I'll do it.'

Whatever it was he did to calm the caretaker down, I don't know, but he did, and the festivities continued and next thing I passed out, one arm hanging out of the bed.

Next morning we woke up in this wreckage of a dorm, with orange and Duvel and Ian's piss everywhere, hungover to shit, desperately needing something to eat and ending up in what we thought was a burger bar. There we spent the last of our money on seven burgers, which they handed us to eat raw. Turned out be horse meat and of course none of us could eat it so we went hungry.

Which served us all right, I suppose.

That was our Belgium jaunt. On our return home we went straight back on tour with the Buzzcocks, but somewhere in the middle of all that madness we found time to record what would go on to become one of our best-known tracks, 'Atmosphere', which we did for *Licht und Blindheit*, a French-territory-only EP. Who puts one of their best songs on a limited-edition single available only in France? Us, that's who.

'Atmosphere' is a massive song. A lot of people say it's their favourite Joy Division song but it's not mine; it reminds me too much of Ian, like it's his death march or something, and it figures that it's one of the most popular songs to play at funerals: Robbie Williams has got 'Angels' for weddings and we've got 'Atmosphere' for funerals. Becky says that when I die she's going to play 'Atmosphere' at my funeral – but by Russ Abbott. Thanks, love.

So no, 'Atmosphere' isn't my favourite. If you were to ask me what was, it would have to be 'Insight'. I mean, it might change tomorrow, but it's 'Insight' right now because it's just so simple but so powerful – and it doesn't have a chorus. That was one of the things I really liked about Joy Division, that the songs didn't have to have a chorus or a middle eight. I used to love it about New Order, too, until we started to get all formal about the writing, until by the end every song had a verse, chorus and middle eight, which to me just made everything bland.

But 'Insight' doesn't have all that. To me it's the sound of a group of young musicians working out the possibilities of what they can do, and working them out together. Changing the world. It reminds me of a time when writing music was easy but most of all fun.

The release of the 'Transmission' seven-inch in October had proved to be a disappointment for Tony Wilson, who had hoped that its chorus of 'Dance, dance, dance to the radio' would win it radio airplay. Plans to hire a radio plugger were shelved at the insistence of Rob Gretton and Martin Hannett, who felt that to promote the single went against the Factory ethos. As a result, and despite critical acclaim, just 3,000 of the 10,000 copies ordered by Wilson were sold. Rob Gretton was to orchestrate the band's next act of commercial defiance, striking a deal with French label Sordide Sentimental. Set up in France in 1978 by Jean-Pierre Turmel and Yves Von Bontee, it had piqued his interest with a superbly packaged release of Throbbing Gristle's 'We Hate You (Little Girls)', and a deal was made to release two Joy Division songs in similar fashion: 'Atmosphere' and 'Dead Souls', produced by Martin Hannett during sessions at Cargo in October. Finally released in March 1980, The Licht und Blindheit EP was limited to just 1,578 copies, mail order only, with most fans having to content themselves with taping it from the John Peel programme.

The tracks that Throbbing Gristle put out on Sordide Sentimental were never going anywhere else. I mean, they were harsh even by the standards of Throbbing Gristle. Whenever I put that EP on my cat used to run out of the room. Us? We put two of our best songs on it. On a limited edition that we never even got any money for. The run was 1,578 copies; I found out years later that 1578 was also the last date the French beat the English in a war.

Having said that, it didn't bother us at the time – this came during a period when we were continually writing great songs, so it didn't seem like such a big deal, to be honest. And, looking at it in terms of the whole Joy Division story, well, it's just 'us' isn't it? That special attitude championed by Rob and accepted by Tony that was either total naivety, utter stupidity, incredible foresight or a weird mix of all three. I honestly don't know. I mean, people said we were mad at the time – other bands and their managers, I mean. But Rob loved it. He loved being bloody-minded and contrary and he liked nothing better than winding up Tony.

'Atmosphere' was originally written in two halves. The bass and drums was one idea – me and Steve came up with it together. The vocals and the keyboards was another idea. We'd been working on them separately, just tinkering with them, really, then put them together and got the song that we called 'Chance', featuring our Woolies organ borrowed from Barney's gran.

It would be a few years yet before we got overdrawn at the riff bank. This was the time, after all, that we also wrote 'Love Will Tear Us

Apart' and ended up recording it for the first time as part of a second John Peel session in November. It was a song we'd written during rehearsals at TJ's. I had the riff, Steve built the drum part and Ian mumbled some words then said he was going to go home and write some lyrics for it, which he did, using the bass riff as the melody for the chorus. But Christ, if he'd written that song about me I'd have been heartbroken. I'm not sure who it was written about. I never asked. But whoever it was deserves all of his money just for that.

'He's possessed by the devil, that twat'

Still with the Buzzcocks tour, we were travelling further afield in the UK and Ian began having more fits. He had a really bad one in Bourne-mouth. He was so tired by the time we got there. We all were, of course – absolutely knackered – but the rest of us weren't on heavy medication. We didn't have a wife and a baby, and our affairs of the heart weren't quite so complicated.

After a gig in Guildford the night before, Rob had shaved the band's hair with clippers. Ian, Bernard and Steve got sheared; only I got away with it. We were staying at a B&B where Bernard had to go and sleep in the bathroom to get away from Rob's snoring – the start of a regu-lar habit for him – there was a lot more booze involved and it was all a bit of a riot one way or another. The upshot being that by the time we reached Bournemouth we were shattered – especially Ian. Most of the seizures he had occurred towards the end of gigs but this one was near the beginning of the show, which we had to stop. It lasted about an hour and a half, with me and Rob taking turns holding him down in the dressing room; once again with me holding his tongue in his mouth to stop him swallowing it. Christ, it was scary.

He came round and was looking at us, his eyes all glassy.

'Ian,' I said to him, 'Can you hear me, mate? We're going to have to get you to the hospital.' He shook his head: he understood me all right but he didn't want to go to the hospital. Never did; didn't want to be a bother. That was him all over.

'Look, Ian, mate; it's not right; you've been fitting too long. We're taking you whether you like it or not.'

He was still dead reluctant to go and in a funny sort of way he was right. You take a guy who's just had an epileptic fit to casualty and the nurse looks at you like you've just dropped in from Venus. And that's exactly what happened when we'd bundled Ian into the car, got him to the nearest hospital and waited hours for our turn to be seen.

They did at least have the good grace to take him into a consulting room, while we hung about in the waiting room. After a while he came out. A bit pale, bit downcast. Otherwise okay.

'You all right, Ian?'

'Yeah, yeah, I'm okay. Don't worry about it.'

He went back to the gig, where the Buzzcocks had only just come on, and there was no sign of Twinny anywhere. After searching for a while I found him in a cupboard, all curled up in a ball like he was hiding from something.

'What the fuck are you doing in here?' I said.

'He's possessed by the devil, that twat.'

'Get up, you soft bastard,' I said, dragging him out. 'Stop fucking around. Go and see him. He's back to normal now.'

Whatever 'normal' was. For Ian 'normal' was getting hardly any rest, eating shit food, getting pissed, travelling all the time, driving from city to city. The precise opposite of everything he should have been doing. I look back and keep seeing where we should have stopped. It's the part of doing this book that's the hardest. Writing it all down, I can pinpoint the moments where we should have said 'enough is enough' – because now they seem so obvious. But at the time he just carried on and so did we. Selfishness, stupidity, wilful ignorance and a refusal to accept what was going on right in front of our noses – we were all guilty of it, even Ian. Because this was what we'd worked and waited for. All that freezing in TJ's and fighting with the Drones and feeling ignored and overlooked was paying off at last. I wish sometimes I could tell the younger me, 'Slow down, mate, what's the big hurry? You've got another thirty or forty years of this,' knowing that the twenty-two-year-old me would curl his lip and tell the old me to fuck off, because when you're twenty-two it feels like if you don't seize the moment then it'll be gone in a puff of smoke.

Even so, I find it mind-boggling that someone didn't slap Rob Gretton and the rest of us and drag Ian off home to bed. But nobody did. Things just got more and more manic. On the Buzzcocks tour the practical jokes continued. Unsuspecting victims would open doors and get wastepaper bins of rubbish or water dumped on their heads. Or they'd sit in chairs we'd balanced on Coke cans so they'd topple over.

Of course there were times it got right out of hand. One night, around about the time of fireworks night, the whole lot of us – me,

Terry, Dave Pils, Rob and Steve – burst in on Ian and Barney, who were with a couple of girls in a hotel room, Barney in one bed, Ian in the other. Dave lit a couple of bangers and threw them into the room, where one of them landed on Barney's shirt and set it on fire.

Barney went berserk – absolutely wild. After he'd put the shirt out, he was calling us all sorts and shouting at us to fuck off and waving his burnt shirt around. In return we were giving him the Vs and telling him he could fuck off and that he deserved it (although I'm not sure he did, actually; it was probably jealousy on our part, but there you go). Ian thought it was hilarious and these two girls, both completely naked, were absolutely terrified, poor things, the room suddenly full of Northerners chucking fireworks around, setting clothes alight and swearing at each other. Hardly the erotic feast they might have been hoping for.

We would have spent all night screaming at each other had the hotel porter not arrived and kicked off. As he was shouting at us, Barney stormed out of the room, giving it all, 'Right, you fuckers, I'll show you,' as a parting shot, and we were like, 'Yeah, yeah, fuck off,' as he went.

Everything calmed down. Most of us went to the bar for a drink, gave the girls a bit of privacy at last, and as we were sitting there Barney came in, still raging.

'Where've you been?' we said.

'You'll see,' he was saying. 'You'll fucking see, you bunch of bastards.'

We were like, 'Fuck off, twatto,' finishing our drinks. Only to discover the following morning that the stupid twat had let all four tyres down on the car.

I was like, 'What you do that for?'

'You burnt my fucking shirt.'

'But you've japed yourself. You have to travel in that car as well, you stupid twat.'

Of course it took us hours to get the four tyres pumped up. We had to buy a foot pump then take it in turns. We were all sweating like bastards, including Barney.

A lot of the japes took place between us and the Buzzcocks and their crew, and in the run-up to the last gig of the tour, which was at the Rainbow at Finsbury Park, their guys were telling us that they were going to spring something really big on us, really nasty, for our last night.

'Oh, we're going to get you. We're going to get you,' they were saying. 'When you're on stage, mate, mid-performance. We got something very special in mind for you.'

But fuck 'em: they were messing with the kings and straight away we formed a council of war to concoct our retaliation. What we came up with involved the purchase of twelve live mice – we wanted rats but we couldn't afford them – ten pounds of live maggots, ten cans of shaving foam and five dozen eggs. That was all we could afford. A fortune was spent on this jape, but it was going to be worth it.

The plan was to get the Buzzcocks with the maggots during their performance. They'd think that was all we had to offer, but in the meantime we'd have put the live mice inside their tour bus and used the shaving foam on the doors and windows. They'd deal with the shaving foam, board the bus, see the mice, run screaming off the bus and we'd egg as they came out. Brilliant. We were as good as inventing japes as we were at writing songs.

So it got to the gig. Even though we knew we had something lined up we were still worried about what they'd do to us. Their crew were all sniggering. We'd been threatened with the jape to end them all. All week they'd been leading up to this. What would they have come up with? What horrors lay in store for us?

They put some talcum powder on the snare drum.

That was it. That was the full extent of their world-beating jape. A bit of talcum powder on the snare drum. I didn't even notice at the time. As we were coming off I said to Steve, 'What's happened to the Buzzcocks' jape, then?' and Steve told me that they'd put a bit of talc on his snare drum and when he'd hit it a little cloud had come up. That was it.

What a bunch. Oh dear: our response was going to look a bit on the disproportionate side. Still, more fools them for doing such a lame joke, we thought, and seeing them chortling away, thinking they'd been dead funny with their talc-on-the-snare-drum trick, just made us even more determined to set about our reply as planned. We waited until they came on and launched phase one of the plan: the maggots.

Ten pounds of them, we had. That's a lot of maggots. That's five bags of sugar's worth of maggots. Towards the end of their set, as they started playing 'Boredom', we livened things up by creeping up behind the crew with our bags: a couple of bags of maggots each, emptying them first on to the flight cases where the Buzzcocks' crew sat to watch the set, then on to the Buzzcocks' backdrop, which the maggots began crawling up, just as we'd hoped they would, and then on to the fold-back desk.

Barely holding it together we retreated to watch the mayhem from a safe distance, watching the maggots advance. The crew noticed something first. A tide of maggots had made its way from the flight cases up the backs of the crew, then into their hair. We watched as first one then another started to scratch and a horrible realization dawned on them. The next wave of maggots had by now worked their way up the backdrop and were falling on the Buzzcocks' drummer, John Maher. Now the guys on the fold-back desk were running around screaming. So were the rest of the crew. John Maher finished 'Boredom' in a shower of maggots and the band came off, furious with us.

That was it, they thought. Jape over. How wrong they were. They had two buses outside, one for the band and their girlfriends and another one for the crew. We'd prised open the windows, dropped in the mice, coated all the door handles in shaving foam then returned to the Rainbow for an end-of-tour party.

Sarge let us into the dressing room. At last. Allowed inside the sacred dressing room. And what a riot that turned into, everybody pissed. Their lot were laughing about the talc on the snare drum – ho ho, what a funny jape – and we were laughing about the maggots, letting them think that was the end of it but secretly anticipating the carnage we'd prepared for when they got to their buses.

One food fight later and it was time to leave, so we scarpered out quick and piled into Steve's Cortina, parking up beneath an underpass or railway bridge or something, oblique to where the coaches were and across the road, each coach primed with six live mice in it and the windows and door handles coated with shaving cream.

So we watched ... And out came the Buzzcocks and their girlfriends and, in hysterics, we then watched them cursing us and wiping off the shaving cream. They saw us over the road and started screaming at us, but didn't even bother trying to get us – we'd have been out of there while they were still doing the Green Cross Code. We cradled our eggs as we watched them clean off the last bits of foam and board the bus, then we waited for them to come running out as soon as they saw the mice.

But they didn't. The bus drove off. We looked at each other. Shit. Still, at least we had the crew to come. Sure enough, a little bit later, out came the crew; they now saw their coach with shaving cream all over it, started wiping it off, spotted us, and were shouting insults while we sat there killing ourselves and holding on to our eggs, watching them clean up and board their coach.

This time it worked a treat. Seconds after the coach door had shut it opened again and out poured the road crew, falling down the steps, screaming, 'Rats! Rats!'

Brilliant. We were already out of the car and legging it across the road, where we started pelting the lot of them with eggs. It was all over in seconds. We covered them in egg then scarpered back to the Cortina, busting a gut with laughter – only to find a couple of coppers standing there.

Behind us over the road was complete mayhem, with the crew only just recovering from the egg attack, their coach covered in egg and shaving foam, and shitting it about the rats inside. One of the coppers pointed over. 'You do realize that's vandalism?'

Then, for some reason, Dave Pils went, 'Is this 'cause I'm black?'

Which was funny, because he isn't black.

'But you're not black, Dave.'

'It's 'cause my girlfriend's black.'

Jasmine was black – he was right about that.

'Dave ...'

'It is, isn't it, you racist bastard?'

'*Dave.*'

We managed to calm the police down but it took us about fifteen minutes, by which time the Buzzcocks' crew had got rid of the mice, got in their bus and fucked off back to the hotel to meet up with the band.

'Fucking Joy Division put rats in our bus. Did they get you?'

'No,' said the band, 'they wouldn't fucking dare put rats in our bus.'

But Sarge told us later that he'd been in the bus, and Steve Diggle was in there chatting to his girlfriend when Sarge had looked down and seen a mouse in her handbag.

'I thought I was tripping,' he told us later. Looking around he saw a load of beer cans in the corner, and another mouse. Then another. And another. But he'd decided to keep it to himself, guessing that all hell was going to break out if anyone noticed. Instead he just waited till the band got to their hotel and ushered everyone off as quick as he could before dealing with the mice by stamping on them. We didn't like that – we were animal lovers – but I wasn't going to argue. The idea of the Buzzcocks unaware that their coach had been overrun with mice was somehow just as funny as them finding out.

I've got to say, that was a great end to what had been an eventful year to say the least. At the beginning of December we played at Eric's, which was quite a landmark gig, really, because it was the first time Gillian ever joined us on stage. There had been the usual horse-play, with us hanging around the venue in between the sound-check and the doors opening and working our way through a crate of beer that Roger had given us. Barney and Rob had been play fighting, mess-ing about with beer bottles, and one of them cut a finger open. Just our luck it was Barney, who couldn't play the gig because of it. I think it was Rob who suggested that Gillian join us on guitar, because she'd played guitar in the Inadequates – he was always a bit sweet on her, to be honest.

Fortunately Barney was okay for our next gig, at Les Bains Douches in Paris, where Steve told us that he'd be able to negotiate our way around because he had an O Level in French.

'Oh,' he said, 'I used to love speaking French. Really good at it, I was.'

He never spoke a word of French the whole trip. Not even in the petrol station, the bit he had been practising: 'Fill her up, mate' was all that came out.

Anyway, so we got on the ferry and, fuck, the waves were enormous. They were so big they were actually spinning the boat; the captain had to let it drift. Like a bunch of twats, me, Dave Pils and Twinny went out on deck to have a look. We were the only passengers stupid enough – the wind was howling, there were huge waves slapping against the side of the ship and pouring rain.

We made it to the stern, hanging on to the rail, grinning maniacally. It started getting too rough even for us and we made our way back to the door, got there and pulled ourselves in – just as the biggest wave I've ever seen in my life engulfed the whole of the stern where we'd been standing, taking everything that wasn't bolted down. We just stood there, shaking, knowing that another second and it would have been us.

Rob, meanwhile, was down in the casino, pissed and gambling, swearing that he wasn't gambling with the band's money; because, as he always said, 'I keep the band money in this pocket, and me own money in this pocket.'

But by the end of the night it looked to me as if both pockets were empty, pulled out like an elephant's ears. Things got even more interesting after that. When we arrived at the gig we discovered that an ex-girlfriend of Steve's had followed us over, trying to win him back from Gillian. The venue was an old Turkish baths, an early design by Philippe Starck, actually, quite weird: all the baths were still in place, and some still had water in, so people could – I don't know – throw money in them, make a wish or paddle or something.

So anyway, we were playing this gig, two numbers into the set, when suddenly the backstage door opened and Steve's ex, Stephanie, appeared. She stuck her head out and started calling him.

'Steve! Steve!'

Oh dear – he nearly died. He went bright red and kept his head down and then, as she carried on shouting at him – 'Steve! Steve, I love you!' – started played faster and faster.

As if keeping up with Steve wasn't exhausting enough, afterwards we had to make a dash for it in order to avoid her. Eventually we ended up looking for this street Rue St. Denis, which we'd heard was full of hookers. Not to partake, just to gawp. And this is one of my lasting impressions of Ian – an image I have in my head of him, like the image of him chasing the drum down the motorway or pissing in the ashtray. It's of Ian, who liked to read Burroughs and Kafka and discuss art with Annik, asking this French guy where all the girls were. 'Girls,' he was saying. 'Where are all the girls?' Holding his arms to his chest and waving them up and down like a pair of jiggly boobs. 'Where are all the girls?'

UNKNOWN PLEASURES
TRACK BY TRACK

CP 1919   318 MHz

⊢20 ms ⊣

Fig. 2. – 100 consecutive pulses from the pulsar CP 1919. Time increases from bottom to top. Pulsar period is 1.34 seconds.

I really recommend listening to the record while you read.

'Disorder'

I've got the spirit, but lose the feeling ...

Because we recorded *Unknown Pleasures* so quickly there wasn't the time to re-record much (with the exception of Steve's drums, obviously) so there are a few bum notes on the album, most of which are courtesy of yours truly. The ones that are most noticeable – and these are the only ones I'm going to point out – are on 'Disorder', where it sounds like it could be Bernard's guitar but it's not, it's me. The funny thing is, though, they're now part of the song, even though they're bum notes. It's where I was playing the lower string and catching the A and D with my plectrum, which has given it that guitar sound. Playing it back, I can't imagine 'Disorder' without those sounds. Some of the low notes are a bit wild too but, hey, we were young. Like Pete Saville's theory, now we'd stop and go, 'Hold on, Hooky's played a wrong note. He's caught the strings, we'll have to fix that!' It's a mistake, but it ended up being a good mistake; to me it sounds really interesting.

'Day of the Lords'

This is the room, the start of it all ...

We'd only ever played these songs live before, never demoed them. I think the only ones we'd demoed were 'She's Lost Control' and 'Insight'.

'Day of the Lords' is a slow song, but it's a great song. The guitar's loud and swept along by the bass. Martin overdubbed the keyboards. At the time we were all like, 'What? keyboards? If we want fucking keyboards we'll get a fucking keyboard player.' So he overdubbed them when we weren't there. We didn't even hear it until he'd done the mix. He played us the mix and me and Barney were pulling faces behind his back because he was putting keyboards on things. He was right, though, Martin. The keyboards sweeten it and make it better. Bleeding keyboards, soon to be the bane of my life. Great snare sound.

'Candidate'

I campaigned for nothing, I worked hard for this ...

Martin needed two more songs so he said to me and Steve, 'You've not got enough songs. You need to go in and write more songs.'

We were like, '"Go in and write"? We can't "go in and write"! What do you mean?' That just wasn't the way we came up with songs. We jammed them as a band; we didn't write them like that.

'Just go in there and write two more songs.'

'Oh, for fuck's sake!'

So we took ourselves off and started 'writing' – well, jamming. We got 'Candidate' immediately – and also 'From Safety to Where', which ended up not making it on to the album. If you listen closely to 'Candidate' it has that feel of a song that's not quite finished – well, it does to me, anyway, because I know that it's a jam that Ian went and put a vocal on. A great song, yes; but, like I say, not completely worked out. Great for that reason, though.

So we had these two tracks and Martin said, 'Right, Bernard, go and put some guitar on those songs; they're really good, these.' So Bernard went and was sitting there with his guitar for ages, not playing on the tracks – well, hardly playing at all – because he didn't like them. This was the guitarist's equivalent of a huffy teenage strop. Like when you tell a kid to tidy their room and two minutes later they go. '*Happy now?*' That's what I mean when I talk about his 'economical' playing. He's a brilliant guitarist but woe betide you if he didn't like the song; he'd either refuse point blank to put guitar on it or do such half-arsed guitar you wish you hadn't bothered.

Martin decided to turn the twenty-four-track tape over and play the track backwards, pushing him to play over it forwards, which he seemed to quite like; he perked up a bit and we did actually got some good guitar. Martin then spun the tape back over so the guitar's backwards. It actually worked. 'From Safety to Where' was Barney's economical guitar playing at its very best.

'Insight'

Reflects a moment in time, a special moment in time ...

'Insight' is one of my favourite songs and also one of my favourite bass riffs. I mean, the great thing about Joy Division was that we used the bass to write the songs. Most bass players are just used to back up a song, to fatten it up: to 'follow the root notes', as they say. I don't do that. I remember, very early on in our career, Barney turning round to me and saying, 'Can't you just follow the guitar?'

'No, I can't. You follow me. Ha!'

The lyrics are wonderful and there's no chorus. There's repetition in the lyrics, but no chorus. That sound at the beginning is the creaky old freight lift in Strawberry that Martin had mic'd up and recorded, adding fantastic atmosphere to the track. Steve's snare has such great presence. It's well known that Martin used a lot of echo plate and digital delays on *Unknown Pleasures*, which gives it a very unique sound. The very sound me and Barney hated for years – that was 'HIS' sound. There was a rumour that he'd recorded the lead vocal down a telephone line to get the distortion just right, but I doubt that's true; in those days it would have been very difficult to achieve. I reckon he would have 'pumped' the vocal. This was a technique he pioneered, where you used an external speaker in a very ambient room. Using a fader on the desk, you'd send the signal out into the room at a suitable volume and bring it back through a microphone into the control room to mix in with the original track. A great trick. Martin used it on the piano on 'Transmission', putting a speaker underneath the strings and recording it back then adding it into the track as ambience. We also used it to great effect on the bass drum on 'Blue Monday' at Brittannia Row.

'New Dawn Fades'

A change of speed, a change of style ...

'New Dawn Fades' is the track that most people say is their favourite. This seems an odd choice to me, because it's very, very simple and very economical, certainly from my point of view, because the bass is pretty much constant all the way through.

This riff reminds me of my old amp. I had a 100-watt Marshall Lead Amp, wired for bass. I don't know what the difference is – something to do with the frequencies – but it had a fantastic, rich, warm sound, especially when you played high. All the songs on *Unknown Pleasures* were written and played on it; it sounded great. It used to sing to me, that amp: such sweet distortion. It was wonderful. I had to sell it because I needed to pay the gas bill. Rob said we didn't have any money, so I advertised it in the *MEN* and this kid answered. I even took the amp round to his house in its flight-case.

He said, 'You in a band?'

'Yeah, we're called Joy Division.'

'Never heard of you.'

I went, 'Yeah, well, you know, we're up and coming.'

'I'm in a band,' he said, gloating. 'Six hundred quid a week, on the cruise ships, on the liners. Fucking great. It's full of old biddies; knuckle-deep in Lily of the Valley, me, mate. Hundred and sixty-five, yeah.'

I was like, 'Whatever.' He took my amp off me, my *beloved* amp. Me and Iris were going to have our gas cut off otherwise.

So I went back to Rob. 'Right, you'll have to buy me an amp now, out of the group's money, because I haven't got one. I've sold it.'

'You stupid twat,' he said. 'I would have bought it off you. I would have given you the money.'

'Well I asked and you wouldn't give it me.'

'Oh don't be so fucking soft, Hooky.'

What the fuck was 'soft' about that I don't know and never will. But anyway. That was the story of the amp. It really did contribute to the sound of the album, without a shadow of a doubt. I wonder where it is now. While we're on the subject of amplifiers a mention must go to Barney's acquisition of the Vox UL730, a wonderful find. This amp has a fantastic sound and was his pride and joy, and again added a lot to the album. Even Martin loved it. It famously took over a whole PA at Liverpool Eric's once. We'd all been complaining about how loud it was, so Barney had bought an Altair power soak, which supposedly enabled you to have the same sound only quieter. I don't want to get too technical, but the idea was you used the Altair to quieten the amp then took a DI from it to the PA. This we did, but the UL730 obviously had ideas of its own and took over the whole sound system. You could hear nothing else. This amp was stolen with all the gear in America on the first New Order tour. Even I grieved.

'She's Lost Control'

She walked upon the edge of no escape . . .

They used an aerosol to create some of the drum effects – another of Martin's many innovations. He liked to record different sounds that he'd work on to sound like drums but different. For one of the tracks he recorded us kicking a flight-case in time. Also I suspect a Ring Modulator on the real damped snare. The other thing you hear on this track is Steve's Synare, which was a drum synthesizer with a white-noise generator that he used on both 'She's Lost Control' and 'Insight'. He was one of the first drummers to use them, if I'm not mistaken. That was one of the great things about him – and Barney, actually. They're both very experimental, always wanting to try out new things, which I must admit I resisted because I was always like, 'Let's just play. We play great together. What do you want to add stuff for?' In Barney's case it was a bit of a two-edged sword because, while it was great that he was always on the lookout to do things differently, you did tend to feel that he wasn't entirely happy with you. He loved all this new technology, and always did the whole time I knew him, but the technology was reducing the need for players. They say that's why drum machines were invented, so the lead vocalist didn't have to talk to the drummer. Bass synths so that the singer doesn't have to talk to the bass player. You could just programme them yourself and find yourself in your own little world while we're all hanging on for grim death. I never believed in any of that. I always believed that in a group the strength comes from the camaraderie, the chemistry, the people playing together. You should never exclude anybody; you should encourage rather than exclude. No song is worth alienating a group member.

Ian was apparently moved to write this lyric after an incident at work. It's about an epileptic young lady who was having problems finding and keeping a job, who eventually died while fitting. That must have been terrifying for him. The first I knew of that was when Bernard mentioned it on a Joy Division documentary. Again, I wasn't really paying that much attention to the lyrics. It's teamwork. You just see your teammate doing his bit; he looks and sounds up to speed, so, great, that leaves you to concentrate on your own side of things. There's no analysis going on. Nobody was going, 'Let's have a look at your lyrics, Ian. Let's have a talk about them. Let's dissect the lyric.' He probably would have just gone mad and told you to fuck off. He delivered his vocals with the perfect amount of passion and spirit, exactly what we wanted. Saying that, reading the lyrics now, his use of repetition and onomatopoeic delivery is startling.

Now, of course, Ian Curtis is recognized as one of music's greatest lyricists, a fact that wasn't established during his lifetime. In interviews all they seem to pounce on was the Nazi aspects. That just used to upset him. It's a funny thing with interviews. When you're a struggling band nobody wants to know, so you just live without the press. You don't even consider it to be important. All of a sudden you're popular and everybody wants to talk to you. Then it seems vital.

'Shadowplay'

As the assassins all grouped in four lines dancing on the floor ...

This was the song that Barney wanted to sound like 'The Ocean' by Velvet Underground. Again, the lyric doesn't repeat until the end and it has no chorus, which is something that I think Ian was very, very good at – the way he played with the structure of the lyrics but without ever losing what it was about the song that makes it strong. You don't listen to it and think, *Ah, what an interesting lyrical structure.* But it's all in the song. His love of art was showing here. The way he wanted to slightly subvert the normal conventions of rock and pop.

'Wilderness'

I travelled far and wide to stations of the cross ...

I'm blowing my own trumpet here, but this is a fantastic bass line. I watched John Frusciante of the Red Hot Chilli Peppers play it acoustically at their gig at the MEN Arena. I think I can safely say that, of the 19,000 people there, 18,950 didn't know what it was – but I did, and it brought a tear to my eye, definitely. Monster bass line. A bass line that every bass player dreams of and I got it, so thank you.

It's Ian's sideswipe at religion, the futility of religion, the things that are done and perpetrated in it name. It's poetry. Once you unlock the meaning of the lyrics, or at least what you think is the meaning of the lyrics, you can lose yourself in them. Each one of his lyrics is like a wonderful little story in itself. Rob didn't like this track.

Great guitar, too. The two instruments interplay very well. I do think that Barney's guitar playing is underrated. He's a fantastic guitarist. One of the things that puzzled me when he started working with Johnny Marr is why he gave up the guitar. I prefer his playing. Maybe it's that thing about always wanting to move on to something else, whereas I've always been quite happy to capitalize on what I've got. This reminds me of when I got Donald Johnson of Certain Ratio to teach me how to do slap bass. Everyone was doing it and I was feeling the pressure, shall we say. I tried once, one lesson; he just laughed, squeezed my arm and said, 'Hooky, stick to what you're great at!' Lovely guy.

'Interzone'

Four twelve windows, ten in a row ...

Me singing the main vocal while Ian does the low, backing vocal. Ian was very good like that; there seemed to be no ego with him. He was perfectly happy to let you sing, to let anyone sing. In fact he'd encourage you to do it. He was very, very generous in that respect. Strangely enough we were always trying to get Barney to sing but he was never interested.

This was the song that they tried to get us to do at RCA. The cover of 'Keep On Keepin' On' – well, not the actual song itself but the inspiration for it – and you can hear the riff in it a little.

'I Remember Nothing'

Violent more violent his hand cracks the chair ...

We had been playing this one for a while very loosely; it had no real order. So we jammed it in the studio and Martin added the shattering glass and other effects. This was also Barney's first foray into using the Transcendent 2000. He'd bought *Sound Engineer* magazine, or *Sound International* or something, and you got a free piece of electronic kit every week – the idea being to build your own synthesizer, which is what he'd done; he soldered together the Transcendent 2000. Built it himself: quite an achievement. It's used a lot on the track. One of the interesting things about Joy Division is that people can never tell who's playing what; is it guitar or bass, keyboard or bass or guitar? This is a great, atmospheric track and came together very quickly. In the New

Order days, especially towards the end, we'd hammer our tracks to death. Budgeting a month a track to record. You'd try everything bar the kitchen sink and end up mainly coming back to exactly what you started with. Then it was blighted by the huge waste of time and money. Ending up with everyone in the group hating each other. We should have just looked at *Unknown Pleasures* and made every album that way. We'd probably never have split up. But people change. Ah well, last thing is the notable use of the Frank Sinatra lyric 'Strangers'.

TIMELINE FOUR:
JANUARY–DECEMBER 1979

January 1979

The *A Factory Sample* EP (FAC 2) is released, priced £1.50. Recorded at Cargo Studios, Rochdale. Produced by Martin Hannett. Track list (Side A (Aside)): Joy Division, 'Digital'; Joy Division, 'Glass'. (Vinyl etching: 'EVERYTHING'.) Track list (Side B (Beside)): the Durutti Column, 'No Communication'; the Durutti Column, 'Thin Ice (Detail)'. (Vinyl etching: 'IS REPAIRABLE'.) Track list (Side C (Seaside)): John Dowie, 'Acne'; John Dowie, 'Idiot'; John Dowie, 'Hitler's Liver'. (Vinyl etching: 'EVERYTHING'.) Track list (Side D (Decide)): Cabaret Voltaire, 'Baader Meinhof'; Cabaret Voltaire, 'Sex in Secret'. (Vinyl etching: 'IS BROKEN'.)

6 January 1979

Kevin Cummins takes his famous Princess Parkway shots of Joy Division.

"I remember it was really cold and I borrowed that coat that I had on. I think I borrowed it off Steve, actually. They were done really quickly. Kevin freely admits he only took seven shots. He was lucky. He didn't have any money either – didn't have money for any more film. He had one roll and he had to do four or five groups on it. Quite punky really. I mean, now, you sit there, they take fucking thousands of shots and wade through them to get one. But in the old days you had to get it finished and get it out. You know what I'm going to say, don't you? That's right. I liked it much better that way."

12 January 1979

Joy Division play Wythenshawe College, Manchester.

13 January 1979

Ian Curtis appears on the cover of the *NME*; the shot of him smoking was taken during the Kevin Cummins session on 6 January.

23 January 1979

Ian Curtis diagnosed with epilepsy.

26 January 1979

Joy Division play the *A Factory Sample* EP release party, the Factory, Russell Club, Manchester, with Cabaret Voltaire and John Dowie.

31 January 1979

Joy Division's first John Peel session, produced by Bob Sargeant for the BBC. Tracks recorded: 'Exercise One', 'Insight', 'Transmission', 'She's Lost Control'.

"We weren't quite as green as we used to be in terms of being in the studio, so, instead of just sitting around watching other people get on with it, we were a bit more hands-on, happy that we were getting to use this great studio and were being treated well with a trip to the subsidized canteen. I loved that session. I love working for the BBC, actually."

2 February 1979

Sid Vicious found dead of a drugs overdose.

10 February 1979

Joy Division play the Institute of Technology, Bolton, supported by the Curbs.

"Little Hulton's right next to Bolton so I had to drive all the way to Salford to get the gear, pick everybody up and then drive past my house to do the gig. At the end of the night, when we'd finished, I had to drive past my house, drop everybody off, go all the way to Salford and then back home. Fuck me. Who'd be the driver, eh?"

16 February 1979

Joy Division play Eric's, Liverpool, supported by Cabaret Voltaire.

28 February 1979

Joy Division play Nottingham Playhouse as unbilled support for John Cooper Clarke.

Joy Division were late appearing, so John Cooper Clarke went on first, then introduced Joy Division (his distinctive accent leading at least one fan, Dominic, writing on joydiv.org, to expect 'Geordie Vision'); John Cooper Clarke then played a second time.

"We were using Sad Café's PA, which was operated by my cousin, Chas Banks – who was the first person to ever give me a guitar to hold, when I went round to his house in Stretford. I was fourteen. Fantastic guy, a real legend. We were waiting for the PA to turn up – you can't do anything until the PA turns up – and I remember being at the back door when Chas appeared, bruised and battered, and went, 'Just crawled in from a motorway wreck; let's get on with it.' We went out and the van was fucking hammered. It had been in a huge crash on the motorway. All the gear was trashed and everyone was frantically trying to put it back together. Proper rock 'n' roll. That was why John ended up going on twice: because we weren't ready."

1 March 1979

Joy Division play the Hope & Anchor, London. Admission: 75p. 'Cellar bar re-opening. Now with real ale!'

> "This was the gig where Dave Pils and his girlfriend, Jasmine, introduced themselves to us. They ran Walthamstow Youth Centre, which is why we ended up playing there. Dave would become a big part of our lives. He became our roadie and friend and stayed with us for years. Every time we played in London we crashed at their place, which saved us a lot of money. A pair of lovely people. I wonder where they are now ..."

4 March 1979

The Genetic Records demo session, Eden Studios, London. Produced by Martin Rushent. Tracks recorded: 'Glass', 'Transmission', 'Ice Age', 'Insight', 'Digital'.

4 March 1979

Joy Division play the Marquee, London, supporting the Cure. Set list: 'Soundtrack' ('Exercise One'), 'She's Lost Control', 'Shadowplay', 'Leaders of Men', 'Insight', 'Glass', 'Digital', 'Ice Age', 'Transmission'.

> "There's a set list from this still knocking around, written by Steve: it starts with a track called 'Soundtrack', which became 'Exercise One'; we thought it sounded soundtrack-y ... It was exciting being in the Marquee, for obvious reasons, and it was really crowded, but the night was ruined by the fact that we had to drive home afterwards. The Cure never even acknowledged us. Everyone was rocking

except us: we just played then got dragged off to drive home, which was a bit of a downer.

13 March 1979

Joy Division play Band on the Wall, Manchester, supported by the Fireplace. A Musicians' Collective gig. Possible set list: 'Walked in Line', 'She's Lost Control', 'Shadowplay', 'New Dawn Fades', 'Day of the Lords', 'Insight', 'Disorder', 'The Only Mistake', 'I Remember Nothing', 'Sister Ray'.

"A band with a name like the Fireplace could only be in a collective."

14 March 1979

Joy Division play Bowdon Vale Youth Club, Altrincham, supported by Staff 9 (featuring Paul and Steve Hanley and Craig Scanlon, who later join the Fall). Set list: 'Exercise One', 'She's Lost Control', 'Shadowplay', 'Leaders of Men', 'Insight', 'Disorder', 'Glass', 'Digital', 'Ice Age', 'Warsaw', 'Transmission', 'I Remember Nothing', 'No Love Lost'.

"Absolutely cracking. A fucking great set list, that one. I wouldn't put 'Disorder' after 'Glass', mind you; I'd change that bit round. But that's a great set list. Maybe it's a bit up and down, though, come to think of it... So maybe it's not that great a set list. Great songs, though."

'She's Lost Control', 'Shadowplay' and 'Leaders of Men' were filmed by Malcolm Whitehead for his Joy Division short film, which was premiered at the Scala London on 13 September as part of The Factory Flick *(FAC 9). The footage was also later released on the 'Substance' video.*

"That was very exciting, being filmed. Malcolm was a lovely geezer. His idea was to use us in a film he was doing, but in the end the film became more about us than anything else. There are photographs of that gig, too, taken by a very young Martin Ocomin, who started crawling round the stage while we were playing, right up into the drums. I kicked him up the arse and told him to piss off. Photographers, they think they're it. If you want to annoy one just say 'shared copyright' – that should see them off."

I met him years later and we laughed about it; he wanted an auto-graph, and I wrote, 'I told you to fuck off.'

'No,' he said, 'You told me to piss off.'"

30 March 1979

Joy Division play the Walthamstow Youth Centre.

Dave Pils' girlfriend, Jasmine, was a youth worker looking after kids in Walthamstow, presumably trying to keep them on the straight and narrow or whatever, so it was a weird crowd. Very young kids there, running about, ignoring us, like a school-hall-type gig. I do remember being horrified when we saw the poster, though. Dave had designed it: a bunch of Nazis on a tank. We were hoping to put all that stuff behind us! Dave was also the singer in SX, the support band.

31 March 1979

Joy Division start recording *Unknown Pleasures*, Strawberry Studios, Stockport. Tracks recorded: 'Disorder', 'Day of the Lords', 'Candidate', 'Insight', 'New Dawn Fades', 'She's Lost Control', 'Shadowplay', 'Wilderness', 'Interzone', 'I Remember Nothing', 'Autosuggestion', 'From Safety to Where', 'Exercise One', 'The Kill', 'Walked in Line'.

16 April 1979

Natalie Curtis born, Macclesfield.

2 May 1979

The *Unknown Pleasures* recording session ends, Strawberry Studios, Stockport.

3 May 1979

Joy Division play an Amnesty International Benefit, Eric's, Liverpool, with the Passage and Fireplace. Admission: 75p.

When Joy Division left the stage I felt emotionally drained. They are, without any exaggeration, an Important Band.

Ian Wood, *NME*

11 May 1979

Joy Division play a Factory Records night, the Factory, Russell Club, Manchester, with John Dowie, A Certain Ratio and Orchestral Manoeuvres in the Dark. Admission: £1.20; tickets available from Discount Records and Pandemonium.

> "I liked OMD a lot as a group. I always thought they were really, really good; nice guys, too. Although it was those two who got me into cocaine, the bastards, at the premiere of *Pretty in Pink*. And come to think of it, wasn't one of them responsible for Atomic Kitten?"

17 May 1979

Joy Division play *A Factory Sample* night, Acklam Hall, London, supported by John Dowie, A Certain Ratio and Orchestral Manoeuvres in the Dark. Admission: £1.50 on the door or £1.25 in advance from Small Wonder, Rough Trade and Honky Tonk record shops.

> "This would have been the first gig for Final Solution, which was Colin Faver, who went on to become a big DJ – one of the house music pioneers in the South of England – and Kevin Millins, who went on to run Heaven for Virgin and became a great friend of ours. It led to some great gigs, more for New Order than Joy Division. Acklam Hall became a club later on, and Davina McCall used to do the door. I have a wonderful memory of her bending over the table in my hotel room, with her silver hot-panted bottom stuck right up in the air. I always remind her of it whenever I see her.
> OMD also had a guitar stolen and were very upset."

23 May 1979

Joy Division play Bowdon Vale Youth Club, Altrincham, supported by John Dowie and A Certain Ratio (OMD pull out).

4 June 1979

Joy Division play Piccadilly Radio session, Pennine Sound Studios, Oldham. Produced by Stuart James. Tracks recorded: 'These Days', 'Candidate', 'The Only Mistake', 'Chance' ('Atmosphere'), 'Atrocity Exhibition'.

"Stuart James went on to become New Order's roadie. I saved his life once in Texas."

7 June 1979

Joy Division play the F-Club, a.k.a. the Fan Club, Leeds, with OMD.

14 June 1979

Unknown Pleasures (Factory Records FACT 10) released. Produced by Martin Hannett. Engineered by Chris Nagle. Recorded at Strawberry Studios, Stockport. Cover design by Joy Division, Peter Saville, Chris Mathan. Track list: 'Disorder', 'Day of the Lords', 'Candidate', 'Insight', 'New Dawn Fades', 'She's Lost Control', 'Shadowplay', 'Wilderness', 'Interzone', 'I Remember Nothing'.

16 June 1979

Joy Division play the Odeon, Canterbury, supporting the Cure, with Back to Zero. Set list: 'Disorder', 'She's Lost Control', 'Shadowplay', 'Wilderness', 'New Dawn Fades', 'Glass', 'These Days', 'Something Must Break', 'Interzone', 'Atrocity Exhibition'.

"I don't think the Cure liked us. I think they resented us in some way, because we'd managed to stay cool, credible, and independent and they'd, well, sort of sold out a bit. The problem was on their side; it wasn't on our side. But I think they thought, *Wish we were Joy Division.*"

17 June 1979

Joy Division play Royalty Theatre, Kingsway, London, supporting John Cooper Clarke, with Fashion. Set list: 'Atmosphere', 'Disorder', 'Digital',

'I Remember Nothing', 'Candidate', 'New Dawn Fades', 'These Days', 'Interzone', 'Transmission'.

> "We did a series of three gigs with Fashion, both of us supporting John Cooper Clarke, and the idea was that we'd switch: Fashion would open one night then us the next. They were pretty big at the time but I hated their music. It was awful. They were supposed to open in London and us in Manchester. But we ended up being stiffed in London. They left us off the bill then insisted we went on first. It was bedlam backstage that night. Rob threatened everybody. The upshot was that we ended up going on before the doors had even opened. It was either that or don't play. We played 'Atmosphere' and 'Disorder' to a completely empty room. Three people came in during 'Digital'. The place was beginning to fill up when we finished our set."

19 June 1979

Joy Division play the Nuffield Theatre, Lancaster University, Lancaster, supporting John Cooper Clarke, with Fashion.

> **"Horrible gig. Fucking Fashion. I fucking hated 'em."**

22 June 1979

Joy Division play Good Mood, Halifax.

25 June 1979

Joy Division play the Free Trade Hall, Manchester, supporting John Cooper Clarke, with Fashion.

> **"They went on first. HA!"**

1 July 1979

The first 'Transmission' demo session, Central Sound Studios, Manchester. Produced by Martin Hannett. Tracks recorded: 'Transmission', 'Novelty', 'Dead Souls', 'Something Must Break'.

"Quite a pleasant session, this one. I remember Martin being very nice and helpful."

5 July 1979

Joy Division play Limit Club, West Street, Sheffield, supported by OMD.

"This was the first time we ever went over the Snake Pass and the van was so knackered it was really struggling up the hills. Twinny was really annoyed and reckoned he could run faster. So we took him up on it and he jumped out of the van to race us. Of course we beat him up the hill easy. By the time he joined us up at the top he was huffing and puffing, all red-faced, calling us bastards for not stopping. Me and Terry had eaten all his sweets while we waited. He didn't talk to us all night for that.

If I remember rightly Phil Oakey and the other lads from the Human League helped us load in. They were very nice. I met the drummer from Manicured Noise here. It was her twenty-first. Stephanie. Lovely girl. She had a pet rat."

11 July 1979

Joy Division play Roots Club (Cosmo Club), Chapeltown, Leeds. Set list: 'Dead Souls', 'Shadowplay', 'She's Lost Control', 'Candidate', 'These Days', 'Disorder', 'Interzone', 'Glass', 'Transmission', 'Atrocity Exhibition', 'No Love Lost'.

"I'm pretty sure this was where Right Said Fred supported us."

13 July 1979

20 July 1979

Joy Division appear on *What's On* for Granada TV, playing 'She's Lost Control'.

27 July 1979

Joy Division play a Year of the Child benefit concert, the Imperial Hotel, Blackpool, with OMD, the Final Solution, Section 25, the Glass Torpedoes and Zyklon B. Promoted by Section 25. Set list: 'Dead Souls', 'Glass', 'Disorder', 'Autosuggestion', 'Transmission', 'She's Lost Control', 'Shadowplay', 'Atrocity Exhibition'.

"I remember looking out the dressing room window and seeing a Ford Escort sat outside with the *Unknown Pleasures* logo on its bonnet. Cool, that was. This was also the gig where we met Section 25, who became great friends of ours. Ian and Rob took a shine to them and ended up producing their first single, which came out on Factory. That must have been a scream and I would have loved to have been there, because Rob and Ian were both hopeless at that sort of thing. Rob's only advice when you were recording was, 'Make it go *Woomph*.' That was it. 'Make it go *Woomph*.' And Ian, well, he had the ear but he was useless at anything technical.

You may or may not know, but Larry out of Section 25 died recently, in 2010. Very sad. I'll tell you one story about him that made me laugh so much. I mean, he was a proper 'character', and enjoyed fully the rock-'n'-roll lifestyle and some of its foibles, shall we say. His one true love was those flight simulators you get on the computer. What he used to like doing was staying up all night flying long-haul flights in real time. His brother Vinny was telling me that he'd done one where he'd been up all night, flying to New York from London, off his head, and crashed on landing. It had taken him eleven hours to get there! I tell you what, heaven's got to be a lot livelier with that lot there. Him, Ian, Tony, Rob and Martin. What a crew.

But yes, the relationship between us and Section 25 was really very solid, much more so than with A Certain Ratio. They never had the acclaim we had and that was something that I think never bothered Section 25, whereas I think A Certain Ratio got annoyed because they felt in our shadow."

28 July 1979

Joy Division play the Mayflower Club, Manchester, a Stuff the Superstars Special, with the Fall, the Distractions, John the Postman, the Frantic Elevators, the Hamsters, Ludus, Armed Force, Foreign Press and Elti Fits. Admission: £1.50.

It's almost impossible to match a recording as good as theirs with an equally good performance. Joy Division pulled it off. THEY WERE BRILLIANT, I MEAN BRILLIANT!

City Fun fanzine

"There was always intense rivalry between us and the Fall. They started the same time as us and did a lot better than us more quickly than we did. So we were a bit jealous. There always is rivalry between groups. Never with DJs but always with groups."

28 July–4 August 1979

The second 'Transmission' demo sessions, Strawberry Studios, Stockport. Produced by Martin Hannett. Tracks recorded: 'Transmission' (single version), 'Novelty' (single version).

2 August 1979

Joy Division play the YMCA, Prince of Wales Conference Centre, London, with Teardrop Explodes and Echo & the Bunnymen. This is the first show of a four-night alternative rock festival at the Prince of Wales Conference Centre. Set list: 'Dead Souls', 'Disorder', 'Wilderness', 'Autosuggestion', 'Transmission', 'Day of the Lords', 'She's Lost Control', 'Shadowplay', 'Atrocity Exhibition', 'Insight'.

The truth is they were phenomenal – the most physical hard rock group I've seen since Gang of Four.

Adrian Thrills, *NME*

"It was a great gig, that one, and it's where the famous pictures of us come from – where we're drinking backstage, post-gig, out of cans, and where Ian's got the cig and we're sat on the step. They're all from backstage at the YMCA, very famous, nice pictures. We all look very happy."

8 August 1979

Joy Division play the Romulus Club, Birmingham, supporting Dexy's Midnight Runners.

"Dexys were diabolically dressed, like something out of Star Trek. This was way before theirs became a big name, of course, but Kevin Rowland still swanned around like he was a God. They were playing jokes on a reel-to-reel tape recorder in between songs: very strange. This was the night I ripped my favourite blue shirt that Rob bought me, on my own bass cab. I was devastated. Stayed in a mad B&B afterwards, complete with a saucy landlady."

11 August 1979

Joy Division play Eric's, Liverpool (matinee and evening shows), with Swell Maps. Admission: £1.10 for members. Set list (matinee): 'Transmission', 'Untitled', 'Disorder', 'New Dawn Fades', 'Glass', 'Shadowplay', 'Colony', 'Interzone', 'Ice Age'. Set list (evening): 'Insight', 'Autosuggestion', 'Digital', 'She's Lost Control', 'Day of the Lords', 'Wilderness', 'Atrocity Exhibition', 'Transmission', 'New Dawn Fades' (instrumental), 'Interzone', 'Dead Souls'. Ian has a fit during 'New Dawn Fades' and is carried from the stage. He returns during 'Interzone'.

13 August 1979

Joy Division play the Nashville Rooms, London, with OMD and A Certain Ratio. Set list: 'Atmosphere', 'She's Lost Control', 'Exercise One', 'Disorder', 'Colony', 'Candidate', 'Autosuggestion', 'Ice Age'.

"Annik Honoré saw the band for the first time and met us briefly. This was the night of the van crash, of course. But it was a great gig. Look at that set list, starting with 'Atmosphere'. It didn't have the connotations then that it does now that it's sort of Ian's death march. Back then it was a good song to start with – well, we thought so anyway because we were awkward bastards. We liked to come on and defy expectations by starting with something slow and reflective, before building up to the faster songs."

24 August 1979

Joy Division play the Walthamstow Youth Centre, London. Afterwards Annik interviews the band at Dave Pils' and Jasmine's flat.

27 August 1979

Joy Division play Leigh Open Air Festival, Plank Lane, Leigh, with the Distractions, Echo & the Bunnymen, OMD, A Certain Ratio, Teardrop Explodes and Lori & the Chameleons. Billed as 'Zoo Meets Factory Half Way', this is the last day of the festival. Admission: £2. Set list: 'Disorder', 'Leaders of Men', 'Colony', 'Insight', 'Digital', 'Dead Souls', 'Shadowplay', 'She's Lost Control', 'Transmission', 'Interzone'.

"I remember being really upset by Martin Moscrop of A Certain Ratio at that gig. We did 'The Sound of Music' at the sound-check and I had a bit on the song where I sang, 'Hi, hi, hi, hi, higher'. Martin turned round to me at the end and said, 'You sounded like the fucking laughing policeman, mate, ha, ha, ha.' I've never been able to think of that song in the same way since. He ruined it for me in that one moment. 'The Sound of Music' was one I played guitar on and Bernard played bass. But yeah, ruined for me from then on."

31 August 1979

Joy Division play the Electric Ballroom, London, with A Certain Ratio, Scritti Politti, Monochrome Set. Set list: 'The Sound of Music', 'Wilderness', 'Colony', 'Day of the Lords', 'Shadowplay', 'Transmission', 'Interzone', 'Disorder', 'She's Lost Control', 'Insight'.

"Great gig, this one. I was very impressed that the Monochrome Set's singer was an Indian Prince."

8 September 1979

Joy Division play the Queen's Hall, Leeds, third on the bill, with A Certain Ratio, Cabaret Voltaire and OMD, and with Public Image head-lining. This is the opening day of the three-day Futurama Festival. Set list: 'I Remember Nothing', 'Wilderness', 'Transmission', 'Colony', 'Disorder', 'Insight', 'Shadowplay', 'She's Lost Control', 'Atrocity Exhibition', 'Dead Souls'.

> "This was a great concert too. We went down an absolute storm. It was our first gig with John Keenan, who was a very interesting man to work with financially, and our first indoor festival."

13 September 1979

Premiere of *The Factory Flick* (Factory FAC 9, 1979), the Scala cinema, London. This 8mm film comprises: *No City Fun – Joy Division* (12 min), by student filmmaker Charles Salem, featuring three tracks by the band; *All Night Party – A Certain Ratio* (3 min); *Red Dress – Ludus* (3 min); *Joy Division* (17 min), by Malcolm Whitehead, featuring footage of 'Shadowplay' and 'She's Lost Control' shot by Malcolm Whitehead at Bowdon Vale Youth Club.

15 September 1979

Joy Division appear on *Something Else*, playing 'She's Lost Control' and 'Transmission'.

22 September 1979

Joy Division play the Nashville Rooms, London, supported by the Distractions. Admission: £1.25. Set list: 'Atmosphere', 'Wilderness', 'Shadowplay', 'Leaders of Men', 'Insight', 'Colony', 'Transmission', 'Disorder', 'She's Lost Control', 'Atrocity Exhibition', 'Glass', 'Exercise One'.

> "Terry couldn't make it so Twinny said to me, 'Can I bring my mate as a roadie?' and I was like, 'Yeah, course,' thinking that was nice.

Around the time of our
first gigs. They come back
to haunt you, eh?

Bowdon Vale Youth
Club. We were definitely
finding our way now.

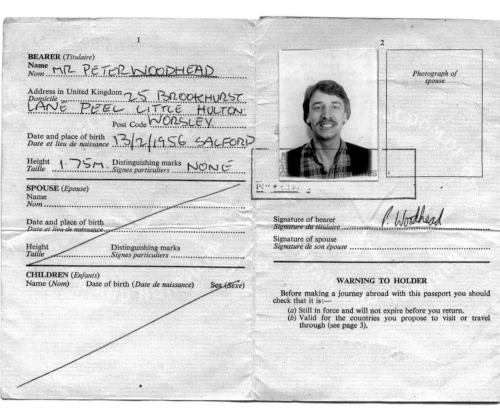

My first passport, so we could play in Belgium.

Me and the van on holiday on route to Benidorm. Hardly dressed for it!

Bloomin' heck! This is what a couple of years in a band does to you. Love the old glam rock top.

The morning after the night before . . . what a mess!

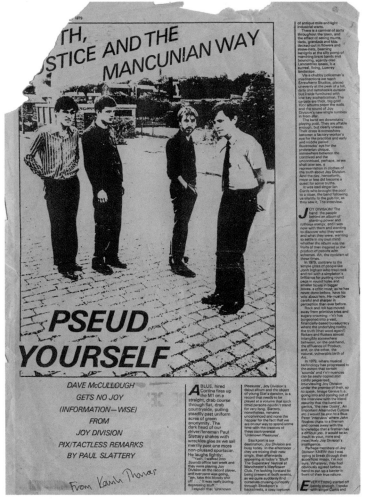

Old Sounds interview.
Our first I think?

European Tour again
just messing around

This would have been our digs for the night. Left to right: Steve, Ian, Rob, me, Mark Reeder (an old friend) and Harry De Mac, our English sound guy, hiding in the corner.

The Mighty Sarg. YOU AIN'T COMIN' IN DICKHEAD! PISS OFF!

Walthamstow's Dave Pils, gets his gold watch off New Order. A great roadie!

Me and Terry Mason in Tractor Music in Rochdale's re-opening.

roof we used to get on! Y.M.C.A. London I think. Very smart! Steve has gone for fags!

No wonder the Head chased us out! He's behind you!

In TJ Davidsons. Mean and moody. Great pic Kevin.

Then his mate turned up and he was on crutches. I took Twinny to one side. 'Look, he's on crutches. How's he going to help if he can't walk?'

Twinny was like, 'Oh come on, Hooky, he's a nice guy. He needs a night out.' I was just shaking my head. I mean, what a liability: some kid on crutches along for the ride. Anyway, at the end of the night we couldn't find him – he kept us waiting for ages – and when we eventually did he was snogging the face off some girl. So not only had he turned up on crutches, done fuck all and drunk all our rider, but he'd ended up copping off as well, the lucky bastard."

28 September 1979

Joy Division play the Factory, Russell Club, Manchester, with Teardrop Explodes and Foreign Press. Set list: 'Atmosphere', 'Wilderness', 'Shadowplay', 'Insight', 'Colony', 'Twenty Four Hours', 'Interzone', 'She's Lost Control', 'Transmission' (encore; fight occurs), 'Atrocity Exhibition' (encore, minus bass).

"The big fight. I was ashamed."

29 September 1979

Joy Division play the Mayflower, Manchester, with Foreign Press (formerly Emergency).

October 1979

The *Earcom 2* compilation (Fast Products FAST 9b) released. It features two Joy Division tracks, recorded by Martin Hannett as part of the *Unknown Pleasures* session: 'Autosuggestion' and 'From Safety to Where'.

October 1979

The 'Transmission'/'Novelty' seven-inch single (Factory Records FAC 13) released. Produced by Martin Hannett. Sleeve design by Peter Saville. Later re-released as a twelve-inch with new cover (FAC 13.12).

October–November 1979

The Sordide Sentimental session, Cargo Studios, Rochdale. Produced by Martin Hannett. Tracks recorded: 'Atmosphere', 'Dead Souls', 'Ice Age'.

2 October 1979

Joy Division play Mountford Hall, Liverpool University, as part of the Buzzcocks tour. Set list: 'Wilderness', 'Ice Age', Candidate, 'Shadowplay', 'Insight', 'She's Lost Control', 'Twenty Four Hours', 'Disorder', 'Transmission', 'Warsaw'.

3 October 1979

Joy Division play Leeds University as part of the Buzzcocks tour.

> 'The anguished singer had achieved total physical self-expression by the climax of "She's Lost Control" and, evidently having lost control, he was helped offstage at the conclusion of a set which, for practical reasons, could not be extended.'
>
> Des Moines – *Sounds*.

4 October 1979

Joy Division play City Hall, Newcastle, as part of the Buzzcocks tour. Set list: 'Disorder', 'Shadowplay', 'Colony', 'Day of the Lords', 'Glass', 'Transmission', 'She's Lost Control', 'Atrocity Exhibition'.

5 October 1979

Joy Division play Apollo, Glasgow, as part of the Buzzcocks tour.

> **"I remember freaking out at the height of the stage: it was one of the highest I've ever played on."**

6 October 1979

Joy Division play the Odeon, Edinburgh, as part of the Buzzcocks tour. Set list: 'Leaders of Men', 'Digital', 'Day of the Lords', 'Transmission', 'Shadowplay', 'She's Lost Control', 'New Dawn Fades', 'Disorder', 'Transmission'.

7 October 1979

Joy Division play Capitol, Aberdeen, as part of the Buzzcocks tour.

> "Sarge threw a kid out of the backstage area for having a Scottish accent. He was trying to say he had an interview with Pete Shelley for a fanzine. 'I can't understand a word you're saying, dickhead, OUT!'"

8 October 1979

Joy Division play Caird Hall, Dundee, as part of the Buzzcocks tour. Set list: 'Atmosphere', 'Wilderness', 'Interzone', 'Colony', 'These Days', 'New Dawn Fades', 'Transmission', 'Shadowplay', 'She's Lost Control'. Ian collapses.

10 October 1979

Joy Division gig at Ulster Hall, Belfast, cancelled. Part of the Buzzcocks tour.

11 October 1979

Joy Division gig at Kelly's, Portrush, cancelled. Part of the Buzzcocks tour.

13 October 1979

Joy Division gig at City Hall, Cork, cancelled. Part of the Buzzcocks tour.

16 October 1979

Joy Division play Plan K, Brussels. Set list: 'Love Will Tear Us Apart', 'Wilderness', 'Disorder', 'Colony', 'Insight', 'Twenty Four Hours', 'New

Dawn Fades', 'Transmission', 'Shadowplay', 'She's Lost Control', 'Atrocity Exhibition', 'Interzone'.

18 October 1979

Joy Division play Bangor University, as part of the Buzzcocks tour.

20 October 1979

Joy Division play Loughborough University, as part of the Buzzcocks tour.

21 October 1979

Joy Division play Top Rank, Arundel Gate, Sheffield, as part of the Buzzcocks tour.

22 October 1979

Joy Division play the Assembly Rooms, Derby, as part of the Buzzcocks tour.

23 October 1979

Joy Division play King George's Hall, Blackburn, as part of the Buzzcocks tour.

> **"The Blackburn Lot ended up being great supporters of both New Order and the Haçienda. Mad football fans."**

24 October 1979

Joy Division play the Odeon Theatre, Birmingham, as part of the Buzzcocks tour.

25 October 1979

Joy Division play St George's Hall, Bradford, as part of the Buzzcocks tour.

26 October 1979

Joy Division play the Electric Ballroom, London, supported by the Distractions and A Certain Ratio, during a break from the Buzzcocks tour. Set list: 'I Remember Nothing', 'Love Will Tear Us Apart', 'Wilderness', 'Colony', 'Insight', 'Day of the Lords', 'Shadowplay', 'She's Lost Control', 'Transmission', 'Disorder', 'Atrocity Exhibition', 'Interzone'.

> "Something I remember about the Buzzcocks tour is that they played the same set every night, whereas we always varied ours. We did it to keep ourselves interested, so that all the songs got an airing, to try to find that ultimate moment and sometimes, again, just to be bloody awkward. If the audience were really wild, we'd start with 'I Remember Nothing', just to wind them up. One thing that punk taught you was to be challenging – always try to break the rules, to forge your own way. Being on Factory reinforced those ideals. It was like, whatever the game was we weren't going to play it. Whatever was expected of us we did the opposite. I was really inspired by Throbbing Gristle back then. Genesis P-Orridge, what a man. I loved how awkward they were – how they used to try to drive their audience away every night. I wouldn't have minded us being a bit more like Throbbing Gristle, actually."

27 October 1979

Joy Division play the Apollo Theatre, Manchester, as part of the Buzzcocks tour. Set list: 'Dead Souls', 'Wilderness', 'Colony', 'Autosuggestion', 'Love Will Tear Us Apart', 'Shadowplay', 'She's Lost Control', 'Transmission'.

28 October 1979

Joy Division play the Apollo Theatre, Manchester, as part of the Buzzcocks tour. Set list: 'The Sound of Music', 'Shadowplay', 'Colony', 'Day of the Lords', 'Twenty Four Hours', 'Disorder', 'Walked in Line', 'I Remember Nothing', 'Transmission'.

29 October 1979

Joy Division play De Montfort Hall, Leicester, as part of the Buzzcocks tour.

30 October 1979

Joy Division play the New Theatre, Oxford, as part of the Buzzcocks tour. Set list: 'Walked in Line', 'The Only Mistake', 'Leaders of Men', 'Insight', 'Ice Age', 'Love Will Tear Us Apart', 'I Remember Nothing'.

November 1979

A photographic session with Anton Corbijn results in yet more iconic images of the band and sees the start of a relationship that will eventually culminate in the multi-award-winning film *Control*, Corbijn's biopic of Ian Curtis.

"What I loved about Anton was that he did the pictures really quickly, with no fuss, no fucking about: bang, bang, bang and it was over. At the time, I thought, *Now, that's how a photo shoot should be*. Those shots he took of us in the tube station: absolutely brilliant. The way that he works, he almost does it like a throwaway gesture. When he did New Order in America was with us for four days, pissed as a fart, having a great time; when we were all sat on the grass outside the gig on the afternoon of his last day he went, 'Oh, I'm sure there's something I've forgotten. What have I forgotten?' Then the colour drained out of his face and he went, 'Oh my God, I've forgotten to take any pictures.'

All his gear had gone to the airport so he rushed to a garage across the way, bought a couple of instamatic cameras and took us into a fairground opposite the venue, where he got Steve to wear these daft glasses and did the photo shoot. He'd been there for four days and did the shoot as the car was waiting to take him to the airport. Class. And this is the thing – they were brilliant. The guy is either a fucking genius or somebody up there likes him, without a shadow of a doubt. He's a nice guy as well, really easy to be with. He's sweet and patient – one of those people that you feel so comfortable with and happy to be with – which is a gift for a photographer. He did a great job of *Control* and I knew he would. He is a perfectionist, though, and in that respect working with him wasn't easy. Doing the soundtrack was the last nail in the coffin for New Order. I realized after that me and Barney were poles apart, too far apart, and no one seemed able to bring us back together. I thought our management were useless and Steve seemed lost. It was awful. The music was great, though. Typical: you're always better when you're full of anger. One thing I was happy about was that Natalie Curtis was included in the publishing for the songs. The credits are 'Curtis-Hook-Morris-Sumner'."

1 November 1979

Joy Division play the Civic Hall, Guildford, as part of the Buzzcocks tour. Set list: 'No Love Lost', 'These Days', 'Disorder', 'Candidate', 'Shadowplay', 'Autosuggestion', 'Warsaw', 'Transmission', 'The Sound of Music'.

> "This was the night that Pete Shelley slipped Twinny (£3.50) to get the key to his room so he could play a practical joke on Dave Pils. Dave was awoken by a drunken Buzzcock tickling his feet under the covers. Dave ran away screaming."

2 November 1979

Joy Division play the Winter Gardens, Bournemouth, as part of the Buzzcocks tour. Set list: 'I Remember Nothing', 'Love Will Tear Us Apart', 'Interzone', 'Colony', 'Insight', 'These Days', 'Digital', 'Transmission', 'Atrocity Exhibition'. The set is cut short because Ian has a fit and is taken to hospital.

3 November 1979

Joy Division gig at Sophia Gardens, Cardiff, cancelled. Part of the Buzzcocks tour.

4 November 1979

Joy Division play Colston Hall, Bristol, as part of the Buzzcocks tour.

5 November 1979

Joy Division play the Pavilion, Hemel Hempstead, as part of the Buzzcocks tour. Set list (possibly incomplete): 'Dead Souls', 'Wilderness', 'Twenty Four Hours', 'New Dawn Fades', 'Digital', 'Disorder', 'Interzone'.

> "The practical jokes went up a gear here. The Buzzcocks' road crew told Terry that swallowing a huge lump of dope would give him a mild buzz. He was incapacitated. We arrived to find him leaning against a wall outside the venue, whimpering. We put him tenderly in Steve's car to recover and sleep it off, then Twinny, me and Barney took it in turns to shove lit bangers up the car exhaust and repeatedly scared him to death. Rob did the sound for the gig."

7 November 1979

Joy Division play the Pavilion, West Runton, as part of the Buzzcocks tour. Set list: 'Colony', 'These Days', 'Autosuggestion', 'Twenty Four Hours', 'Love Will Tear Us Apart', 'The Sound of Music', 'Atrocity Exhibition'.

9 November 1979

Joy Division play the Rainbow Theatre, London, as part of the Buzzcocks tour. Set list: 'The Sound of Music', 'Shadowplay', 'New Dawn Fades', 'Colony', 'Insight', 'Love Will Tear Us Apart', 'She's Lost Control', 'Transmission'.

10 November 1979

Joy Division play the Rainbow Theatre, London. The last date of the Buzzcocks tour. Set list: 'Dead Souls', 'Wilderness', 'Twenty Four Hours', 'Day of the Lords', 'These Days', 'Interzone', 'Disorder', 'Atrocity Exhibition'.

26 November 1979

Joy Division record their second John Peel session, BBC Studios, Maida Vale, London. Produced by Tony Wilson (not the same one). Tracks recorded: 'The Sound of Music', 'Twenty Four Hours', 'Colony', 'Love Will Tear Us Apart'.

8 December 1979

Joy Division play Eric's, Liverpool (matinee and evening shows), with Section 25.

18 December 1979

Joy Division play Les Bains Douches, Paris. Set list: 'Passover', 'Wilderness', 'Disorder', 'Love Will Tear Us Apart', 'Insight', 'Shadowplay', 'Transmission', 'Day of the Lords', 'Twenty Four Hours', 'Colony', 'These Days', 'A Means to an End', 'She's Lost Control', 'Atrocity Exhibition', 'Interzone', 'Warsaw'.

31 December 1979

Factory office party at Oldham Street, Manchester.

> "Rob bought about 200 cans of beer for 25p each – the idea being to sell them for 50p and make back the money that we paid for the PA and the lights, so we'd break even. It was a nice idea; quite forward-thinking, actually. Rob said, 'Right, I'll sell the fucking beer. I can't trust you bastards. I'll do it.' But what he didn't do was get a float, so when the first kid came up with a pound note to buy a 50p drink Rob had no change. So he said, 'Fucking have two cans.'
> The kid said, 'I don't want two cans. I want one.'
> 'Look, we've got no change.'
> 'Well, give me the beer then.'
> 'Come back later and get your 50p.'
> 'No, no, I'll come back later and give you 50p.'
> Rob was like, 'Oh, fucking hell!' and gave him the beer.
> Anyway, so the next kid came up: same story. Rob had to keep

231

giving the beers away and in the end he got so fucking fed up he just went, 'Fuck off the lot of you; you can have it.' And he just walked away and left the bar open.

That was when we discovered that it was easier to give drink away than it was to get people to pay for it – an important lesson, that, and one we made great use of during the Haçienda years."

PART FIVE

'Ceremony'

Failures of the Modern Man

Dont speak of the safe Messiah
Failure of the Modern Man
To the centre of all lifes desires
As a whole not an also ran

Love in a hollow field
break the image of your fathers son
drawn to an inner feel
he was thought of as the only one

He no longer denies
all the failures of the Modern Man
He no longer despies
No now he cant pick sides
sees the failures of the modern man

Wise words and sympathy
tell the story of our history
New strength gives a real touch
Sense and reason make it all too much

With a strange fatality
breaks the spirits of a lesser man
some other   could see
in his way he was the only one

now that its right to decide
in his time he was the total man
taken from Ceasars side
kept in silence just to prove us wrong.

I. Curtis(November, 1977).

'A right mother hen'

Joy Division began the new decade with a ten-date, eleven-day tour of Europe, where Ian was joined by Annik.

As I've said, I liked Annik. She really, really cared for Ian and she looked out for and after him. Being Belgian she seemed impossibly exotic. She was strong, independent, very into her music, intelligent and pretty into the bargain.

But none of that could make up for the fact that she was a royal pain in the arse on that tour. She didn't like us being at all laddish and was always pulling us up on our manners. God help you if you farted in the minibus or something. She disapproved of us chatting up girls and generally being dirty bastards, and didn't like our bad language. She was a right mother hen, in other words, clucking round us all the time.

Ian seemed to love it, of course, but that's because he changed when he was with her – that chameleon aspect of him coming out again. Was he more himself when he was with Annik, or more himself when he was pissing about with us? There's the eternal question. All I can remember is that with her he became a bit ... Well, Barney probably put it best when he said 'poncey'. With us: chasing groupies and pissing in ashtrays and looking at turds in toilets. With her: talking about Burroughs and Dostoyevsky. The perfect friend or partner for Ian would have combined all those things, but if that person exists they were nowhere near our social scene, so he had to be the chameleon, moving from one to another. You have to say he was bloody good at it. In her book Debbie says he would have made a good actor, and I think she's spot-on there.

So the tour was hard. Not just because of Annik, though she hardly helped, of course. But because we had no money, we were hungry, it was cold and miserable, we were driving around in a minibus and we really got on each other's tits, and the gigs were small too.

Worst of all, there was never any privacy. Nowhere could you go to be by yourself for a bit. I'd not been abroad for any length of time, had a bit of my mother in me when it came to food, and wouldn't touch anything that wasn't 'English'. So at the end of a gig when the promoter brought us Chinese, I went hungry. Never had rice, you see. I was in my early twenties and had never had rice. Well, maybe rice pudding. So I just used to sit there, tummy rumbling, watching that lot eating and going hungry. If it wasn't Chinese then it would be lentils – most of the promoters were hippies – and just the sight of lentils used to turn my stomach. So again I ate nothing.

Added to the hunger was the cold. The van was freezing. You'd spend the whole journey twisting and turning, hugging yourself trying to keep warm, with everyone bitching and moaning around you ... Jesus.

I just wanted to go home. To warmth, and the cat, and proper food. When we got to Antwerp it was like heaven because we had a hotel lined up and we were looking forward to getting a proper wash and a decent bed for the night, rather than kipping on a promoter's floor.

But on our arrival at the hotel any thoughts of luxury were well and truly dashed when the promoter announced that we weren't allowed to check in until after 1am. Huh? What kind of hotel can't you check into until one o'clock in the morning? Annik was grumbling off about that, quite rightly on this occasion, because Ian was ill and she'd made it her job to ensure he was as comfortable as possible – which must have been especially hard for her, considering his policy of behaving like nothing was wrong. She was on damage limitation, I suppose you'd have to say.

Either way, we went off, did the gig then returned to the hotel just after midnight. Perhaps they'd take pity and let us in before one.

But of course they didn't. So we had to wait in the freezing cold, moaning about the van and watching people coming and going from the hotel. There were some right choice fuckers coming out of there, I'm telling you. Tarty women and fat geezers.

Then all of a sudden Annik sat bolt upright and went, 'I know what ziss is – eet's a brothel.'

Me and Barney were like, 'Really?' looking forward to getting in there even more. But she started having this flaming row with Rob.

'You peeg,' she was saying. 'You peeg. You are deesgusting to bring us to ziss brothel,' which the rest of were cracking up about – right up until she announced that there was no way we could stay there, no way.

Then we stopped laughing. Because let me tell you we'd been really looking forward to a bed for the night. It didn't matter to us that it was a brothel. It was the wash and bed we were desperate for. But she was really kicking off about it, shouting at Rob and calling him immoral or something, which was the wrong thing to say because Rob squared up to her, pushed his glass up his nose and said, 'I'm immoral? *I'm* immoral? I'm not the one fucking a married man with a kid.'

Which wasn't strictly speaking true, of course. Ian's medication meant that fucking anybody was out of the question; and, like I say, it's public knowledge that he and Annik never – what's a nice way of saying it? – *consummated* their relationship. Even so, what Rob said was close enough to the bone to shut Annik up and she agreed that we could go in, which we did, only to discover that it was indeed a brothel. Everything was neon and there were neon strips everywhere – under the tables, which looked really good. (Come to think of it, I'll have it to suggest that to Becky for our house.) And in every room there was a speaker under the bed, so that when music was playing it vibrated (but I won't suggest that).

Oh, and there was hot water and a mattress. The fourth date of the tour and it was the first time I'd had a proper mattress. Fucking luxury.

Annik still didn't like it, though. She and Ian ended up with the promoter at his house and when we all met up the next morning there was, shall we say, an atmosphere in the van.

Things took a weird turn the next night, after the gig in Cologne, when this guy gave one of our entourage – all right, you've twisted my arm, it was Steve – a tab of acid. A 'red star', this guy called it. I think he'd got the idea from an interview that Steve was into hallucinogenics – which obviously wasn't that far from the truth, because Steve said, 'Thank you very much,' and swallowed it.

At which point the Dutch guy's eyes widened and he went, 'Oh my God, you Mancunians are *wild.*'

'What do you mean,' said Steve. 'Why?'

'You've just taken *five* hits of acid in one go. You're supposed to break a corner off to take it.' And the guy walked off shaking his head at how wild we Mancunians were, while Steve sort of looked around at us, the colour draining from his face.

To paraphrase Hunter S. Thompson, we were at the promoter's house when the drugs began to take hold.

It had a mezzanine section, this house, where we were all sleeping. You got to it by climbing up a ladder, and Steve was getting more and more fucked by the second. Barney could see the writing was on the wall, grabbed his sleeping bag and escaped down the ladder. Which left me, Twinny and Steve, who by now was a proper space cadet and was starting to talk about how he was going to get an axe and chop me and Twinny into little bits.

Twinny, you'll recall, is easily spooked at the best of times, so the next thing you know he'd fucked off as well – except that because he was so freaked out by all the talk of Steve chopping us up with an axe he moved the ladder so Steve couldn't get down into the main bit of the house. But then again neither could I.

It was the beginning of a very long night. Stuck alone with Steve, who had reached a kind of zoned-out, off-in-another-world stage of this trip, I'd nod off and every time I woke up he'd be staring intently at me and I'd go, 'Fuck off, Steve. Stop staring.'

He was still spaced out the next morning. Much to our relief he was okay to play, but he didn't speak – not a word for three days – which was quite weird. We'd be in the bus and you'd look and Steve would be staring at you.

Then the next time you looked he'd be staring at Barney and it would be Barney's turn to feel uncomfortable. Thank God there was no axe available, that's all I can say.

Still I wasn't eating. By the time we reached Rotterdam I could have eaten the hind legs off a rotten donkey, I was that hungry, and it was bloody Chinese again. They'd taken us to a Chinese restaurant, where I sat feeling sorry for myself until this waitress who spoke really good English came over to ask why I wasn't eating.

I was a right little kid, going, 'I can't eat it. I don't like it. Me mam says it's dirty.'

Evidently she was taking pity on me and said, 'What *can* you eat?'

'English food.'

'Ah,' she said. 'That's a shame because we only have Dutch food – steak and chips, egg and chips, sausage and chips.'

Oh God, it was like I'd died and gone to heaven. My deep affinity with the Dutch began that night as I ate like a lord – two steaks, two full dinners. It was brilliant. It was all my mother's fault, of course. That's how deep the indoctrination went. Even though all the rest would be tucking greedily into their Chinese and somehow managing not to fall down dead, and despite the fact that I was fucking *starving*, I still couldn't accept the evidence of my own eyes and eat some special fried rice or whatever. When I did – I must have been at death's door to do it, but I eventually did – it tasted incredible. I loved it. I was like, '*Mother* ... !'

The same thing happened years later with New Order, when we went for a meal with Cabaret Voltaire. There I was, heart sinking as we pushed open the door to a Sheffield curry house, knowing I was going to have to order whatever was the one dish they had for unadventur-ous bastards like me: Maryland Chicken, which tasted like they hated making it. One of the Cabs had this amazing-smelling curry.

'Can I have a taste?' I said.

'Yeah, course ...'

It was delicious. Fabulous.

'*Mother* ... !'

But that moment in Holland ended up being among the best of the tour. It was funny, though, because then more than ever – because of the discomfort, probably – we played some of our best gigs. We always loved playing so much and during that tour in particular it felt like the only refuge – from the cold, the hunger, Annik's clucking, the band bickering – was being on stage. We'd play and be brilliant and really click as musicians, then come off stage and immediately resume our former positions at each other's throats.

What was at the root of it all, I'm not sure. Definitely we felt a bit frustrated that, with our album doing so well (it had featured in a load of best-of-year lists from 1979), and us being such a hot band, we could still be so cold, freezing in a minibus and on people's floors. I'll tell you this for nothing: I've never been so happy to return to Manchester as I was when we got back.

'We carried on'

We played a lot with Killing Joke around that time. They were a tough bunch to work with but we became friends, and years later they were the only group ever to ask me to join them. Primal Scream almost did, just changing their minds right at the end: they were worried they'd sound too much like New Order. Anyway, Killing Joke got back together after a long time apart to make an album, *Pandemonium*, but their bassist Youth was getting into production and didn't want to tour, so I got the call: did I want to play bass on tour with Killing Joke?

Because New Order had split up, and I'd finished doing Revenge, I was at a bit of a loose end; so I decided that at the very least I could listen to the album they wanted me to play. Plus the wages they were offering were very good: a grand per gig. *Per gig.*

We were actually working together on a German concept album, *Freispiel*, in Cologne's Stadgarten Studio, it was a collaboration of rock and avant-garde musicians. We worked with Rüdiger Elze (guitar) and Rüdiger Braune (drums) both from the group Kowalski. Afterwards I ended up back at the lads' hotel. I was drinking then, and doing whatever else was going round – and there was plenty of it going round that night.

In the room were me, Geordie and Jaz and two girls. We all sat down to listen to their new album and when it was over they stopped, looked at me and said, 'Well? What do you think?' Now, because I was completely off my tits, I said, 'I can't play that shit.'

But I didn't mean like 'shit', like the music was shit. I meant shit, as in 'that shit', meaning the bass, which was the normal, low-end, chord-following rumble, which is just not what I do; I don't play bass like that. I can't play bass like that. Not that the album was shit. Far from it. Just that I don't play 'that shit'.

Being off my face, though, I couldn't get this point across. But Geordie and Jaz were just as wasted as I was, and they weren't getting it either. They thought I was talking about the album. I wasn't.

The more I tried to dig myself out of it, the worse it went, until the atmosphere had become really heated and we were getting to our feet. If it wasn't for the girls breaking it up we'd have ended up fighting there and then – and they would have kicked the shit out of me. Meaning 'the shit'.

Anyway the situation was defused thanks to the feminine intervention and a couple of weeks later I was surprised to find that the offer still stood. By this time I was thinking that a grand a gig was simply too good an offer to pass up. Fuck it, I'll follow chords for a grand a gig. So I decided to swallow my pride and play that shit. I got my head round it, too, and was starting to look forward to being on the road with Killing Joke. Then I spoke to either Jaz or Geordie and they said that Youth had changed his mind: couldn't bear to have someone else playing his bass lines, apparently. Yeah, me, I know …

Anyway, as a result of all that me, Jaz and Geordie decided to do a bit of work as a side-project, and we put six or eight tracks together. We even had meetings with their management, E.G., about setting up a band together. Never got as far as a name, but we were thinking about who we were going to have drumming for us, and I'd even persuaded Jaz that he should do more singing, rather than his normal, more shouty style, when suddenly it all went quiet. Never heard from them, never got a postcard, a phone call whatever – complete media blackout. Until one day I started getting PRS on a weird song that I'd never heard of and didn't remember playing on and it was a Killing Joke song. They'd used me on one of their albums, the cheeky buggers. Saying that, I do hold Jaz and Geordie in the absolute highest regard; not being in a band with them is one of my only regrets in music.

So that was that. They always were a right bunch, though, to be honest, and they'd be jockeying for position on the bill all the time. They were very ambitious and driven; ruthless. I mean, that night at the ULU, they were trying to fuck things up for us. They were trying the old Fast Breeder trick of being the support but going on late so it looked like they were the headliners. Meanwhile we were having trouble with another support group, from Manchester, called the Smirks, who were aptly named because they were a right bunch of arrogant smirkers. That almost ended in fisticuffs too.

Plus my bass amp blew up while were sound-checking. Of course in those days you didn't have somebody who would come and fix your gear. You didn't have a 'guitar roadie'. And you didn't carry spares. What you did was get your manager to ask the support group if you could borrow their amp. Oh, but our support were Killing fucking Joke and the Smirks, and Killing Joke were doing their level best to fuck us right up with all their time-keeping shenanigans, and I'd almost had a fight with the Smurfs, so of course they both refused to help.

It was quite funny, really: because I'd done so badly at school I knew nothing about electronics when I joined the band, and when I had to fix the gear I did wish I'd paid more attention in physics. But there I was – I had to take the whole cab apart, hundreds of screws, check the wiring, which was okay. Shit, one of the speakers had blown.

As I was doing that Killing Joke came on. I was stuffed in the back of the cab, with the Joke sound-checking more loudly than usual, it seemed, me holding a soldering iron and trying to see with a fag lighter. I ended up rewiring the cab and managed to get through the gig. Fuck me, that was traumatic.

Not quite as traumatic as what happened next, though, because it was around this time that Ian started cutting himself up.

After getting back from the European tour he'd apparently downed a bottle of Pernod and slashed himself with a knife – a fucking kitchen knife. We talked to him about it in practice afterwards.

'What the fuck did you do that for, Ian, you daft bastard?'

'Oh, it was just one of those things,' he said, shrugging. 'I got pissed and got carried away. You know ...'

'Yeah, yeah ...'

But, actually, no. I didn't know.

Of course – you know what I'm going to say. We brushed off the fact that he'd added self-harming to the list. We avoided the subject. We carried on like everything was all right and pretended that Ian wasn't ill, wasn't struggling with the responsibility of the band and didn't have some heavy, heavy affairs-of-the-heart stuff to contend with. We carried on. With Ian's blessing we carried on; Ian, who out of all of us most wanted us to taste the fruits of success and didn't want his illness to get in the way; Ian, who always buoyed us up after a bad review or a shit show. Who, even though he was the frontman and the focal point, always insisted that we were a group, who used to say, 'All I do is the words and sing. The others do the music.'

Because that's the thing, and I can't say it enough: nobody wanted the group – *the whole group* – to do well more than Ian did. So he lied. Either to us, or to himself, or both. He lied when he said that it was no big deal to get pissed and start carving away at yourself with a knife.

He was fitting more frequently, too. He'd fit at gigs. There was one when he just froze, mid-strum on his guitar. Another one when he fell into the drum kit and was thrashing around; Steve played on as Ian kicked his drums out from beneath him and Twinny and Terry rushed on to haul him off the stage. Another where he kicked the flight-case the synthesizer was on and sent it spinning off the stage. More than anything Ian hated having a fit on stage and I can see why. Being at your most vulnerable, just flipping out like that, with some of the audience laughing, some scared, some cheering, some thinking you're a freak. It must have been horrible. But we'd stop him swallowing his tongue and he'd get up, tell us he was fine and, well, you know the rest.

It got so that recording our next album was almost a break. Almost.

'He thought we were pricks – and how right he was'

By now plans were being made to tour America, and Joy Division were due to record their second album at Britannia Row studios in London. Things were going less smoothly for Ian Curtis, however. During a confrontation in which Debbie smashed his copy of Bowie's Low, *he admitted his affair with Annik. Despite assuring Debbie that he would break it off, he didn't, and continued writing to Annik, his letters to her reflecting his inner turmoil. He told her about the obligations and responsibilities that weighed heavily upon him; that his epilepsy seemed to be worsening, the attacks growing more frequent and more intense; and that his dog, Candy, was to be sent away. Finding it increasingly difficult to cope with Candy during Ian's absence, not to mention the cost, and with Ian unwilling to either contribute or discuss the issue, Debbie felt she had no choice and had made arrange-ments for the dog to live on a farm in Rochdale. Ian, meanwhile, was taking barbiturates for his epilepsy, which have a numbing, deadening effect.*

Next the band decamped to London for the recording sessions, leaving Terry Mason and Twinny at home and using Dave Pils as a roadie. He stayed at home in Walthamstow, Martin Hannett in a hotel, while Rob Gretton and the band rented two flats in York Street. The cost of this, how-ever, meant that band members had very little to live on.

We had enough to get some food and maybe a pint, the usual. Both Sue and Iris worked, so at least me and Barney didn't have to worry about providing, but Ian had a wife and kid back home, so, just like everything else in this story, it was harder for him.

It's funny really, when you look at it like that, because nowadays if we'd released an album like *Unknown Pleasures* we'd have been nomi-nated for the Mercury, be swanning around Glastonbury fighting off mates of Kate Moss and sitting on sofas with Fearne Cotton. Back then things moved much more slowly. Independent music stayed under-ground. Ian on the cover of the *NME* was as big as it got. We never felt like we were stars at all, and we never acted like it.

For a start we didn't have any money, hadn't really earned any yet.

We let Rob take care of all of that and he did it very well, keeping it all close to his chest. One of Tony's favourite sayings was: 'Always keep your bands poor. That way they make great music.' He may well have been right. There's nothing like sudden fame and wealth to turn a band's heads.

But just every now and then it would have been nice to have tested his theory instead of being forced to prove it.

It made us a better band, though. I mean, Rob, you'd have to say, was very good at keeping you grounded, making sure your feet stayed firmly on the ground. His thing was: just get on with it, play live and record. That was how we went in to record *Closer*. We were keen to do an album as good as *Unknown Pleasures* but it wasn't like there was huge pressure – not from Rob and not from Factory. All the pressure we felt came from within and we were brimming with confidence back then. Ian's illness was the only black spot on the horizon. Otherwise we were rocking.

By that time we'd already recorded 'Love Will Tear Us Apart' at Pennine but weren't happy with it so had another crack in Strawberry. Martin was up to his old tricks. He'd stay up till two in the morning then phone Rob and go, 'Right, I'm going in the studio now with Chris to mix "Love Will Tear us Apart",' and Rob would phone me up and go, 'You're nearest: fucking get down to Strawberry now, Hooky; they're mixing,' and I'd go, 'Fucking hell, it's two in the morning.'

He'd just say, 'Fucking get down there.' Because he didn't have a car, you see. So I'd drive to the studio at half-two in the morning, buzzing the buzzer for hours before they'd let me in, and Martin would say, 'Oh, you turned up, did you?'

'Yes, why are you doing it now?'

'Oh, it's the only time we could get.' But it wasn't – it was just so you weren't there, so you didn't turn up. Because one of the most famous things about Martin was that he hated having the musicians around during the mix, so he'd make it really difficult. The night he did 'Love Will Tear Us Apart' the air conditioning was cranked up as usual. I was freezing while Martin and Chris sniggered. He may well have been a genius, Martin, but that didn't stop him being a right twat sometimes.

All of which didn't bode well because we were due to record our second album with him, a prospect we might well have been dreading but for the fact that we were going to London to record it, in Britannia Row studios, owned by Pink Floyd, just like proper rock stars.

Our families didn't like it, of course. We got a lot of grief: 'Why can't you just record at Strawberry?'

I think Rob liked the idea of getting Ian away for a bit and of course Ian loved it because he got to shack up with Annik. Martin wanted to use Britannia Row because it was state of the art at that time and he did like his toys. Chris Nagle got the elbow, though. Martin wanted to use this other guy he'd met, John Caffery, who wasn't wildly imaginative but was a nice bloke, while the tape operator was Mike Johnson, who later became New Order's engineer on everything we ever did. We liked him and really got on with him; he was very imaginative and willing to try anything.

So we decamped to London, where Rob had hired two flats above a shop, which were opposite each other across a corridor, both two-bedroom. They were probably quite small but they seemed huge to us at the time, with open-plan kitchens and everything. Ian and Bernard had one side – with Annik in with Ian when she stayed over – while me Steve and Rob had the other side. Our flat wasn't as cosy – it was a bit bigger, colder and more sparsely furnished – but was still okay.

Martin was in a hotel because he wanted to be as far away from us as possible because he thought we were pricks – and how right he was.

Then there was Brittannia Row itself. The studios we'd used in Manchester were a bit old fashioned. All wood-panelling and heavy drapes and cork tiles on the walls. Britannia Row was like something out of *Star Wars* in comparison. It was a bit more austere and clinical than anywhere we'd been at home. It had an enclosed spaceship atmosphere, with the control room in particular really packed full of stuff. There wasn't much room for anybody else; we had a bench seat against the wall. Me and Bernard would position ourselves one either side of Martin, looking over his shoulder.

He was in his element there, Martin was. He loved the airless quality of Britannia Row. He loved how it felt sealed off from the outside world and started working at night to take advantage of it at its most silent and dead. Listen to the finished product and you can hear all of that in the album.

There were offices, too, so loads of staff hanging around – Pink Floyd's staff, I think – and there was a PA company based there, plus they had a recreation room with a pool table in it. Islington was a very interesting area. There was a famous taxidermy shop called Get Stuffed full of very exotic animals and a military shop on the corner where I used to stand staring in at the window, looking at these really expensive World War II flying jackets, lusting after them.

Every day we'd clamber into Steve's car and drive the few miles from York Street to Islington, Martin arriving in his old beat-up Volvo. He'd ripped the speakers out and replaced them with two Auratone monitor speakers, studio speakers that are very flat but faithful. Martin said if we could make the mix sound good on the Auratones then it would sound good on anything. Nobody in their right mind would listen to Auratones for pleasure because they sound rotten; they soak up all the reflections and echo and wetness on a track, make everything sound dead dry and boring. But that was Martin's scheme: make the record sound good on them and it'll lop your head off on a set of decent speakers. Listening to a mix with him meant getting in his car and having him drive you around while you checked out how it sounded. He hadn't bothered screwing them down, these speakers, so they just used to roll around the floor of the Volvo, and because Martin was such a terrible driver they did a lot of rolling around.

But of course we weren't using him for his skill as a driver. As a producer he was getting the best out of us, and at the same time we were learning from him. It was him who encouraged us to use the piano; they had a grand piano at Brittannia Row. He put it on 'The Eternal', trying it on nearly every track. He showed Bernard how to use keyboards properly, how to layer them to give the sound a real richness and depth. Christ, he used to get pissed off with us, especially me and Barney: we were about as welcome as a dog at a game of skittles.

'Oh, Martin, what do you reckon about making the high hat a bit brighter?' one of us would say, strictly taking turns.

He'd scream at us. 'Fucking shut up, you pair of twats.'

I've since discovered that Martin was on heroin then, and that one night he drove to Manchester and back to score, he was that desperate for it. But to be honest there was no evidence of that in the studio. He was smoking a lot of dope, as he always did, but otherwise really efficient and really creative. He introduced us to the ARP synthesizers and sequencers, which he and Bernard used a lot, and to audio gates, used so that the drums would trigger synthesizer sounds and sound really crisp and powerful.

Martin's big thing was still clarity. He always said that for a recording to have lasting effect and impact it had to have clarity and separation. Now, remember: me and Barney still didn't like the sound of *Unknown Pleasures*. I mean, I suppose that by then we'd grudgingly accepted that it was a great album, and knew that part of that was down to the work Martin had done, but it still wasn't how we heard Joy Division. We wanted a harder, harsher more metallic sound, like a group playing in a garage with metal walls, like the Stooges or Velvet Underground. He wanted us to sound like – how did he describe it? – adult gothic music or something.

Well, he was right and we were wrong. Sorry, Martin, if you're up there. But it didn't stop us bitching at the time because he'd make us play the song then take it apart.

'Right, let's concentrate on this bit,' he'd say, and would do a lot of work adding effects and synth parts. He spent many a happy hour messing about with the synths and the sequencers, too – much to the studio manager's delight, because it was an expensive studio, Britannia Row, around £40 an hour; considering I was only earning £12 a week, this was an absolute fortune.

So workwise it was great. As far as socializing went, this was when a division appeared in the band. The first, I suppose you'd have to say. It was caused by Ian finding his arty feet and us not handling this all that well.

By finding his arty feet I mean behaving a little bit pretentiously. There were other influences in his life now and he was soaking them up. One of these was Genesis P-Orridge out of Throbbing Gristle. Now I like Genesis, and I fucking love Throbbing Gristle, but I can't get on with the whole none-more-arty attitude that goes with that scene. Genesis wrote the book on all that.

Then of course there was Annik. Although she had her flat in Parson's Green she and Ian had set up house in his room in the flat across the way and were acting like a right pair of arty Bohemian types. Every five minutes they'd be announcing that they were off to some art exhibition or some gallery, with their noses in the air, making it perfectly clear that whatever they were doing wasn't for the likes of us.

The fact that in return we gave it loads and called him all sorts of pretentious tossers wasn't very nice of us, of course. If I'm honest, we were pretty horrible to him about it. So what if he wanted to go to an art gallery with his new beau? It was really none of our business.

But you know what it's like. Young lads, their mate suddenly going off with his new girlfriend, taking on airs and graces: they rip the piss. I've no doubt that the likes of Genesis and Annik thought they knew the 'real' Ian, and that he was most at home in 'their' world. But we thought we knew the 'real' Ian. Probably Debbie did, too. What I've realized in the years since is that the truth was a lot more complex and in-between than any of us really knew at the time. Thinking about it, I bet even Ian didn't know who the 'real' Ian was.

About halfway through the recording Rob announced that we should get our other halves down, and sent them money for train tickets. Debbie didn't come, much to Ian's relief. She used the money to pay a bill. I can't remember the sequence of events, but that's because it was a day best forgotten. For a start, we left them waiting around at the station for a couple of hours. Then they had to hang around while we finished in the studio, which didn't exactly improve the mood. Later I accidentally blabbed to Iris about Annik being with Ian all of the time. Me and my big mouth. She kicked off, which added to the general air of gloom. She then told Lesley.

In short, the day was a complete debacle, because it was really expensive and everybody was as miserable as sin and I don't even know why that day was chosen, because we were in the studio anyway, which didn't help matters. So you had Sue, Lesley, Gillian and Iris all twiddling their thumbs, dead fucking pissed off at being dragged to London only to have to sit around, and fuming that they were apparently banned from the whole process while Annik was hanging around.

We breathed a big sigh of relief when it was all was over, I can tell you, and Rob celebrated by putting cornflakes in everybody's bed. However, in order to escape suspicion, he put them in his own bed as well and was walking around scratching his head, going, 'Well if we've all got cornflakes in our beds, then who's fucking done it, then?'

A few days later the truth emerged and we were like, 'You barmy bastard. What's the point in japing yourself?'

Another night we overheard Ian and Annik getting ready go out, and Annik saying, 'Ian, Ian, hurry and do the i-ron-ing.' Just like that. 'I-ron-ing'.

And there stood Ian, all done up ready to go out, doing Annik's ironing with a fag hanging out of his mouth.

We were like, 'I-ron-ing. I-an, have you done the i-ron-ing?' which really pissed him off and he got really angry. Me and Barney noticed that they had a teddy bear in the eiderdown in their room and laid into him about that, too.

He was like, 'Fuck off, you pair of twats. Just fuck off and leave us alone, would you?'

I feel terrible about it now, of course. Now I'm older and wiser, and now I've looked at his lyrics and worked out what a tortured soul he was. We should have left him alone to have his love affair but we didn't because he wasn't tragic Ian Curtis the genius then. He was just our mate and that's what you did with your mates up North: you ripped the piss out of them.

One particular evening we got back before Ian and Annik, who were still out somewhere, probably at a gallery or an exhibition or something, and Barney said, 'Come on, let's jape their room.'

So we went in and the first thing we did – what a bunch of bastards – we took out the bed. No mean feat. Then we unfolded the i-ron-ing board, made the bed over the i-ron-ing board and tucked the teddy in the top. We hid in Barney's room, looking through the keyhole waiting for them to come back. Didn't have long to wait. A few minutes later the front door opened and Ian and Annik came into the flat and then went into the bedroom.

Next thing you know, she screamed. 'Ian, Ian, what have zey done to our room?' We pissed ourselves laughing. Then Ian kicked off. Really kicked off. Shit. He heard us laughing from the other side of Barney's door and launched himself at the door, screaming, 'You fucking cunts, you fucking bunch of twats,' kicking hell out of the door.

We weren't laughing any more. We were scared, because let me tell you, he was going mental. Absolutely mental. What if he had a fit? What if he smashed the door in?

He calmed down enough for us to make our escape. But of course we still had their bed, which was in bits in the other flat. As we scarpered across there we had Annik on our tails and she launched herself at the door.

'You peegs,' she was screaming. 'You fooking English peegs.' Kicking the glass window in the door.

Of course we were in fits again, which just made it worse. God knows how we got the bed back together.

Part of the problem was that we were jealous of Ian, I think. Annik was fit and exotic, and Ian was living with her in the flat while we were all slumming it. Or that's how it felt anyway.

Plus he was Martin's favourite. As far back as *Unknown Pleasures* Ian had developed a special relationship with Martin – the two of them seemed to feed off each other creatively – and I think we sort of resented that, too, like Ian was the teacher's pet or something. Especially as Martin treated the rest of us like shit.

Ian would say to Martin, 'Do you need me for a while, Martin?'

Martin would say, 'No, mate, you're all right; come back at eight.'

So Ian and Annik would happily go off together, whereas me and Barney were always 'that pair of bastards'. We'd play the tracks with Steve and Ian would do a guide vocal but then he'd return to record the proper vocals at night, when it was quieter in the studio. Which is fair enough – it's a normal thing to do – but it did create a bit of a them-and-us situation.

It went both ways, of course. It's a well known fact that we totally pissed him off during the making of *Closer* because he wrote a letter to someone – Rob, I think – saying that he wasn't happy with the album, partly because of us lot, 'sneaky, japing tossers', he called us. But in his letters to Annik he says he was very happy with the album: strange.

You've got to say he had a point. I remember being in the flat one night and A Certain Ratio were round having a smoke with Rob. Me and Barney didn't bother with all that so Barney was going, 'What shall we do to them? Come on, we got to do something …'

So they're all sitting there, squinting at us through clouds of dope smoke, going, 'What are you up to, lads?' as we set about our plan. First we smeared their minibus handles and windscreen in jam and marmalade, and tied toilet rolls to their exhaust; then we prepared eggs and pots and pans full of water.

When ACR finally made their way out we were waving goodbye to them from the flat windows, watching as they got to the bus and found the jammy traps. Next thing we were pelting them with water and eggs and killing ourselves as we watched them trying and failing to wrench open the doors and get out of the line of fire. Finally they managed it and tore away, with two long trails of pink bog paper hanging off the back off the bus.

So Ian had a point. We *were* sneaky, japing tossers. Not long before he would have been a part of it too. So if we resented him for being Martin's favourite and having a fit foreign girlfriend, well, maybe we also thought, *We're losing our mate here.*

His illness hung over us, though. One night we were in the studio. He was working on his vocals and he seemed a bit rattled about something and went off by himself. We were waiting for him to do a vocal and after a while Martin was going, 'Where is Ian? Where the fuck is Ian? Hooky, go and find out where Ian is and drag him back here.'

So off I trotted and found him in the toilet, where he was sparkled on the floor, big gash in his head. He'd gone to the toilet, had a fit, fallen forward and banged his head on the sink, which had knocked him out.

Guess what? We brought him round, he said he was all right and we carried on. I should call the book that, shouldn't I? *He Said He Was All Right So We Carried On.*

The other thing I remember is recording one afternoon and a bloke calling in to reception to see Martin. There was a group with him, a young group. They wanted to talk about Martin producing their first single.

So Martin went off to talk and of course, being nosy, I poked my head around the door to get a look at these kids, who it turned out were called U2. I don't know if it had been raining outside but they looked like something the cat had dragged in, and they were sitting in reception staring at Martin with complete awe. Very funny.

They were huge fans of Joy Division, it turned out, and wanted Martin to produce their first single, '11 O'Clock Tick Tock', which he did.

Years later I got the shock of my life when Tony told me one story about Bono. It seems that after Ian had died Tony met Bono somewhere, and Bono was telling Tony not to worry because he would take over from where Ian left off.

Very strange. But nice ... Well, he did in a way, didn't he? We may have been laughing at them in reception that day, the star-struck young pretenders, but just look at how our two careers went. Seven years later we'd been stung with a tax bill for nearly a million quid and losing all our money on a nightclub, while they'd gone off and made *The*

Joshua Tree, become the biggest band in the world and hadn't opened a nightclub. And we all know how they feel about tax. They did everything right, in other words.

For the cover of Closer, *as well as the twelve-inch of 'Love Will Tear Us Apart', Peter Saville showed the band a series of photographs taken by Bernard Pierre Wolff of crypts in Genoa's Staglieno Cemetery. Of course, these images would later take on an extra, tragic significance.*

'I guess it worked for Ian,' said Saville. 'Perhaps if I'd been sent a draft of the lyrics, and had any kind of sensitivity, I might have thought, I'm not going to indulge that route. Let's have some trees …'

The 'Love Will Tear Us Apart' single cover was done before *Closer*. We went to Peter's studio in Portobello Road. He'd just seen an article about a photographer who'd taken some photographs of a cemetery on the outskirts of Genoa that was used by rich Italian merchants. These rich families had got into a macabre competition with the tombs, each building more and more elaborate monuments.

I loved the images and I loved Peter's cover. I was always fascinated by the way the apostrophes both go the same way. They don't frame the word *Closer* as you expect them to. I did ask him recently what that was all about, and it turns out that what I thought were apostrophes are actually full stops from the second century BC, and the reason they go that way is to do with the angle the original stone mason leaned when he was tapping out the words and punctuation marks. So there you go.

It's a beautiful cover. We all loved the pictures, especially Ian. I wonder: when he chose them did he realize how symbolic they would be? I don't know; nobody does, I suppose. In my gut I think not but I do think that he saw them and saw how they fitted perfectly with the music on the album – which itself was a kind of soundtrack to his suffering, I guess. Quite shocking really. By the time we chose those pictures he had less than two months to live.

'His mum got the blood out by washing it in a bath of salt water'

With the American tour due to begin on 21 May at Hurrah nightclub in New York, Joy Division next embarked on a busy schedule of UK dates partly aimed at raising funds, including a Factory mini-residency at the Moonlight Club in Hampstead, as well as a prestigious support slot for the Stranglers at the Rainbow Theatre in Finsbury Park.

Prior to this gig, however, the Stranglers' frontman Hugh Cornwell was sent to Pentonville Prison for possession of heroin, cocaine and cannabis, and the show was instead reconfigured as 'The Stranglers & Friends' with other well-known artists (Toyah, Hazel O'Connor, Robert Smith and Richard Jobson among them) filling in for Cornwell.

The night would also prove eventful for Joy Division, who were scheduled to perform there before returning to the Moonlight in Hampstead for the last night of the Factory residency. On stage at the Rainbow, Ian had a fit triggered by strobe lights and collapsed into the drum kit but recovered enough to play the Moonlight just over an hour later. He then had another fit during that set – though the performance was still rated a triumph by the NME's Neil Norman, who wrote: 'Unlike the Fall, who make me want to go out and kick a cat, Joy Division convince me I could spit in the face of God.'

Though the pressure was evidently becoming intolerable, and Ian spoke of opening a bookshop with Annik and even, according to Genesis P-Orridge, hatched plans with him to form a breakaway group, Ian nevertheless insisted to his band mates that they continue with the schedule.

It got chaotic now. Really, really busy. First off we had this label residency at the Moonlight Club in Hampstead, loads of Factory bands playing over three nights: Section 25, Crawling Chaos, John Dowie, A Certain Ratio, Kevin Hewick, Blurt, Durutti Column, X-O-Dus and the Royal Family.

And us. Being the biggest, it fell to us to attract the punters. Factory were apparently nervous that the other bands wouldn't be enough of a draw but I found that hard to believe, because the venue was tiny.

Anyway, we'd stayed down in London after recording *Closer*, and went on to do the first two nights of the Hampstead gig, the second and third of April, which went well – as in we turned up, played, did good gigs. One of the nights was attended by this A&R guy from Polydor called the Captain, who's a bit of a legend in the industry. He's a very tall, broad guy with a military bearing, hence the name, but a nice bloke. I've since met him many times over the years. He looks after U2 now, and was a big help in their career, but before all that he came to see us, which Ian was dead excited about.

'Oh God, Hooky,' he was going, 'there's an A&R man from Polydor here. He's called the Captain. He's great. Come and meet him – we might get some free drinks.'

Great. Free drinks. Well up for that. So after the set the band and Rob went to meet the Captain and discovered, firstly, that he was dead posh – 'Hello. How are you, Peter?' – like that; and secondly that he was going to get a round of drinks in: 'Now, what can I get everybody?'

We were like, 'Fucking great,' and really took the piss, ordering triple vodkas and orange and two beers – each. But he just looked amused, said, 'Fine, fine,' went to the bar, ordered the drinks and handed them out.

'Tuck in, everybody, tuck in. It's all you chaps deserve after such an excellent gig.'

Then he turned to the barmaid. 'How much is that, my good woman?'

'Eight pound fifty, darling,' she said.

The Captain reached into his jacket and pulled out a chequebook. At which point the barmaid looked absolutely incredulous, as though he was offering to pay with a huge purple marrow, and said to him, 'We don't take cheques, darling.'

So the Captain turned to us, looking suitably embarrassed and said, 'I'm terribly sorry about this, but can anybody lend me eight pounds fifty to pay for the drinks?'

I think it was Ian who lent him the money to get the round in and the guy made a cheque out to him for the round of drinks, then slunk off as soon as he could.

Then came the gig at the Rainbow, where the Stranglers' crew behaved like complete bastards. Before the doors opened I was on stage ogling Jean-Jacques Burnel's set-up, which was split into high/mid/bass, like a proper PA. Oh, it was great. He had a really huge rig and I had a really small, cheap set-up in comparison. I was jealous. The problem was their crew wouldn't let us move any of it so we could sound-check. That day the Stranglers' crew were swanning about as if they owned the place because there were all these 'pop stars' hanging around, like Toyah and what have you. It was as though it had suddenly become this huge event or something. They were recording it to release as an album, too, which didn't help.

All day the crew were just rude, to be honest. Because Jean-Jacques Burnel was one of my heroes I'd been really, really, looking forward to that Rainbow gig, so for them to treat us so badly was gutting and I held a grudge about it for a long time. Same with Rob.

It was at that gig, in fact, that we swore to ourselves that we'd make sure we never treated a support band the way the Stranglers had treated us, and thus a policy was born – one that arguably got out of hand in the Haçienda years, when visiting bands were treated like royalty. I used to moan and whinge about it at the time, but Rob would always remind me of that Stranglers gig.

He'd say, 'Treat your bands how you want to be treated.' And he was absolutely right.

The crew problem went right across the board, including the lighting guys. At most gigs Rob would position himself in the lighting booth so that if the technician went to the strobes he was there to sort it out straight away. We'd always know about it on stage because the lights would kick in then stop almost immediately, and you could just imagine Rob pushing his glasses up his nose and telling the technician to kill them or else. But that night we didn't even get a sound-check so there was no way Rob was going to get in the lighting booth. Sure enough, during 'Atrocity Exhibition' the guy went to the strobes.

They were blasting away and not stopping like normal, and I thought, *Uh oh*, and no doubt so did Barney and Steve, and the next thing you know Ian's dancing had fallen out of time and suddenly he'd lost it; his legs went, he stumbled back and into the kit and the lighting guy realized something was wrong and brought the lights down just as Twinny and Terry dashed on and me and Barney took off our guitars and went to help Ian, who was fitting in the drums.

We carried him off, got him to a room backstage and stayed with him for a while until he'd recovered. He was going, 'Thanks, lads. Sorry, lads. I'm all right now. Let's get over to the Moonlight, eh?'

We were telling him, 'No, mate, no you're not fucking going on again tonight. They can manage without us.'

Tony was down to see us that night but bollocks to that – even Rob was adamant that Ian needed to rest. But Ian insisted. You know why? Because he was a man of his word, simple as that. He wasn't a wimp. You put Ian on a battlefield and he'd be the guy still fighting with his arms hanging off. He said, 'Don't worry, I'll be fine. A couple of Aspirin, no problem. Let's go.'

Definitely his own worst enemy. So we went to perform at the Moonlight, and of course things didn't get any better. We were as good as our word. We played. But Ian collapsed again. He was really, really tired by this point, almost weary. But instead of resting, which of course he should have done, we went to Malvern the very next night, did a storming gig with Section 25, drove home that night and dropped Ian off. The next day, I got a phone call from Rob to tell me that Ian had tried to kill himself.

It was on Easter Sunday that Ian took an overdose of phenobarbitone at home in Macclesfield. It's been suggested that after taking the pills he had second thoughts, fearing the possibility of brain or liver damage rather than death, or that his attempt was a cry for help. Whatever his reasons, he alerted Deborah and was immediately taken to hospital in Macclesfield and had his stomach pumped.

The following day, Easter Monday, Tony Wilson, Alan Erasmus and Rob Gretton took Debbie to visit Ian in hospital. There it was suggested that Ian stay with Tony and his wife, Lindsay Reade, at their cottage in Charlesworth in order to ease Ian's marital pressure. It was agreed that the stay would begin the following day, Tuesday 8 April.

Meanwhile, Rob Gretton had decided that the next day's gig, at Bury Town Hall, was to go ahead as planned, only without Ian. Alan Hempsall of Crispy Ambulance, a big Joy Division fan, was asked to stand in and duly began learning lyrics. When he turned up on the night, however, he was surprised to find Ian Curtis at the venue. Gretton had apparently

*visited Ian in hospital and persuaded him to perform – for at least one
or two songs ...*

We should have cancelled of course. I mean, looking back now, you
start to see the gigs we should have got rid of. That Stranglers support
at the Rainbow, for one, and that one at Bury Town Hall for another.
But we decided to go ahead with it for whatever reason. Whether we
needed the money for the American tour or would have been penal-
ized financially for pulling out, I don't know, but we went ahead with
them.

I hate to say this, but in an awful sort of way it was quite exciting,
really, to consider being able to play a gig without worrying about Ian
for once. Because, after the initial shock of him trying to top himself, you
felt like, *Right, okay, that's a fucking scary thing, but at least he* didn't *go
through with it. He pulled back in time. He changed his mind. He chose not
to die. He wants to live.*

So you felt that he'd turned a corner somehow. He'd had a go at the
suicide thing, decided he didn't like it and that would be that. Plus, to
sound very, very callous for a moment, it was nice to think of playing a
gig without the fear of one of the band collapsing on stage. We could
actually enjoy the music for once. Yeah, that does sound callous. Maybe
I should take that out.

It was a lovely venue, actually, Bury. There was a large, ornate chandelier that hung above the stage, and a covered grand piano that had
been pushed up to the stage. Of course they're kidney-shaped, aren't
they, those pianos, so muggins here stepped on to it, thinking it was part
of the stage, and shot straight through to the floor and nearly killed
myself, which was my only brush with death for the day – or so I
thought at the time.

So anyway, Minny Pops played their set, then Section 25 came on, did
most of their set and finished with 'Girls Don't Count', which was the
song that Ian and Rob had produced and was supposed to be released
as a single but hadn't yet come out – delayed because of the sleeve, I
think. So they were playing that, and me, Barney and Steve went on
stage to join them, along with Alan from Crispy Ambulance and Simon
Topping from A Certain Ratio, who would be singing the Joy Division
songs.

Maybe the idea was to try to dazzle the crowd with the amazing array of Factory talent on stage so they'd be so bowled over they wouldn't notice that Ian wasn't there – I don't know. What I do know is that the crowd were getting more and more rowdy.

Now, the venue was sold out and was at capacity: 400. But earlier, after the sound-check, the bands and Rob had gone for a bite to eat and returned to find a bunch of kids hanging around outside the venue. They'd caught sight of Rob and started hassling him to get in, and for some strange reason he took pity on them and put them all on the guest list.

Little did he know that these kids were a right bunch of trouble-makers, and immediately on entering the gig had gone to the fire escapes to let in all their mates – loads of them – which swelled the numbers inside to around 600. The mood, as they say, started getting ugly.

What didn't help matters was Ian coming on to sing 'Decades' and 'The Eternal', but with nothing like his normal spark, which sort of brought the evening down, to be honest. It eludes me, actually, the point of him coming on, because it definitely made matters worse. I mean, up until then it was going all right. I dare say there were plenty in who didn't even realize Ian wasn't on stage. Of course the true fans knew, but then they weren't the ones most likely to cause trouble. When Ian went off again the crowd became even more restless and we played 'Sister Ray' then left, just as it started to get rowdy.

Really rowdy. Most of the bands were backstage when it all kicked off. I found out later that Larry from Section 25 had got caught out there and had to hide behind the curtains. But the rest of us were in a dressing room at the side of the stage, kept separate from the main venue by a huge drape that ran down one side. So we didn't see one of the idiots throw a pint pot that shattered in the chandelier above the stage, showering the stage with broken glass. We didn't see Rob dive into the crowd to try to lamp the idiot who'd thrown the pint pot. Didn't see Twinny dive in after him and get set upon by a bunch of thugs who started kicking the hell out of him. Or Terry grab a micro-phone stand and jump off stage to help them.

Twinny went down, his head smashed open and bleeding badly, and they would have kicked the shit out of him if Terry hadn't smacked a couple of them with the mic stand, which at least gave Twinny the chance to pull himself to his feet and fight back, still bleeding badly.

The thing was: he had my shirt on, the fucker. That afternoon he'd asked if he could borrow it and, even though it was my favourite (after the blue one, of course), I'd let him have it because he promised me he was going to be dead careful with it, and absolutely not get a battering from a load of thugs and bleed all over it.

Later on his mum got the blood out by washing it in a bath of salt water. The salt lifts the blood out, she told me later, and she was absolutely right because the shirt was fine. Little tip for you there.

So anyway, it was all kicking off out in the venue, a proper riot. These guys weren't messing about. Twinny was badly hurt and they were coming back for second helpings, Terry swinging his mic stand around his head trying to keep the crowd off him. He was that scared he actually pissed himself, but luckily he hadn't borrowed my trousers.

Backstage the first we knew of it was when Tony Wilson came bursting into the dressing room, screaming like a girl: 'Oh fuck, it's all gone off. Everyone's getting beaten up.'

Hysterical, he was. Imagine the suave, intellectual Tony Wilson you've seen on telly. Now imagine the opposite and that was how he was.

Next thing, the door opened again. With it open all we could hear was the sound of shouting and glasses smashing from out in the venue: the sound of it all really going off. Then Rob was standing there, out of breath, in complete disarray, saying one word: 'Fuck.'

I was straight out of my seat, 'What the fuck's going on?'

'It's a fucking riot, mate,' he said. 'They're going fucking apeshit out there. Terry, Twinny and Dave are out there. We've got to help them, mate, come on ...'

He opened the door, we poked our heads out and straight away there was a hail of bottles. I'm not kidding, it was like a fucking mortar attack – all these bottles shattering around us. Rob darted out and I grabbed two empty bottles of Pils off the dressing-room table, shoved one at Alan Hempsall, and shouted, 'Come on, let's get out there.'

Alan Hempsall stood there like I was trying to hand him a dog turd. Wouldn't take the bottle. I looked from him to the rest of them.

'Come on, then.'

They all stared at me. The rest of Joy Division, Tony, Lindsay, Iris, all of Minny Pops, A Certain Ratio and Section 25, all of them at the back of the dressing room and staring at me, wide-eyed and shitless.

Well, fuck 'em, I thought, and turned to follow Rob when all of a sudden I was being grabbed from behind, held back, arms going around my waist, someone else grabbing on to my arm.

Tony was holding me, Lindsay was holding me, Iris was holding me; Paul from Section 25, too. One of them had long nails and really hurt me but that was my fault for struggling, I suppose, because I was going mental and the bastards wouldn't let me out; they ended up pinning me down and sitting on me in the dressing room. I was shouting that we could have them if we all stuck together, how we should be out there helping our mates and all that. Calling them all the names under the sun.

They were right, though. I'd have been toast if I'd got out there. A member of the band? The bastards would have kicked seven shades of shit out of me. So I can say that now: they basically saved my life. But at the time all the thanks they got was me struggling and swearing at them and calling them rotten. But save my bacon they did. They held on to me until at last the trouble had ended. Then, like survivors emerging from a nuclear shelter, we ventured outside.

The place was trashed. Twinny had a massive gash in his head, blood all over him. Terry was in a terrible state; they all were.

Ian had disappeared, though, and I found him in a stairwell with his head in his hands, and one of our lot (she shall remain nameless) screaming at him: 'This is all your fault. This is all your fault.'

I was going, 'Will you get the fuck out?' I gave this dick a shove out the way and said, 'Are you all right, Ian?'

He was just like, 'Yeah, I'm all right, Hooky, I'm all right. Just leave me for a minute; I'll be okay.'

Ian wasn't much of a fighter, especially when he was sober. He was obviously really shocked and shook up. Tony came to have a word and I left them to it, went out to see the others who were in the process of calling an ambulance for Twinny. Lindsay ended up taking him to the hospital, telling him on the way that she had stockings and suspenders on, even showing him them at the traffic lights. He just said, 'Under the circumstances, Lindsay, I'm not really interested!' When they got to A&E who else should be there, getting stitched up, but the two lads Terry had battered with the mic stand. Nice one, Terry.

After the Bury gig Ian went to stay with Tony and Lindsay, where he spent a few days listening to records and smoking dope. Debbie attended the next Joy Division concert at the Factory II on 11 April but during the course of the evening learned more about Ian's relationship with Annik – specifically their living arrangements during the Closer sessions. After the concert the couple argued and Ian returned to Charlesworth. However, he left at some point during the weekend and stayed either with Bernard or his parents, missing Natalie's birthday on 16 April. He returned home briefly then departed for Derby, where Joy Division were playing at the Ajanta Theatre on Saturday 19 April.

This was to be the band's penultimate gig. There Ian met up with Annik, and that night the pair stayed at a hotel in Rusholme. The following day they visited Rob Gretton, who by coincidence Debbie phoned during their visit. On Monday Annik returned to London and Ian went home to Macclesfield, but at this point both Ian and Debbie's parents became involved and on Tuesday 22 April there was apparently a showdown involving all concerned – as well as Rob and Lesley Gretton – at the Curtis home in Macclesfield. The same day, Debbie phoned Annik at the Belgian embassy and by her own admission 'screamed' at her that she planned to divorce Ian and would be naming Annik as co-respondent. Though advised to hang on by her parents in order to win a larger divorce settlement when Joy Division were a bigger band Debbie chose not to. 'It was difficult initiating the divorce,' she writes in Touching from a Distance, 'but once I had made the decision it felt wonderful. It seemed as though a huge weight had been lifted from my shoulders.'

For her part, Annik has said that the call forced her to confront the fact that Ian was married – something she had downplayed. 'I realized I was hurting somebody,' she said.

Meanwhile Ian went to stay with Rob and Lesley Gretton, then with Bernard, while the band – despite taking a break from playing live – busied themselves with rehearsals and preparations for the upcoming US tour. Now at new rehearsal rooms, Pinky's in Broughton, they wrote two new songs, the first since the Closer sessions: 'Ceremony' and 'In a Lonely Place'.

'We were so excited about going to America'

Ian saw Annik for the final time on Friday 25 April, at a Factory night held at the Scala cinema in London's King's Cross – where Joy Division had been due to play but pulled out. The following day Annik was scheduled to leave the UK for an Egyptian holiday; by the time she returned, Ian should have been leaving for America with Joy Division.

They left the venue in the early hours then returned to her flat so she could finish packing. Then in the morning went to catch their respective trains, bidding farewell at the station. She never saw him again.

Meanwhile the band pressed ahead with plans to film a video to accompany the single release of 'Love Will Tear Us Apart'.

We'd worked him nearly to death in March. Then we'd done quite a bit of working him to death in early April.

Ian had responded by trying to kill himself.

We'd paid him back with a debilitating riot and then at last – at long bloody last – we pulled some gigs. Every gig, in fact, that we could pull. We did it because of Ian, because he needed a rest.

But sometimes I wonder if it wasn't the gigging break that did him in in the end. At least when we were playing we were away, our minds were distracted. With the gigs cancelled and us staying close to home, Ian also ended up staying so much closer to the source of all his domestic problems.

Not that we were aware of all these troubles, the depths of his problems, at the time, mind you. It's only recently, since the explosion of interest in Joy Division, you might say, and while I've been researching the book, that I've really started to get a clear picture of the kind of shit Ian was going through and the very short timescale involved.

At the time he kept it mainly to himself. As far as we were concerned he was dead excited about going to America, really looking forward to it. Yet you read about him telling people that he didn't want to go. According to Genesis P-Orridge, Ian said he'd 'rather die' than go on tour – and maybe he did say that, but not to us he didn't: no way. With us Ian was bang into the idea and maybe if he'd been spent more time with us, and less at home, and less talking to the likes of Genesis, then he'd have been buoyed up by it all. I think he'd have gone to America, where, looking at it, the schedule wouldn't have been exhausting, and I think he would have loved it.

I'm not saying his problems would have gone away, of course. Just that they wouldn't have been crowding in on him quite so much. I really think that if he'd made it to America he'd have lived.

Or maybe I'm just talking out my arse again. Barney always said that it was his medication that made him suicidal, and that could have happened anywhere – Macclesfield or New York.

Anyway, what else could we do but stop? Ian was exhausted, his illness getting worse. He *had* to rest. Even though, in a funny kind of way, he did the exact opposite: he was drifting between staying at his mum and dad's and with Barney; he had Debbie and everyone on his case; he went to London to say goodbye to Annik, so was probably upset about all that. Then, a couple of days later, we were recording the 'Love Will Tear Us Apart' video, and that seemed to take forever.

We'd arranged to film it in T. J. Davidson's, even though we weren't really using it any more. Looking for more basic comforts we'd ended up in Pinky's near Broughton Baths (quite near North Salford Youth Club, actually, the second youth club I ever went to, with Barney; I got chased away from the first, South Salford) but it wasn't big enough to make the video.

Now, it probably won't surprise you to learn that we hated the whole idea of a video where you mimed or acted to the track. In fact we were never into it, all through New Order. God, you feel like such an idiot miming. So what we decided to do was hire a PA and a mixing desk, play 'Love Will Tear Us Apart' and record while we filmed, so the video would be a live performance of the song.

We set up for the filming with a long runway so the cameras could come in and out on a track, like a mini-railway. Then off we went and did a few run-throughs, trying to get the sound right. But we couldn't, because there wasn't a separate room in which to mix the sound. It was confused with the racket that we were getting off the instruments and through the amps. It didn't really work, and the tape we ended up with, the soundtrack to the video, sounded pretty rushed and bad, to be honest. Nor could we overdub any backing vocals – or anything else, for that matter.

Even so, we were very happy with it as it happened. It was raw, dirty and arty. We liked that: it was us all over, of course. As usual it never really occurred to us that anybody else might have a problem with it. If they did, well, that was their problem. Trouble was, hardly anybody we sent it to would play it. It got shown a little, but not nearly as much as we'd hoped, so it had seemed a bit of a waste of time.

Ah, but then we heard that it had gone down well in Australia, and of course we thought, *Good on the Aussies. They've got good taste, they have. They know art when they hear it*. And thus began an affection for our like-minded brethren down under.

It wasn't until years and years later that we visited Australia – as New Order, of course – and discovered the truth. Somebody at the Australian record company had simply laid the actual record over the film, and it wasn't even properly synchronized. It looked well dodgy, actually – well, we thought so. But this became the version that ended up being the 'official' (for want of a better word) version. Now of course it's perfect, capturing us at our youngest and freshest with a great soundtrack.

I suppose you could say it was yet another of those slightly questionable self-defeating decisions, to do the video that way: like insisting on performing 'Blue Monday' live on *Top of the Pops* (which they're not set up for) and seeing it go ten places down the charts as a result. But we didn't care, not really. Our ultimate aim was just to be ourselves, to do things the way we wanted them doing, and we'd insist out of sheer bloody-mindedness. Rob was always in our corner. Tony was always in our corner. You might call them mistakes but at least they were mistakes made on our own terms. Mistakes that then became legends.

A few days later we played Birmingham. We didn't know it then, of course, but it would be our last-ever gig as Joy Division.

It was a good one, too. We later released it on the album *Still*. Ian had a bit of a wobble during 'Decades' but was fine for 'Digital'. Even so, it was one of those gigs – like all of them were around then – where you were looking at Ian wondering if, or *when*, it was going to happen, and that was because it was now happening at every show. With hindsight you can look back and say he probably wasn't going to be right at any gig, whether in America or outer space. Even so, the idea of cancelling or rescheduling America never came up.

We were so excited about going, so wound up about it and desperate to do it. Ian, the fan of the Doors and Lou Reed and Iggy Pop and Burroughs, especially. I don't care what Genesis P-Orridge says, he was looking forward to going. I mean, we had so much going for us then. The word was getting out that we were a great group to see live. We had 'Love Will Tear Us Apart' up our sleeve. We were on the way up.

That's what always gets me about what he did. Sometimes you can see just why he did it, and it makes a kind of sense.

Other times, it just makes no fucking sense at all.

'I never said goodbye'

Ian killed himself in the early hours of Sunday morning. The last time I saw him was on the Friday night, when I gave him a lift back to his mum and dad's in Moston, just past where my house on Minton Street was. You drove to the top of the road and his mum and dad lived in Failsworth, literally a quarter of a mile from my house. So, yes, I drove him home that Friday night and he was cock-a-hoop, full of it. We'd had a great practice and I was dropping him off. We were laughing and joking and every now and then one of us would go, 'I can't believe we're fucking going to America!' We were screaming in the car, jumping up and down on the seats, properly shouting, whooping, hollering: 'Yeah! America!'

No 'rather die' about it.

This was on the Friday night. We were due to leave after the weekend. If the silly bugger hadn't killed himself we would have been on a plane to America on Monday. If he'd known all along that he planned to kill himself, as some say he did, was he just putting it on, all that excitement? Was he *that* good an actor?

Barney spoke to him on Saturday. There was a phone at his mum and dad's, whereas he didn't have a phone at home, so you were able to phone him there but not in Macclesfield. Barney rang to see if he wanted to come out but Ian said no, because he was going to go to Debbie's, and of course that's what he did. He went up to Debbie's. They had an argument and she went to work.

And he went and hung himself.

Before he was supposed to leave for America, Ian had been staying with his parents and seemed well, according to his mother, Doreen. On Saturday morning he received a letter regarding his divorce and told his mother he wanted to go to Macclesfield to see Natalie, to say goodbye. Doreen and Kevin, Ian's father, gave him a lift to Piccadilly Station, and the last they saw of him he was waving to them from the station approach. Natalie was staying with Deborah's mother, but Debbie saw Ian at the house on Barton

267

Street on Saturday afternoon before she went to work behind the bar at a wedding reception, promising to return after work to see him. She did, finding that he'd been drinking spirits and coffee, having watched the Werner Herzog film Stroszek, *and they continued discussions about the future of their relationship. Ian told her that he had spoken to Annik earlier; he also asked Debbie to drop the divorce. As he became more and more worked up, Debbie began to worry that he might have a seizure and offered to spend the night. She then drove back to her parents to tell them she intended to stay. However, when she returned to Barton Street, Ian seemed to have calmed down.*

He asked her to leave and to give him her assurance that she wouldn't return to the house before ten the next morning, when he was due to leave for Manchester. After she left, he listened to The Idiot *by Iggy Pop on repeat, drank more coffee and spirits, then wrote a long letter to Deborah, in which he said that he wished he was dead but made no mention of any intention to kill himself.*

At about eleven thirty the next morning Deborah returned to the house to find Ian dead, kneeling on the kitchen floor with a rope around his neck, the other end tied to the kitchen clothes rack attached to the ceiling. A neighbour cut him down.

I was having Sunday lunch with Iris when I heard. I got up from the table to answer the phone. It was the police, detective sergeant somebody, who said, 'We're sorry to have to inform you that Ian Curtis took his own life last night. We're trying to get in touch with Rob Gretton. If you speak to him, could you ask him to ring us, please?'

I said, 'Right,' and went numb. (I stayed numb for days, actually, as though my brain was frozen.)

In that state I went and sat back down at the dinner table, picked up my knife and fork and carried on eating. I didn't say anything to Iris. Just sat back down and continued eating my food, except not really tasting it now, feeling all of a sudden like I was no longer in my own body. As though I was looking down on myself.

After a while Iris said, 'Who was that on the phone, by the way?'

'Oh, that,' I said. 'That was the police ringing to tell me about Ian.'

'What about him?'

'He's killed himself.'

I don't remember anything then. I don't remember anything for a long time after that. I mean, I remember that we spent a lot of time together sitting in a pub: me, Barney, Terry and Twinny, just sitting having a drink, playing darts, spending time together, going to see Rob, talking to him, sitting round, trying to make sense of it all. There was no shouting or crying, just a perpetual stunned silence that being together seemed to make bearable. Steve was in Macclesfield, but the rest of us, we kind of huddled together for warmth: Just stayed together because we were all going through exactly the same thing. Gradually the details of Ian's death began to seep through: the divorce, hanging himself, the whiskey, Iggy Pop. All the stuff that we discovered in dribs and drabs and absorbed with that same sense of numbness.

He was lying in state at the chapel of rest but I didn't go to see him. Steve and Rob and Tony and all that lot went, but me and Barney were like, 'No, we don't want to see his body. We're going to the pub.'

I really regret that now and always will. We acted like kids in a way, but it seemed okay. It was sort of allowed because it was like the grown-ups were sorting it all out, Tony and Rob and everyone else.

I hired a car for the funeral.

There were loads of people there for the funeral. But the funny thing is I don't remember much about it. Just that there were loads there, all the bands, the guys from Factory Benelux, but not Annik, obviously, because of Debbie and the family. I remember sitting at the back at the funeral and Ian's sister screaming really loudly when the curtain closed behind his coffin. But it all seemed surreal; I felt strangely detached. Afterwards we went to the pub down the road: me, Steve, Gillian, Barney, Rob and Terry. Twinny couldn't face it, so he didn't go. We sat and had something to eat, had a couple of pints. That was when Rob said, 'Don't worry. Joy Division will be really big in ten years' time.' He was right, of course. Ten, fifteen – twenty, too. Not that any of us gave a shit at that precise moment in time. We finished the afternoon off watching the Sex Pistols' film at Factory's office, a kind of wake. A truly dismal affair.

Afterwards we made arrangements to go back into the practice room on Monday. I remember writing the intro and verse to 'Dreams Never End' on my six-string bass in the back bedroom of Minton Street over the weekend. The beginning of our new life as New Order. It was as though a film of Factory records had paused for a moment while Ian was scrubbed out of the picture. Then the film started again

269

and continued as though nothing else was different. In the end it would be years before we would start talking about Joy Division, and Ian, and start to face up to it, to ask ourselves what went wrong. What we could have done differently. How we might have saved him.

Oh, and I remember going to the inquest later, with Rob, and maybe Steve, which was even more surreal because there was bad feeling towards us – towards the band. Like his mum and dad thought we were responsible. I can vividly recall Debbie's dad giving evidence about Ian, saying, 'He was on another plane.' I was thinking, *Fuck, I wish it had been that plane to America*. They were talking about him as if he were a stranger and the inquest found that he'd taken his own life under the influence of alcohol.

Me, I felt guilty. Guilty that I never went to see him when he was lying in state. Guilty that I never said goodbye. Guilty that, like everybody else, I went along with Ian when he said he was all right; that I was so wrapped in my own bit of me, of the band, that I never took the time to listen to his lyrics or him and think, *He really needs help*.

So, yes, I felt all of that, and still do. I'm sure I'm not the only one. In a way we're all of us to blame, but none of us are. Years later I remember Dave Pils telling me that when we'd last stayed with them in Walthamstow Ian had left his mac behind, the famous mac he always wore. Dave had grabbed the mac and gone running after the car when we left, but it was too late, we were gone. That was the last time Dave saw Ian.

'What did you do with the mac?' I asked.

'Took it down the charity shop, Hooky.'

I thought, *You silly sod. The charity shop? Who would do something like that?*

But then even later I was talking to one of our roadies, Corky (Mike Caulfield). He was reminiscing about our old practice place in Cheetham Hill and how it used to have Ian's scarf hanging on the back of the door. A proper old man's woolly scarf, it was, brown and grey and black. We'd brought it from the rehearsal room at Pinky's when we moved.

Corky said, 'What happened to it, Hooky, that scarf?'

I thought, *Oh fuck* – because with a sudden jolt I realized I'd taken it to the charity shop. I'd forgotten it was Ian's scarf and donated it. *What an idiot*, I thought. *Who would do something like that?*

Well, I had. I suppose in the end it's almost too easy to look back and say what you should have done, how you might have changed things. How you might have done things differently and ultimately stopped Ian from doing what he did. What's harder – what's much, much harder – is to accept what you actually did do. Accept what you did and live with it. At that point I thought that the worst thing that had happened was me losing a friend, the band losing a member. It took me a long time to realize that a child had lost a father, a mother and father had lost a son, a sister had lost a brother, a wife had lost a husband, a mistress had lost a lover. All a lot more important than me and the band; we paled into insignificance. You're selfish when you're young and I suppose in many ways that's self-preservation. Now I'm embarrassed to have put us first. Even after writing and researching this book I'm no clearer as to why he decided to end it on that night. About what made that night different. The only odd thing I see is the dog story: Candy going to the farm. It seems like such a cliché. Did they have the dog put down, I wonder? Was that what was too much for him to bear on top of everything else? I will never know.

EPILOGUE

Ian Curtis
18th MAY 1980
May He Rest In Peace

We packed everything in a little box once he'd gone, and put it away. Now, of course, Ian's with me all the time, and even this book is as much about him as it is me. But back then – then it was like the group disowned the group. I mean, Joy Division's popularity skyrocketed: 'Love Will Tear Us Apart' came out and was a great success, then *Closer*, but we didn't promote them, didn't play them, didn't read reviews of them, didn't want to know about sales, nothing. Didn't care about them.

The only thing we took from Joy Division – the only two things, actually – were the songs Ian had left us: 'Ceremony' and 'In a Lonely Place'. To each other we said, 'See you on Monday,' and that was it. Me, Barney and Steve got together on the Monday to work on the songs. I took the riff for 'Dreams Never End' into rehearsal. It was weird because I was looking for Ian to tell me if it was any good or not. Realizing that we'd lost our spotter, our mentor. Realizing that suddenly we had to find a new way of working that didn't rely on him. We had to learn to record everything, play it back and pick out the good bits ourselves.

We never considered carrying on as Joy Division, though. We had made a pact years before that if one of us didn't want to do it any more, or if anything happened to any one of us, then Joy Division would be over. The group was finished. I mean, the desire to carry on was uppermost, but as for trying to carry on as Joy Division with one of us lot singing, or even getting in a new lead singer, it never even came up. We just knew that Joy Division was over. But we wanted to continue as a band, to carry on making and playing music. From a purely practical point of view, we did have the core of a band so it seemed right to carry on. There was, of course, the problem of who was going to sing the songs. That wouldn't be resolved for a while. In fact, right up until we played our first gig as a three-piece, all three of us were singing two or three songs each, but we got there in the end.

Then there was the business of finding a new name. We sat down one day to try to come up with one, thinking that we were going to learn our lesson this time, and that whatever name we came up with wouldn't be anything even vaguely Nazi-sounding.

No way, we thought. No fucking way were we going to make that mistake again.

CLOSER TRACK BY TRACK

JOY DIVISION

May

19th	Fly In	
20th	Day Off	
21st	New York	Hurrahs
22nd	New York	Hurrahs
23rd	New York	Hurrahs
24th	Day Off	
25th	Toronto	The Edge
26th	Day Off	
27th	Chicago	Tuts
28th	Madison	Merlins
29th	Minneapolis	Duffies
30th	Day Off	
31st	Day Off	

June

1st	New York	Pop Front
2nd	Fly to San Fransisco	
3rd	Day Off	
4th	Day Off	
5th	Day Off	
6th	San Fransisco	American Indian Hall
7th		
8th	Los Angeles	Flippers?
9th	Day Off	
10th	Fly Home	

I really recommend listening to the record while you read.

'Atrocity Exhibition'

This is the way, step inside ...

Me and Barney were bored writing on our own instruments so we just thought, *Let's swap.* Barney plays bass and I play guitar on 'Atrocity Exhibition'. I was nowhere near as proficient a guitarist as him, mind you, but I like the way it sounds. Great riff. Great bass too.

During the recording Iris had insisted I go home for a christening or a wedding or something, and Martin mixed the first two tracks while I was gone: 'Heart and Soul' and 'Atrocity Exhibition'. I remember coming back and being dead excited to hear them because I played the guitar really heavily on 'Atrocity Exhibition' and I loved it. So there we were, sitting in Martin's Volvo. Barney put the cassette on so I could listen to the mixes and the bass was really low on 'Heart and Soul', very dead and quiet, and I was, like, head in hands, *Oh fucking hell, it's happening again.* Unknown Pleasures *number two.*

As if that wasn't bad enough, he then put on 'Atrocity Exhibition' and Martin had fucking melted the guitar with his Marshall Time Waster. Made it sound like someone strangling a cat and, to my mind, absolutely killed the song. I was so annoyed with him and went in and gave him a piece of my mind but he just turned round and told me to fuck off.

Rob said, 'Fucking hell, Hooky, if you're going to fuck off home you've got to be prepared to take what happens in your absence.'

'Isolation'

Mother I tried please believe me ...

This is an interesting track because it has no guitar on it. If we wrote 'Isolation' now, Barney would not only have played the synth but would have done a guitar part too. We would have done a low part, a medium part, a high part; we'd have done a part you can't hear, a part on the left, part on the right; we'd have killed it. So it was the inexperience involved in us writing 'Isolation' that just kept it dead simple, straightforward and very, very effective. What Martin did was take the original drum track, flange it and effect it through his synth, then get Steve to overdub the drums so they were separate; then he could have them really up front in the mix, not buried in a drum mix. Plus he used the drums to trigger his synth, which was, again, ahead of his time. Barney overdubbed the Arp over the Transcendent, playing the same part, and it sounds current even now. Nice vocal effect. I mean, Martin was a fucking genius, without a shadow of a doubt. The way the acoustic kit comes in halfway through the song is fantastic.

Martin had finished it with a dead stop and the echo going off. But there was a click on it and he wanted to edit it out. But John Caffery got in a right mess – too nervous, I think – and couldn't get the edit to work. And the more he tried to fix it the more he was losing of the take – and this was the only copy of it. Don't forget that editing was done with a razor blade, cutting out the part you didn't want then sticking with tape the bits you did. He was working on the master, so the tape was getting shorter and shorter. In the end Mike Johnson, the tape op/tea boy, had to come in and rescue him, to rescue the edit. That was what impressed us so much about him and why, when we came back in to record as New Order, we got him in as our engineer. That's why 'Isolation' sounds a bit weird at the end. It's a great song, though. If we'd believed in releasing singles off albums then we would have released it, but we always knew 'Love Will Tear Us Apart' was going to be the next single and we were far too bloody-minded to put the singles on the albums.

'Passover'

This is the crisis I knew had to come ...

I'm playing six-string bass on this, the first time I used it, I think. I got it on Barney's recommendation, actually. He'd seen it in Mamelok's music shop on Deansgate and very graciously suggested I go and have a look at it. 'You should get it, you should get it; it's fucking great. You could really use it, because the way you play is guitar-like.' Which was very nice of him.

So I went and tried it out and, lo and behold, something about it got me playing it like a guitar. I suppose, in a way, I've always been a frustrated guitar player who plays bass, but what I've done is stuck with bass and made it a guitar. So getting the six-string bass actually felt quite natural. Around the same time we tried out some effects pedals, again on his recommendation, I got the Electro-Harmonix Clone Theory, because of the fragility of the six-string sound, and that really helped it, fattened it up. Everyone thinks it's a guitar but it's not; it's the six-string bass. It was quite a departure for me. Coupling the chorus with a short eighty-millisecond delay gave me the sound for the next phase of my career. This track has great crescendos and dropdowns and is one of my favourites. Ian's lyrics are insanely good with hardly any repetition.

'Colony'

A worried parent's glance, a kiss, a last goodbye . . .

Great· lyrics. 'Colony' is on the four-string bass. These songs are the product of a great group, without a shadow of a doubt: music chemistry at its best. Steve's drum riffs, the bass riffs and the guitar riffs are all excellent. The whole lot of them on every song are excellent. I shouldn't say it really, because I was in the band, but I love this album. There's not one dodgy track on it. It's very atmospheric, very powerful. If you listen to *Unknown Pleasures* there's a bit of reticence on some songs, but not on this LP. Every song is confident – which is strange, given the fact that most of the music is very melancholic, very fragile but intense.

'Means to an End'

Two the same, set free too, I always looked to you . . .

This is the pop song on the album. It's a fucked-up disco song. We had it worked out a little but finished it in the studio. Martin always liked it when we did that – it meant he could put his stamp on it. Weird: the verse has four ascending notes all next to each other, with no thought to sharps or flats. It's very unusual. I liked that.

'Heart and Soul'

Existence well what does it matter . . .

This is so seductive, a very sexy song that has many layers. I wrote the low bass and we transferred it to the synthesizer. Martin showed Barney how to layer and structure the keyboards, the strings especially, and that's what he's doing here – playing the low bass, while nice and low in the mix you've got my six-string bass. This was another occasion when Martin really took the heat out of it during the mix, downplayed it, but it really adds to the atmosphere. I was upset when I first heard it but he was right and I was wrong.

Barney was moving from guitar to keyboards. Live this had no guitar, but of course in the studio we would overdub some at Martin's request. I have a feeling Ian may have played the chord guitar. We continued with this way of writing, which felt quite natural. Barney would say, 'Oh, why don't we put that low bass on the synth, and you can play over with it with your six string and add high strings for the breaks?' This was what we did and we used it a lot in New Order too. I'd write a bass line then he'd put it on the synth to make it dancey and I'd play over it with the melody. Barney used to call me Mr Melody, in his lighter moments.

'Twenty Four Hours'

Now that I've realized, how it's all gone wrong . . .

Ian had difficulty singing some of the songs he wrote because he didn't have the range in his key, but I've always felt very, very strongly that a great vocalist can write great music and doesn't have to sing it perfectly as long as the emotion's there. The emotion comes from the heart, the soul, the passion, which together make a perfect delivery. When Barney used to strain in his vocals it sounded a hell of a lot better to me than when he started writing them all in the right key. I thought then it became too perfect; I preferred the emotion and the vulnerability of it before. Ian had that too. I mean, I know I keep saying it, but what you want in life is strength and belief, and if someone has that it doesn't have to be technically perfect.

People turn round to you and say, 'God, you'd been hearing these lyrics for weeks – why didn't you realize he was so bad?' You hadn't. He wasn't slumped in the corner with a lone fiddle in the background; he was fucking going for it. I suppose that's the contradiction: on the one hand, he was ill and vulnerable; on the other, he was a screaming rock god. That's what was confusing.

'The Eternal'

Cry like a child though these years make me older . . .

This is a great song. My favourite lyric. So dreamlike. Any band would die to have this under their belt, in their arsenal. It's instrumentally and musically powerful as well as vocally powerful. It's the six-string bass with the clone pedal, which gives you a slight double-track. It just makes it wobble and sound fatter. Barney's playing the keyboards and then at the end using the Transcendent as a white-noise generator. Steve's drum riff is amazing, so simple and strong. And there's a great use of echo plate on the snare by Martin. Listening to it now you can hear how well we played together; the solidity between me, Ian, Steve and Bernard was very, very powerful. I don't think any of us will ever have it again. Classic.

'Decades'

We knocked on the door of hell's darker chambers ...

This is an interesting track. It begins with me playing low bass and, unusually, playing in sync with the bass drum; then there's overdubbing of another bass part, on the six-string, very rhythmic so it sounds like guitar. There's a great Syndrum sound, loads of echo plate in use. There's Barney on the keyboards, again layered wonderfully, and over-dubbed guitar melodies. It's one of the most beautiful songs we ever did. I think it's more beautiful than 'Atmosphere'.

I find *Closer* much easier to listen to than *Unknown Pleasures*. I like it as a musical offering and find myself listening to *Closer* simply for pleasure, which I can't really do with anything else that I've done. Definitely not the New Order stuff, sadly. This is actually one of my favourite albums. My five favourites would be *Chelsea Girls* by Nico, *New Boots & Panties* by Ian Dury & the Blockheads, *Raw Power* by Iggy Pop, *Berlin* by Lou Reed and *Closer* by Joy Division. Oh, I forgot John Cale, *Paris 1919,* and the Sex Pistols, of course ... Oops, that's seven.

TIMELINE FIVE:
JANUARY 1980–OCTOBER 1981

```
                                              Page 4
JOY DIVISION


PROFIT AND LOSS ACCOUNT

FOR THE YEAR ENDED 30 SEPTEMBER 1981

                                      1981        1980
                                       £           £

INCOME

Concert performances, publishing
   royalties etc.                    21,373      14,793

Factory records                     106,667      31,044

Bank interest                         1,366         -

                                    129,406      45,837

EXPENDITURE

Wages                                    -        3,266

Travel, subsistence and tour costs       -       13,045

Equipment accessaries and repairs        -          304

Sundry                                  798       1,615

Telephone and postage                    -        1,229

Professional charges                  1,270       1,665

Depreciation                             -        1,576

Bank interest                            42          -

                                      2,110      22,700


NET PROFIT                          127,296      23,137
```

7–8 January 1980

The first 'Love Will Tear Us Apart' session, Pennine Sound Studios, Oldham. Produced by Martin Hannett. Tracks recorded: 'These Days', ' The Sound of Music', 'Love Will Tear Us Apart' (version one).

11 January 1980

Joy Division play Paradiso, Amsterdam, Netherlands. The start of the European tour. The support band don't play so Joy Division do both slots, performing two different sets for the price of one. Set list ('support' set): 'Passover', 'Wilderness', 'Digital', 'Day of the Lords', 'Insight', 'New Dawn Fades', 'Disorder', 'Transmission'. Set list (main set): 'Love Will Tear Us Apart', 'These Days', 'A Means to an End', 'Twenty Four Hours', 'Shadowplay', 'She's Lost Control', 'Atrocity Exhibition', 'Atmosphere', 'Interzone'.

12 January 1980

Joy Division play Paard Van Troje (the Trojan Horse), The Hague, Netherlands, supported by Minny Pops.

13 January 1980

Joy Division play Doornroosje, Nijmegen, Netherlands.

14 January 1980

Joy Division play King Kong, Antwerp, Belgium.

> When finally the Joy Division company arrives the next day, we immediately bring them to the Boemerang ... in a very friendly and polite way the manager tells us the place is 'too scruffy' and request another place to stay... hell!
> In a hurry we manage to find some rooms in the Appelmans hotel near the central station, and this time the crew and band seem to be satisfied and get in.

All goes well until Annik Honoré, the young girlfriend of Ian Curtis, pops her head in; she sees the red lights, the 'special' furniture and erotic paintings on the wall and screams: 'No way! You're not going to put us in this whorehouse! Don't you know Joy Division is an important band?'

Curtis looks at her and laughs – he doesn't mind sleeping here with the others – but she bursts into tears.'

Excerpt from *The Night Ian Curtis Came to Sleep* by Marc Schoetens, from joydiv.org

15 January 1980

Joy Division play the Basement, Cologne, Germany. Set list: 'Atmosphere', 'Love Will Tear Us Apart', 'These Days', 'Insight', 'Twenty Four Hours', 'A Means to an End', 'She's Lost Control', 'The Sound of Music'. 'Glass', 'Day of the Lords', 'Shadowplay', 'Interzone', 'Disorder', 'Transmission', 'Atrocity Exhibition'.

> "They were good gigs but fucking hell, Europe was cold. Thinking about it, what can't have helped was the fact that I'd gone skinhead. The rest of them were growing theirs back but I'd decided to shave all mine off. Ever since the time they'd japed me into dyeing it blond I'd been different with my hair – so if they cut theirs, I'd be growing mine; if they grew theirs, I'd get mine cut. That was the same all through New Order, too."

16 January 1980

Joy Division play Lantaren, Rotterdam, Netherlands.

17 January 1980

Joy Division play Plan K, Belgium. Set list: 'Dead Souls', 'Wilderness', 'Insight', 'Colony', 'Twenty Four Hours', 'A Means to an End', 'Transmission', 'Atmosphere', 'Love Will Tear Us Apart', 'Digital', 'Warsaw', 'Shadowplay', 'Atrocity Exhibition', 'Sister Ray', 'The Eternal'.

18 January 1980

Joy Division play Effenaar, Eindhoven, Netherlands, supported by Minny Pops. Set list: 'Love Will Tear Us Apart', 'Digital', 'New Dawn Fades', 'Colony', 'These Days', 'Ice Age', 'Dead Souls', 'Disorder', 'Day of the Lords', 'Autosuggestion', 'Shadowplay', 'She's Lost Control', 'Transmission', 'Interzone', 'Atmosphere', 'Warsaw'. The band have some trouble with a bunch of young Rockabillies. Some songs are shot on Super-8 ('Digital', 'New Dawn Fades', 'Colony', 'Autosuggestion') and later appear on the *Here Are the Young Men* film.

19 January 1980

Joy Division play Club Vera, Groningen, Netherlands.

21 January 1980

Joy Division play Kant Kino, Berlin, Germany. Set list: 'Dead Souls', 'Wilderness', 'Colony', 'Insight', 'Twenty Four Hours', 'A Means to an End', 'Transmission', 'The Eternal'.

> "According to Ian's letters to Annik, he and Barney were very depressed after this gig because of the sound. I don't remember that. They had a few posters up advertising forthcoming films and I nicked a few, which we put on the wall in the practice place for inspiration. That's where we got loads of our New Order titles from: they're all old films. Very cheeky."

7 February 1980

Joy Division play a Factory benefit (in aid of the *City Fun* fanzine), the Factory II, New Osborne Club, Manchester, supported by A Certain Ratio and Section 25.

> "I remember that when we came off Ian was dying for a piss so we couldn't go back on and do another encore. He was hopping about trying to find a toilet but there wasn't one backstage, so in the end we were going, 'Oh, just piss in the corner,' and he was

going, 'No, no, I can't! I can't piss in the corner! I can't do it, I can't do it.'

Rob was going, 'Fucking hell, Ian, you know, you're supposed to be going back on,' and Ian was running round like a fucking madman, holding himself.

So in the end Rob went and got a pint pot and ordered him to go into a corner and piss into it so we could go back on.

After an age Ian came back, saying, 'Aw, thanks for that, Rob – I was desperate.' But the pot had only a quarter of an inch of piss in it – something to do with his meds, I suppose.

It was too late to go back on by then, so we didn't. But I do remember that it was nice to be back in Manchester, just to be home. I was the only one whose car wasn't broken into that night. I lived in Moston and knew the area, so I parked right outside the window of the pub opposite. I warned them all. But when everyone – audience included – came to leave they discovered that every single car round the club had been broken into."

8 February 1980

Joy Division play University of London Union, supported by Section 25, A Certain Ratio and Killing Joke. Set list: 'Dead Souls', 'Glass', 'A Means to an End', 'Twenty Four Hours', 'Passover', 'Insight', 'Colony', 'These Days', 'Love Will Tear Us Apart', 'Isolation', 'The Eternal', 'Digital'. This concert appears on CD2 of the September 2007 re-mastered edition of *Closer*.

Mid-February 1980

Debbie confronts Ian about Annik.

20 February 1980

Joy Division play High Wycombe Town Hall, supported by Killing Joke and A Certain Ratio. Set list: 'The Sound of Music', 'A Means to an End', 'Colony', 'Twenty Four Hours', 'Isolation', 'Love Will Tear Us Apart', 'Disorder', 'Atrocity Exhibition'. Both concert and sound-check appear on CD2 of the September 2007 reissue of *Still*.

"The reason that a lot of these gigs were so widely bootlegged was there were these two young lads – quite nice lads, actually – called John and Lawrie, who used to come and tape all the gigs then provide us with a cassette. We'd let them into the sound-checks so they'd do them too, which was quite nice of them – because really they were bootlegging you with your consent, weren't they?"

It was during this period that Ian's self-harming episode occurred.

21 February 1980

Joy Division cancel their gig at Manchester Polytechnic.

28 February 1980

Joy Division play the Warehouse, Preston, supported by Section 25. Set list: 'Incubation', 'Wilderness', 'Twenty Four Hours', 'The Eternal', 'Heart and Soul', 'Shadowplay', 'Transmission', 'Disorder', 'Warsaw', 'Colony', 'Interzone', 'She's Lost Control'.

"We turned up on the day and everything that could go wrong went wrong. The PA was dreadful, our equipment was all over the place . . . Everything, actually, just went completely to shit. But for some reason we embraced it with humour, didn't alaways happen, and it ended up becoming quite funny. You know the way it goes sometimes: when the more something goes wrong the funnier it gets? Well, it was like that.

Years later Tony Wilson put out a bootleg of this gig because he loved it so much because you can hear everything going wrong. It was the beer pump – it kept cutting out the amps. Barney's guitar amp went. Then my amp went. Barney came over and tried to plug into my amp and I was going, 'You're wasting your fucking time 'cause my amp's gone as well.' Then the keyboards went off.

Rob was in the background screaming, 'Play, you fuckers, play!' It's on the bootleg, him screaming at us. Occasionally one of us would go to the mic and say, 'Oh, sorry about this; this has all gone wrong.' It just completely fell apart but the audience didn't seem to mind, particularly. There weren't that many of them there.

There was a wonderful, glorious moment when some girl got up on stage while we were all busy trying to fix our equipment; we were all looking at her thinking, *What's she doing?* She just went up to the mic, grabbed hold of it and said, 'The coach for Blackburn is leaving in five minutes.' That's on the bootleg as well.

We just couldn't get it back then; we'd just lost it, you know, lost the whole gig. Complete disaster. So anyway, afterwards in the dressing room there was a great atmosphere, with everyone laughing and joking, but the promoter came back and was fuming. He said we hadn't played and we could fuck off if we thought he was going to pay us. Then he stalked out of the dressing room.

We weren't having that. The dressing room doubled up as a food store and there was a freezer in there, so I kicked the lock off the freezer. Inside were about thirty frozen chickens that we took as wages. I remember Ian nabbed all these chickens to take home to Debbie – so I think he must still have been living at home with her then. He probably took them back as a peace offering: *Sorry I've got another girl on the go, love. Here are some defrosting chickens.*"

29 February 1980

Joy Division play the Lyceum, London, co-headlining with Killing Joke, supported by Section 25 and A Certain Ratio. Set list: 'Incubation', 'Wilderness', 'Twenty Four Hours', 'The Eternal', 'Heart and Soul', 'Love Will Tear Us Apart', 'Isolation', 'Komakino', 'She's Lost Control', 'These Days', 'Atrocity Exhibition'. This concert features on the *Heart and Soul* box set.

March 1980

'Licht und Blindheit' seven-inch single (Sordide Sentimental SS33022) released: 'Atmosphere'/'Dead Souls'. Produced by Martin Hannett. Limited to 1,578 numbered copies.

5 March 1980

Joy Division play Trinity Hall, Bristol, supported by the Passage.

"Around this time Ian himself started to get very worried about the frequency of his fits, worrying that they would take over his life and that he would not be able to carry on working."

13 March 1980

The second 'Love Will Tear Us Apart' session, Strawberry Studios, Stockport. Produced by Martin Hannett (working sporadically over a period of three weeks beginning 24 April). Tracks recorded: 'Love Will Tear Us Apart' (single version), 'She's Lost Control' (twelve-inch version).

"Tony had visited us at Strawberry and again brought Ian a Frank Sinatra album. Tony tried to encourage Ian to emulate it here: I think he thought the combination of the timbre of his voice and this song would be perfect. I don't think it ended up like Frank Sinatra, though; just sounds like Ian to me.

At the time we all thought he was doing it to wind us up. But I know that in one of his letters to Annik Ian mentions how much he liked Frank Sinatra's voice, so obviously not. But Christ, the recording of 'Love Will Tear Us Apart' was a marathon. We were in the studio overnight on these sessions, everybody was exhausted and it still wasn't done – we ended up finishing it in Britannia Row during the recording of *Closer*. There were loads of different mixes of it, too. Martin kept remixing it and must have done it ten to fifteen times; then Tony pulled the plug on him because it was costing so much money. Martin was never happy with it and kept searching, constantly, for the great mix. He tried different engineers but could never get the definitive mix. Funnily enough, I now don't like the mix he eventually chose for the single. I like the one that's got a dead-loud guitar overdub on it, a radio mix."

18–30 March 1980

Joy Division record *Closer*, Britannia Row, London. The band stay in two flats, the 'party' flat, and the 'intellectual' flat, living the rock-'n'- roll high life on £1.50 a day. Tracks recorded: 'Atrocity Exhibition', 'Isolation',

'Passover', 'Colony', 'A Means to an End', 'Heart and Soul', 'Twenty Four Hours', 'The Eternal', 'Decades', 'Komakino', 'Incubation', 'As You Said'.

2 April 1980

Joy Division play the Moonlight Club, West Hampstead, London, supported by Section 25, Crawling Chaos and John Dowie. Set list: 'The Sound of Music', 'Wilderness', 'Colony', 'Love Will Tear Us Apart', 'A Means to an End', 'Transmission', 'Dead Souls', 'Sister Ray'.

'Sister Ray' features on *Still*, but is wrongly credited to the Moonlight Club.

3 April 1980

Joy Division play the Moonlight Club, West Hampstead, London, supported by A Certain Ratio, Kevin Hewick and Blurt. Set list: 'Love Will Tear Us Apart', 'Glass', 'Digital', 'Heart and Soul', 'Isolation', 'Disorder', 'Atrocity Exhibition', 'Atmosphere'.

4 April 1980

Joy Division play the Rainbow Theatre, London, supporting a unique Stranglers line-up along with Section 25, Fashion and the Soul Boys. Set list: 'Dead Souls', 'Wilderness', 'Shadowplay', 'Heart and Soul', 'Decades', 'She's Lost Control', 'Atrocity Exhibition'.

4 April 1980

Joy Division play the Moonlight Club, London, supported by the Durutti Column, X-O-Dus and the Royal Family and the Poor. Set list: 'Transmission', 'A Means to an End', 'Twenty Four Hours', 'Day of the Lords', 'Insight', 'Interzone'.

2–4 April 1980

After an exhausting run of concerts Ian has a fit on stage. This comes shortly after an incident in which he wounded himself with a kitchen knife.

5 April 1980

Joy Division play the Malvern Winter Gardens, Malvern. Set list: 'Disorder', 'Wilderness', 'Twenty Four Hours', 'Heart and Soul', 'Atmosphere', 'Love Will Tear Us Apart', 'Isolation', 'Interzone', 'She's Lost Control', 'Girls Don't Count', jam with Section 25.

> I met the band backstage. They were all very polite and friendly, apart from Hooky, who was being an arse. Ian was sat on his own. He seemed in good spirits, though looked tired and had a painful-looking shaving rash under his chin. He talked enthusiastically about the 'new songs' and actually thanked me (but I don't know what for!). He spoke in a soft, high-pitched voice, which surprised me. Fond memories indeed!'
>
> Phil (fan), on joydiv.org

6 April 1980

Ian takes an overdose.

8 April 1980

Joy Division play Derby Hall, Bury. Set list: 'Girls Don't Count', 'Love Will Tear Us Apart', 'Digital' (all without Ian), 'The Eternal', 'Decades' (or 'Passover'; both with Ian on vocals), 'Sister Ray' (without Ian). The gig ends in a riot.

9 April 1980

Following the Bury gig, Ian begins his stay with Tony and Lindsay.

11 April 1980

Joy Division play the Factory, Russell Club, Manchester, supported by Minny Pops.

12 April 1980

Joy Division cancel their gig in Bradford (venue unknown).

12–13 April 1980

Ian leaves Charlesworth and spends most of the week away from home, either with Bernard Sumner or with his parents.

16 April 1980

Natalie Curtis' first birthday. Ian is absent, though briefly returns home before leaving for Derby on Saturday.

18 April 1980

'Love Will Tear Us Apart' seven-inch single (Factory Records FAC 23) released. Produced by Martin Hannett. Sleeve designed by Peter Saville. Re-released on twelve-inch with a new cover (FAC 23.12 27.6.80). Track list: 'Love Will Tear Us Apart', 'These Days', 'Love Will Tear Us Apart' (Pennine version).

19 April 1980

Joy Division play the Ajanta Theatre, Derby, supported by Section 25 and XL5. Set list: 'Dead Souls', 'Wilderness', 'Digital', 'Insight', 'Passover', 'Heart and Soul', 'Isolation', 'These Days', 'Transmission', 'She's Lost Control', 'Colony', 'Girls Don't Count', jam with Section 25.

> "I remember that there was a bit of a weird atmosphere to this gig. Also we had a lot of equipment problems. The synthesizer in particular kept going out of tune – and I think if you listen to 'Isolation' on the live tape the whole thing's out of tune – and it was really off-putting. The sound was bad, too, and you felt that Ian was unwell. So I really did get a feeling that something was wrong. With hindsight everything was falling apart."

19–20 April 1980

Ian and Annik spend the weekend at a hotel on Rusholme, going their separate ways on Monday: Annik back to London, Ian home to Macclesfield.

22 April 1980

Debbie calls Annik at the Belgian embassy, warning her of her intention to divorce Ian and name Annik as co-respondent. Debbie and Ian's parents become involved and Ian's parents now learn about his suicide attempt for the first time. Debbie begins divorce proceedings.

25 April 1980

Joy Division cancel their appearance at the Scala cinema, London, because of Ian's poor health. A Certain Ratio, Durutti Column and Section 25 play.

> "We'd cancelled but Ian still turned up at the Scala. He arrived about 1.30am and sat at a table on his own, writing furiously in a notebook while watching Kevin Hewick play. Three songs later he was gone. He hadn't spoken to anyone. Kevin told me that Tony debuted *Closer* that night, playing a tape of the LP in between the live acts."

26 April 1980

Joy Division cancel their gig at the Rock Garden, Middlesbrough.

26 April 1980

Annik leaves the UK for Belgium, then on to Egypt for a holiday.

Late April 1980

'Ceremony' (though as yet unnamed) and 'In a Lonely Place' demo session, Pinky's, Broughton. 'In a Lonely Place' later released in the *Heart and Soul* box set as 'In a Lonely Place (detail)'.

"People say that the recordings of these tracks were from TJ's, but they weren't. The only time we went into TJ's during this period was to record the 'Love Will Tear Us Apart' video. Besides, we'd started taping everything by then, so there might be hundreds of those tapes – it's just that bootleggers get hold of one of them and make out it's the only one of its kind, which is what happened here: Rob lent a tape out to a fan and it got leaked, and then years later these songs are cropping up on bootlegs and now they're on YouTube and whatever. Exactly where the recordings are from – whether it's Pinky's or Graveyard in Prestwich – is difficult to say but I do know this: they're definitely not from TJs."

28 April 1980

The 'Love Will Tear Us Apart' promo video is filmed at T. J. Davidson's, Manchester. Directed by Stuart Orme. The video would be first shown on Granada's Saturday-morning children's show, *Fun Factory*, on 26 June 1980, introduced by Manchester DJ Ray Teret, who said: 'Joy Division isn't a female vocalist; it's a band.'

"That's Rob Gretton's hand you see pushing the door, and the 'Ian C' you see scratched on to the door originally said either 'Ian C is a bastard' or 'Ian Curtis is a bastard' and was scratched there by a girl who Ian had, shall we say, 'spurned' a while back, when we first started rehearsing there."

2 May 1980

Joy Division play High Hall, Birmingham University, supported by A Certain Ratio. Set list: 'Ceremony', 'Shadowplay', 'A Means to an End', 'Passover', 'New Dawn Fades', 'Twenty Four Hours', 'Transmission', 'Disorder', 'Isolation', 'Decades', 'Digital'.

This was Joy Division's last ever gig (it was recorded and later released on *Still*), and when we debuted 'Ceremony'. Ian wrote very positively about the gig – 'It was our biggest crowd ever' – while berating himself for forgetting the last verse of 'Transmission'. He also said that the best number of the night was the new one, 'Ceremony'.

3 May 1980

Joy Division cancel their gig at Eric's, Liverpool.

4 May 1980

Ian is hypnotized by Bernard while staying at his flat in Worsley. The process regresses Ian to his childhood and then several lives before and leaves a marked impression on him.

5 May 1980

Ian moves back to his parents' house.

8 May 1980

Joy Division cancel their gig at the Astoria, Edinburgh.

9 May 1980

Joy Division cancel their gig at the Albert Hall, Stirling.

13 May 1980

Ian goes home to see Debbie and Natalie. He has his picture taken with Natalie: this is the last photograph taken of him.

14 May 1980

Joy Division recording session, Graveyard Studios, Prestwick. Tracks recorded: 'Ceremony', 'In a Lonely Place'. 'Ceremony' is later released on the *Heart and Soul* box set

"I remember doing the session because it was downstairs in Stewart Pickering's house in Prestwich, which was next to a graveyard. (Hence Graveyard Studios.) But Martin was in a weird mood and it was very rushed, the whole thing, and a bit of an unsatisfactory session, which is why it was never used for anything – nothing official anyway. But the plan, had everything turned out all right, was for these recordings to become the next single: the next record was going to be 'In a Lonely Place' and 'Ceremony'. But, of course, this never came to fruition.

I know a lot fans think the 'Ceremony' on the *Heart and Soul* box set comes from the same session as 'In a Lonely Place', but it doesn't; it's from this session. 'In a Lonely Place' is from a rehearsal tape and this isn't and I'll tell you how I know. Those drums are dead loud; it's not ducking the vocal. So I'd say that's a recorded version of a live rehearsal, because the drum sounds as fat as fuck but it's not making the cassette-player compressor duck and that's what had happened. That's the one we did at Graveyard, I swear it, and I can do that in court."

18 May 1980

The day before the band are scheduled to leave for America, Ian commits suicide. The 'joint' North American tour with Cabaret Voltaire would have opened at Hurrahs in New York on 21 May, taking in Toronto, Detroit, Chicago, Minneapolis, San Francisco and Los Angeles after that. Martin Hannett was committed to mix the live sound on this tour.

23 May 1980

Ian Curtis is cremated. Factory hold their own wake at Palatine Road and screen the Sex Pistols film *The Great Rock 'n' Roll Swindle*.

13 June 1980

The inquest into Ian's death is held, Macclesfield.

27 June 1980

'Love Will Tear Us Apart' twelve-inch (FAC 23.12) released.

18 July 1980

Closer (Factory Records FACT 25) released. Produced by Martin Hannett at Brittania Row, London. Engineered by Martin Hannett and

John Caffery assisted by Michael Johnson. Photograph by Bernard Pierre Wolff. Designed by Peter Saville, Martyn Atkins, Chris Mathan. Track list: 'Atrocity Exhibition', 'Isolation', 'Passover', 'Colony', 'A Means to an End', 'Heart and Soul', 'Twenty Four Hours', 'The Eternal', 'Decades'.

18 July 1980

Free giveaway flexidisc (Factory Records FAC 28) released. Produced by Martin Hannett. Initial pressing: 10,000 copies. Track list: 'Komakino', 'Incubation', 'As You Said'.

> "For a while there had been talk of making *Closer* a double album but we dropped that plan because we all hated the idea of a double. This did mean that we couldn't put the other three tracks on the album, so we came up with what we thought was a compromise: releasing a flexidisc with the album. You'd buy the album and get the flexidisc free. But the record stores didn't like that and decided to sell the flexidiscs – they didn't get the giveaway idea. So when you bought the album they'd say, 'Yeah, you can buy the flexidisc as well to go with it: 50p,' or whatever, the rotten devils. Our intention was to give them all away."

2 September 1980

'Atmosphere'/'She's Lost Control' (Factory Records FACUS2/UK) twelve-inch single released. Produced by Martin Hannett. Sleeve photography by Charles Meecham. Typography by Peter Saville.

8 October 1981

Still (Factory Records FACT 40) 2 x twelve-inch LP released. The final Joy Division album, a double LP comprising songs by the band never readily available and some formally unreleased; it also includes a live recording of their final concert. Produced by Martin Hannett. Engineered by Chris Nagle. Sleeve design by Peter Saville. First 5,000 with collectors' hessian cloth cover. Track list: 'Exercise One' (*Unknown Pleasures* session), 'Ice Age' (Oct/Nov 1979, Cargo Studios), 'The Sound of Music' (Love Will Tear Us Apart' Session 1), 'Glass' (Factory sample), 'The Only Mistake' (*Unknown Pleasures* session), 'Walked in Line' (*Unknown Pleasures* session), 'The Kill' (*Unknown Pleasures* session), 'Something Must Break' ('Transmission'session), 'Dead Souls' (from 'Licht und Bleinheit'/Sordide Sentimentale session), 'Sister Ray', 'Ceremony', 'Shadowplay', 'Means to an End', 'Passover', 'New Dawn Fades', 'Transmission', 'Disorder', 'Isolation', 'Decades', 'Digital'. Track 10 recorded live at the Moonlight Club, London, 2 April 1980. Tracks 11–20 recorded live at Birmingham University, 2 May 1980.

'I bought this Joy Division bootleg the other day, and the strange thing was, the first track on it was recorded at TJM practice studios, 'Shadowplay'. I know for a fact we didn't even own a tape recorder, so I don't know how anybody else can have recorded it. When I listened, it wasn't from there, so I took it back and the bloke knocked me a fiver off it because the track list was wrong.'

Peter Hook interview with Jon Savage, April 1994

ACKNOWLEDGEMENTS

Much love and thanks to my beautiful wife, Rebecca, and my beautiful children, Heather, Jack and Jess. I could not have done it without your love, patience and understanding.

301

In memoriam, rest in peace ... Jean Jackson, Derrick Jackson, Dave Dee, Rex Sargeant, Larry Cassidy, Mia Hook, Martin Rushent and New Order.

Special thanks to ... Andrew Holmes and David Sultan. Their hard work in making this book the very best it could be was fantastic. I am in your debt, boys ... forever.

Thanks, in no particular order, to ... Twinny, Terry Mason, Claude Flowers, Lesley Thorne, and all at Aitken, Alexander & Co., Phil Murphy, James Masters (for being a fountain of knowledge) Kelvin Briggs, Mike Jones, Emily Husain and all at Simon & Schuster, Mike and Carol Georgieff-Jones. The people of Manchester and Salford, Alan Erasmus, Aaron Mellor and all at The Factory, Anthony Addis and all at OJK & Co, Stephen Lea, Mike Hall at IPS Law. THE LIGHT ... Jack Bates, Nathan Wason, Andy Poole and Paul (the Bear) Kehoe. Stephen Jones. Pete and Peasy @ Oxygen Management, Steve Strange at X-Ray Agency. The Mighty Sarge. Debbie and Natalie Curtis. The Buzzcocks. Alison Bell, Amanda Dunlop. Dr Hew Jones. Kate King at JMC Office Services. Joanne and all at the Alderley Edge Hotel. Spellcheck, JoyDiv.org. Chris and Tom Hewitt. John Brierley. My brothers, Chris and Paul Hook, and their families. Dianne Bourne and the *Manchester Evening News*. OZ PA. Dave Pils and Jasmine. All at Factory Records. Phil Saxe. Matt Greenhalgh and Anton Corbijn. Electro-Harmonix, Shergold Guitars, Crown Amps, Alembic. AMS Digital Delay, Michael Winterbottom and all the 24 Hour Party People. Kevin Hewick. Peter Saville and Alice Cowling. Paul Fletcher at One Love Music. Warner Brothers Music. Universal Publishing. The Sex Pistols. Roger Eagle. Jean-Jacques Burnel for the sound. Paul Simonon for the strap length. Cockney Rebel for turning me on to music. David Essex and Ringo Starr. The list is endless ...

INDEX

(page numbers in italic type indicate illustrations)

A Certain Ratio (ACR), 115, 130, 206, 214, 218, 220, 221, 222, 227, 251, 254, 258, 260, 284, 285, 287, 289, 292, 293
A Different Kind of Tension, 179, 180
Abraham Moss Centre, 65
Academy, 122
Accelerator, 94
Acklam Hall, London, 214
Acton, Irene (Peter's mum), see Hook, Irene
Adam and the Ants, 68
Adverts, 58, 90
Aherne, Caroline (Peter's ex-wife), 20
Ajanta Theatre, Derby, 262, 291
Albrecht, Bernard, see Sumner, Bernard
Amnesty International Benefit, 213–14
An Ideal for Living, xiv, 74–5, 80, 81, 94, 100, 107, 116, 127, 156, 157
   12-inch version of, 78, 104, 108, 130, 138
   bootleg versions of, 78, 104
   Ian finances, 73, 76–8, 104
'Anarchy in the UK', 88
Anderson, John, 100, 101, 104
Angelic Upstarts, 147
Anti-Nazi League, 81
Apollo Theatre, Manchester, 227
Armed Force, 219
Arrow Studios, 100, 104, 126
'As You Said', 289, 296
Assembly Rooms, Derby, 226
Astoria, Edinburgh, 294
'At a Later Date', 51, 63, 70, 92, 93, 127
Atkins, Martyn, 296
Atkinson-Wood, Helen, 30
'Atmosphere', 106, 117, 160, 161, 188, 189, 215, 216, 220, 222, 223, 224, 225, 280, 282, 283, 284, 287, 289, 290, 296
Atomic Kitten, 214
'Atrocity Exhibition', 161, 177, 215, 217, 218, 219, 220, 222, 223, 224, 226, 227,

229, 230, 231, 256, 276, 282, 283, 285, 287, 288, 289, 296
'Autosuggestion', 213, 218, 219, 220, 227, 229, 230, 284

Back to Zero, 215
Band on the Wall, 108, 109, 127, 128, 129, 130, 131, 147, 212
Banger, Ed, 134
Banks, Chas, 210–11
Barlow, Sue, see Sumner, Sue
Bates, Iris (Peter's ex-partner), 67, 181, 244, 249, 260, 261, 268, 276
Battle of the Bands, 126
Beatles, 110
Bendow, Ian, 17
Benson, Baz, 12
Best, George, 20
Bez (dancer), 164
Bicycle Thieves, 90
Bidet Boys, 133
Big Alex, 51
Big in Japan, 68
Binnick, Bernie, 100
'BL', 51
Blackadder, 30
Blitz Club, London, 144
'Blue Monday', 24, 202, 265
Blurt, 254, 289
Bono, 252
Bontee, Yves von, 189
Boon, Richard, 28, 42, 47, 55
Booth, Dave, 76, 94
bootlegging, 78, 80, 90, 93, 104, 145–6, 286, 293, 299
Bowdon Vale Youth Club, 148, 212, 214, 222
Bowie, David, 30, 49, 55, 244
Boys in Bondage, xiv, 80
Bradley, Mick, 133

Brandwood, Derek, 100, 155
Branson, Richard, 71
Braune, Rüdiger, 240
Brierley, John, 114, 115–16, 130
Brierley, Peter, 20–1
Britannia Row Studios, 202, 244, 246, 248,
    288, 295–6
Brotherdale, Steve, 59–60, 63–5, 70, 75, 91,
    92, 134
    now at McDonald's, 65
Brunel University, Uxbridge, 132
Burnel, Jean-Jacques, 112, 256
Burroughs, William, 185, 186, 234, 266
Butlin's, 17–19, 24
Buzzcocks, 28, 29, 35, 42, 44, 48, 53–4, 55,
    57, 59, 63, 70, 81, 83, 87–9, 90, 92, 101,
    110, 120–1, 127, 133, 135, 144, 167,
    178
    bad behaviour of, 182–4, 192–7
    Joy Division tour with, 179–84, 191–8,
        224, 225, 226, 227, 228, 229, 230
    perform in shower of maggots, 194–5

Cabaret Voltaire, 48, 108, 112, 131, 134,
    185, 186–7, 208, 209, 210, 222, 239,
    295
Caffery, John, 246, 277, 295, 296
Cain, Dave, 13
Cale, John, 280
Can, 109
'Candidate', 153, 201, 213, 215, 216, 217,
    220, 224, 229
Candy (Ian's dog), 244, 271
Captain (A&R guy), 255
Cargo Studios, 114, 115, 116, 130, 189, 208,
    224
Casey, Jayne, 68
Cassidy, Larry, 218, 259
Cassidy, Vinny, 218
Caulfield, Mike ('Corky'), 270
Central Sound Studios, 161, 162
'Ceremony', 154, 233, 262, 273, 292, 293,
    294, 295, 297
'Chance', 160, 189, 215
Check Inn, Altrincham, 133
Cheesehead (guitarist), 130
Chelsea, 121, 133
City Fun, 219, 284
Clapton, Eric, 81
Clarke, John Cooper, 27, 55, 127, 131, 210,
    215–16
Clarke, Margi ('Margox'), 158–9
Clash, 30, 45, 48, 111

Closer, 140, 142, 151, 160, 164, 262, 275–80,
    275, 288–9, 292
    double album mooted, 296
    Ian's death and, 253
    no promotion of, 273
    re-mastered, 285
    recording of, 243–53, 255
    released, 295–6
Coach House, Huddersfield, 112, 129
Cockney Rebel, 24–5, 77
Coleman, Jaz, 240–1
'Colony', 220, 221, 222, 223, 224, 225, 227,
    229, 230, 231, 278, 283, 284, 285, 286,
    289, 291, 296
Colquhoun, Andy, 129
Control, 3, 35, 45, 54, 105, 118, 173, 174,
    228–9
Coogan, Steve, 53
Cook, Paul, 37
Cope, Julian, 68
Corbijn, Anton, 118, 228
Cornwell, Hugh, 254
Coronation Street ('Corrie'), 5, 35, 64, 111,
    158, 159
Cosgrove Hall Films, 50
Crawling Chaos, 254, 289
'Cries & Whispers', 155
Crispy Ambulance, 115, 257, 258
Cummins, Kevin, 35, 55, 98, 208, 209
Cup Cake (teacher), 14
Curbs, 210
Cure, 168, 211, 215
Curtis, Carole (Ian's sister), 269
Curtis, Deborah (née Woodruff)
    ('Debbie'), 36, 43, 51, 67, 73, 77, 104,
    110, 174–5, 181, 191, 261, 287, 294
    birth of, 30
    book written by, 99, 161, 234
    daughter's birth and, 161, 179
    divorce proceedings initiated by, 262,
        267–8, 292
    Ian's affair and, 244, 249, 262, 264, 285
    Ian's attempted suicide and, 257
    Ian's death and, 269
    Ian's epilepsy and, 124
    Ian marries, 30, 31
    Ian's suicide and, 267–8
    pregnancy of, 109
Curtis, Doreen (Ian's mother), 264, 267,
    270, 291, 292, 294
Curtis, Ian, xiv–xvii, 35, 36, 50, 58, 63, 64, 65,
    70, 98, 99, 107, 126, 181, 283, 287,
    291, 293

Index

alcohol and, 61–2
allergies suffered by, 167
Annik's affair with, 173, 174, 181, 198,
    234, 236–7, 244, 246, 248–50, 252,
    262, 263, 264, 284, 285, 288, 292
attempts suicide, 257–8, 290
band tensions and, 109, 110
band worried about, 121, 123–4, 150
Bernard hypnotizes, 294
biopic of, 3, 35, 45, 54, 105, 118, 173, 174,
    228
birth of, 29
at Burroughs signing, 186
chameleon-like nature of, 235
commits suicide, 266, 267–70, 271, 295
death of, 67, 88, 140, 141, 188, 218,
    220–1, 233
'death march' of, 220–1
Debbie initiates divorce proceedings
    against, 262, 267–8, 292
Debbie marries, 30, 31, 47
domestic problems of, 263
education of, 29–30
epilepsy suffered by, 124, 137–8, 175,
    176, 181–2, 191–2, 209, 220, 229,
    243, 244, 252, 254, 257, 261, 265–6,
    268, 270, 288, 289
famous mac of, 270
first EP financed by, 73, 76, 77–8, 104
funeral of, 233, 269, 295
girls/girlfriends and, 29, 30, 173–4, 193,
    198, 293
guitar mastered by, 163
ill health of, 225
inquest into death of, 270, 295
jobs taken by, 30, 50
joins band, 88
joins Warsaw, 47–8
Martin's creative relationship with, 251,
    252
musical tastes of, 109
nature of, 52, 174–5
Nazi associations dog, 205
NME cover of, 209, 244
Peter first meets, 51
Peter praises, 74–5
piles suffered by, 90
RCA deal and, 100–1
reading habits of, 186, 198, 235, 266
references Sinatra in lyrics, 153, 207
runaway drum and, 172
'Rusty' sobriquet of, 30
Sam Riley plays, 45

self-harming by, 242, 286, 289
Sinatra lyrical references by, 288
songs written/produced by, 63, 74–5,
    153, 165, 190, 233, 258, 273, 278
taken to hospital, 191–2, 229
tortured soul of, 52, 250
'US tour' and, 263–4
worrying side of, 60, 61–2
WWII obsession of, 81
Curtis, Kevin (Ian's father), 264, 267, 270,
    291, 292, 294
Curtis, Natalie (Ian's daughter), 161, 181,
    191, 267, 294
birth of, 213
Ian misses birthday of, 262
songs written/produced by, 229

Damned, 45, 47, 48, 88
Davidson, Tony, 167
Davy, Gareth, 127
'Day of the Lords', 156, 200, 212, 213, 215,
    219, 220, 221, 224, 225, 227, 230, 231,
    282, 283, 284, 289
De La Salle Grammar School, 28
'Dead Souls', 161, 189, 216, 217, 218, 219,
    220, 221, 222, 224, 227, 230, 283, 284,
    285, 287, 289, 291, 296, 297
Dean, James, 25
Deano (friend), 17, 24
'Decades', 259, 265, 280, 289, 293, 297
Deep Purple, 25, 91
DeMac, Harry, 49
Den Byrds, 131–2
Devoto, Howard, 35, 70
Dexys Midnight Runners, 166, 220
Dickin, Bernard ('Barney') (later Bernard
    Sumner), 9, 10, 35; see also Sumner,
    Bernard
'Digital', 106, 113, 115, 116–17, 130, 132,
    140, 145, 148, 162, 208, 211, 215, 220,
    221, 225, 229, 230, 265, 282, 283, 284,
    285, 289, 291, 293, 297
'Disorder', 33, 106, 148, 156, 162, 200, 212,
    213, 215, 217, 218, 219, 220, 221, 222,
    224, 225, 227, 229, 230, 231, 282, 283,
    284, 285, 286, 289, 290, 293, 297
Distractions, 93, 167, 219, 221, 222, 227
Dominic (fan), 210
Doors, 109, 266
Dowie, John, 112, 208, 209, 214, 254, 289
'Dreams Never End', 269, 273
Drones, xv, 42, 44, 59, 64, 70–2, 89, 93, 127,
    192

Durutti Column, 28, 107, 112, 115, 117, 126, 128, 160, 208, 254, 289, 292
Dury, Ian, 98, 280
Dust, 130
Duval, Michel, 185

Eagle, Roger, 68, 92, 112
Earcom 2, 223
Eater, 42
Echo & the Bunnymen, 68, 168, 219, 221
Ed (OZ PA), 106
Eden, Ibiza, 94
Eden, Kevin, 108
Eden Studios, 144, 145, 211
E.G. Records, 241
Electric Ballroom, London, 221, 227
Electric Circus, Manchester, 42, 43, 44, 45, 47, 48, 55, 70–1, 88–9, 92, 93, 98, 112, 120
Elephant & Castle, 79, 101–2
Elite, 108, 128
Elti Fits, 219
Elze, Rüdiger, 240
Emergency, 105, 106, 127, 223
En Attendant, 30, 173
Erasmus, Alan, 28, 60, 61, 91, 107, 112, 114–15, 116, 126, 158, 257
Eric's, Liverpool, 64, 68, 92, 112, 127, 129, 131, 158, 197, 210, 213, 220, 231, 294
Essex, David, 16, 17, 18, 25
'Eternal, The', 259, 279–80, 283, 284, 285, 286, 287, 289, 296
'Exercise One', 148, 156, 209, 211, 212, 213, 220, 222, 296

F Club, Leeds, 118, 131, 160, 215
Face, 131
Factory (documentary), 114–15
Factory Benelux, 269
Factory (at Russell Club), Manchester, 29, 61, 91, 107–8, 126, 127, 128, 131, 176, 209, 214, 223, 254, 290
Factory Flick, The, 212, 222
Factory Records, 28, 112–16, 126, 143, 144, 147, 160, 161–2, 168, 214, 215, 218, 227, 231, 245, 254–5, 259, 291, 296
  closes, 150
  fanzine benefit of, 284–5
  Ian's wake held by, 269, 295
Factory Sample, A, 112–18, 130–1, 208, 209, 214
Factory II at New Osborne Club, 262, 284
'Failures (of a Modern Man)', 74, 94, 126, 127, 130

Fall, xv, 35, 48, 59, 70, 89, 109, 127, 133, 212, 219, 254
Farnworth Flower Arranging Club, 91
Fashion, 215, 216, 289
Fast Breeder, 28, 61–2, 63, 91, 93, 98, 107
Fast Cars, 134
Fast Product, 93, 117
Fast Records, 68, 81
Faust, 109
Faver, Colin, 214
Fellows, Graham, 28
Ferry, Bryan, 76
Final Solution, 214, 218
Fireplace, 212, 213
Flemish Weaver, xiv, 66
Foreign Press, 219, 223
Frantic Elevators, 35, 84, 167, 219
Freispiel, 240
Freshies, 28
'From Safety to Where', 153, 213
Frusciante, John, 205
Fun Factory, 293
Futurama Festival, 173, 222

Gang of Four, 114, 115, 219
Garlands, Liverpool, 94
Garrett, Malcolm, 29
Garrity, Ed, 134
Garvey, Steve, 180
Gee, Grant, 114
Generation X, 30
Genetic Records, 143, 144, 147, 211
Geordie Vision, 210
Gilbert, Gillian (Steve M's wife), 67, 121, 122, 124, 198, 249
  Ian's death and, 269
  joins New Order, 84, 197
  Steve M marries, 84
Gilbert, Lesley, see Gretton, Lesley
'Girls Don't Count', 290, 291
'Glass', 115, 116, 130, 145, 148, 208, 211, 212, 215, 217, 218, 220, 222, 224, 283, 285, 289, 297
Glass Torpedoes, 218
Glastonbury, 85
Glen, D. B., 130
Glover, Youth, 240
Good Mood, Halifax, 216
Granada Reports What's On, 28, 110, 113, 129, 165–6, 217
Graveyard Studios, 293, 294, 295
Gray, Iain, 30, 47

Index

Greasy Bear, 27, 115
Great Rock 'n' Roll Swindle, The, 269, 295
Greaves, Bob, 110
Gresty, Martin ('Nidder'), 46, 75
Gretton, Lesley (née Gilbert) (Rob's wife), 29, 64, 249, 262
Gretton, Rob, 29, 49, 80, 89, 94, 99–100, 126, 129, 154, 163, 165, 175, 192, 203, 205, 216, 218, 220, 230, 231–2, 236–7, 244, 251, 260, 262, 265, 286, 293
  bad behaviour of, 197–8
  band tensions and, 109, 110
  band's first gig with, 106
  becomes a skinhead, 167
  death of, 218
  Factory ethos and, 188–9
  Ian's death and, 269, 270
  independent-label deal struck by, 147–8
  jobs taken by, 138
  Joy Division managed by, 67, 103–19, 245–6, 255, 256–8
  Joy Division saved by, 102
  kibbutz life of, 29, 64–5
  money-spending talent of, 109
  'no girlfriend' rule imposed by, 122, 161, 181–2, 249
  'no press' rule imposed by, 157
  'phone-box' offices of, 139
  pro-Manchester leanings of, 142–4
  snoring of, 191
  songs written/produced by, 258
  'unique' managerial style of, 110
Grimmie (Bernard's cousin), 46
Grundy, Bill, 45, 88
'Gutz for Garters', 63, 92

Haçienda, 20, 80, 88, 150, 226, 232
Hamsters, 219
Hanley, Paul, 212
Hanley, Steve, 212
Hannett, Martin, 27–31, 35, 60, 61–2, 65, 71–2, 77, 88, 89, 91, 112, 114, 116, 117, 130, 145, 160, 163, 200, 201, 202, 208, 215, 216–17, 219, 223, 224, 244, 245–8, 276–7, 278, 279, 280, 282, 287, 288, 291, 294, 295, 296
  death of, 218
  driving 'skills' of, 247
  drugs and, 150, 153–4, 247
  Factory ethos and, 188–9
  Ian's creative relationship with, 251, 252
  tyrannical nature of, 153–5
  uses 'musicians' as swear word, 156

see also Zero, Martin
Happy Mondays, 12, 164
Hardrock Concert Theatre, 30
Harley, Steve, 24–5
Harpoon Gags, 90
Harris, Sean, Sean Harris plays, 45
Harry Hack & the Big G, 58, 90
Hassell, Sven, 81
'Heart and Soul', 276, 278–9, 286, 287, 289, 290, 291, 296
Heart and Soul, 145, 287, 292, 294, 295
Heartbreakers, 56, 57, 89
Heat, 94
Heaven, 214
Hempsall, Alan, 257, 258, 260
Hendrix, Jimi, 84
Here Are the Young Men, 284
Hess, Rudolf, 70, 81
Hewick, Kevin, 254, 289
Hitler Youth, 75, 81, 104
Honoré, Annik, 220, 221, 268, 283
  birth of, 30
  Ian's affair with, 173, 174, 181, 198, 236–7, 244, 246, 248–50, 252, 262, 263, 264, 285, 292
  Ian's death and, 269
  Ian's letters to, 284, 288
  joins European tour, 234, 236–7
  leaves UK, 263, 264, 268, 292
Hook, Chris (Peter's brother), 3, 21, 159
  education of, 6
  emigrates to Jamaica, 5–7
  parents' fighting and, 7
Hook, Ernest William ('Bill') (Peter's step-father), 3
  drunkenness of, 7
  first marriage of, 4
  Irene marries, 3, 5
  unpaid taxes of, 8
Hook, Granddad (paternal step-grandfather), 4
Hook, Heather (Peter's daughter), 301
Hook, Irene (née Acton) (Peter's mum), v, 7, 16, 20, 21, 23, 39, 41, 235, 238, 239
  Bill marries, 3, 5
  honest nature of, 10, 11
  Peter's bleached hair and, 111
Hook, Jack (Peter's son), 301
Hook, Jess (Peter's daughter), 301
Hook, Peter ('Hooky'), 35, 87
  alcohol given up by, 24
  bad behaviour of, 176–7, 182–4, 192–7
  band formed by, 39, 45, 87, 88, 159

Hook, Peter ('Hooky') – *continued*
  Bernard meets, 9, 10
  Bernard's arguments with, 66, 69
  BBC payments to, 139
  becomes a skinhead, 12, 23
  being tone deaf, 74
  birth of, 3, 29
  bleached hair gimmick and, 111
  bullying and, 10
  Burnel influences sound of, 112
  careers advice given to, 14
  childhood of, 3–8, 39
  Corrie and, 5, 35, 64, 159
  Dansette owned by, 23, 75, 76, 77,
  DJing of, 85–6, 94
  earliest memories of, 3, 5
  education of, 5, 6, 8–9, 10–14
  11-plus passed by, 8–9
  emigrates to Jamaica, 5–7
  epiphanies experienced by, 16, 17–18, 25
  exams taken by, 14, 16
  expired van MOT of, 118–19
  family and, live in Jamaica, 5–8, 39
  favourite albums of, 280
  favourite blue shirt of, 110, 166, 220, 260
  favourite Joy Division song of, 188
  favourite lyric of, 279
  fetish party attended by, 128
  first brush with celebrity, 159
  first guitar of, 40
  first record bought by, 23–4
  first record player of, 23
  food tastes of, 235, 238–9
  girls/girlfriends and, 71–2, 181
  grandmother of, 3, 5, 8
  Ian's death affects, 268–71, 273–4
  Ian first meets, 51
  interest in pop music starts, 23–4, 25
  jobs taken by, 14–16, 17–20, 24, 50, 97,
    100, 117, 160
  Killing Joke records with, 240
  low audiences of, 84–6, 112
  mother's support for, 82
  new band considered by, 241
  parents' divorce and, 3
  parents' fighting and, 3, 7
  piles suffered by, 90
  press/media and, 157, 163–4, 299
  pubbing/clubbing of, xiv, 22
  punk movement and, 25–6
  RCA deal and, 101
  reggae discovered by, 23
  Revenge records with, 240

  scooter owned by, 16
  Sex Pistols inspire, 22, 25, 31, 35, 36–9,
    44–5, 76, 280
  sleeping habits of, 137–8
  songs written/produced by, 51, 63, 75,
    153, 164, 189, 229, 269, 276
  Spanish holiday of, 20–1
  spiders feared by, 6, 9
  tells Larry's flight-simulator story, 218
  thieving nature of, 10–12, 23–4
  van stories of, 11, 48, 58, 90, 104–5,
    118–19, 122–3, 137–8, 148–9, 158,
    164, 168–9, 172, 217, 220
  works at George Best's desk, 20, 21
Hope & Anchor, London, 121, 134, 211
Houghton, Stuart, 24, 25, 66
Houldsworth Hall, 42
House of Dolls (Ka-Tzetnik 135633), xiv, 74,
  80
Howlett, Mike, 127
Hubbard, Mr (teacher), 82–3
Hucknall, Mick, 35, 38, 84, 167
Human League, 147, 217
Human Menagerie, The, 24
Hurrah, New York, 295

'I Remember Nothing', 148, 153, 206–7,
  212, 213, 215, 216, 222, 227, 228,
  229
I Swear I Was There (Nolan), 35
Ian Dury and the Blockheads, 98, 280
'Ice Age', 101, 126, 145, 211, 212, 220, 224,
  228, 284, 296
Iggy Pop, xv, 30, 47, 63, 74, 82, 99, 100, 101,
  266, 268, 269, 280
Imperial Hotel, Blackpool, 218
'In a Lonely Place', 154, 262, 273, 292, 294,
  295
Inadequates, 84, 85
'Incubation', 286, 287, 289, 296
'Inside the Line', 63, 92
'Insight', 109, 145, 148, 202, 209, 211, 212,
  213, 215, 219, 220, 221, 222, 223, 224,
  225, 227, 228, 229, 230, 231, 282, 283,
  284, 285, 289, 291
Institute of Technology, Bolton, 130, 210
'Interzone', 100, 126, 206, 213, 215, 216,
  217, 220, 221, 223, 225, 226, 227, 229,
  230, 231, 282, 283, 284, 286, 289, 290
Invisible Girls, 27
Iris (punk), 62
'Isolation', 276–7, 285, 287, 288, 289, 290,
  291, 293, 296, 297

Jackson, Martin, 47
James, Dougie, 97
James, Stuart, 215
Jasmine (Dave's girlfriend), 30, 213, 221
Jean, Auntie (Peter's aunt), v, 3, 8, 14
Jobson, Richard, 254
John (fan), 286
John the Postman, 35, 44, 55, 90, 219
Johnny Seven (toy), 39
Johnny Thunders & the Heartbreakers, 45,
    48
Johnson, Donald, 206
Johnson, Mike, 246, 277, 296
Jones, John Paul, 25
Jones, Rebecca ('Becky') (Peter's wife), 188,
    301
Jones, Steve, 37
Joy Division (formerly Stiff Kittens, then
    Warsaw, later New Order, q.v.), 9, 30,
    163, 170–1, 295, 301, 303
  Annik interviews, 30, 173, 221
  bad behaviour of, 176–8, 182–4, 192–7
  band members of, drift apart, 67
  band members take turns to manage, 98,
    105
  band rivalry and, 44, 70–2, 99, 103,
    120–1, 133, 215, 219, 221, 241, 242,
    256
  bleached-hair gimmick and, 111
  branded 'Iggy Pop imitators', 99
  Buzzcocks' relationship with, 179–80
  cancelled gigs of, 291, 292, 294
  classic songs of, 106
  debut EP of, 73–7, 79
  drugs and, 179
  'elephants' conspire against, 150, 151
  end of, 274
  European tour of, 234–9, 242, 282
  Factory mini-residency of, 254
  fans of, 112, 133, 167, 168, 173, 176–7,
    189, 210, 219, 226, 252, 257, 284–5,
    287, 290, 293
  favourite songs by, 188
  fights at gigs of, 176–8, 223, 259–62
  films about, 3, 35, 36, 45, 54, 99, 105,
    114–15, 118, 228
  final album of, 265, 285, 289, 293, 296
  first EP of, 80, 81, 94
  first gig as, xiv–xvii, 97, 126
  first TV appearance of, 110–11, 175
  flexidisc, 296
  formed, 35
  girls/girlfriends and, 173–4, 181, 193, 198,
    234
  at Glastonbury, 85
  Ian's attempted suicide and, 257–8
  Ian's death affects 'ear' of, 140–2
  Ian's death and, 67, 269, 269–70, 273–4
  Ian's suicide and, 267
  independent-label deal struck by, 147–8
  John Peel sessions, 139, 190, 209–10, 231
  join MMC, 108
  Killing Joke's relationship with, 240
  last-ever gig of, 293, 296
  low audiences of, 84, 112, 129
  missing master tapes of, 145–6
  Nazi associations dog, 70, 75, 81–2,
    101–2, 103, 104, 129, 163, 205, 213,
    274
  'no girlfriend' rule imposed on, 122
  Oldham Tower Club gig of, 84–5, 164
  overdrawn riff bank of, 140, 189–90
  penultimate gig of, 262
  popularity of, skyrockets, 273
  press/media and, 99–100, 112, 123, 131,
    133, 134, 157, 160, 163–4, 165–6,
    168, 219, 219–20, 224, 254
  Princess Parkway shots of, 208
  RCA Records sign, 100–1
  Rob becomes manager of, 67, 167
  royalties received by, 125
  Section 25's relationship with, 218
  self-promotion and, 80
  Sex Pistols inspire, 35, 36–9, 41–2, 44–5
  short film of, 148, 212
  Sinatra lyrical references by, 153, 207,
    288
  Sordide Sentimental deal with, 189
  'sound' of, 83, 115–16
  'stop-the-press' moment of, 106
  tax affairs of, 80–1, 252
  tensions within, 69, 82, 109, 110, 156,
    164–5, 173–4, 185, 186–7, 192–3,
    234–9, 248–52
  TJ's practice room of, 83–4
  touring with Buzzcocks, 179–84, 191–8,
    224, 225, 226, 227, 228, 229, 230
  touring with Rezillos and Undertones.,
    120–1
  trademark lighting of, 182
  U2 fans of, 252
  unreleased-album sessions of, 126
  'US tour' of, 244, 254, 262, 263–4, 266,
    267, 270, 295
  Velvet Underground influences, 140
  violence at Bury gig of, 257–62

Joy Division – *continued*
  Warner not impressed by, 147
  Yorkshire Ripper investigation and,
    118–19, 131
Joy Division (documentary), 99, 114, 204
*Joy Division and New Order – A History in
  Cuttings 1977–1983*, 89
Joy Division (sex-toy company), 80
Joy Division (short), 222
Joy Divisions, xiv
joydiv.org, 132, 210, 283, 290

Ka-Tzetnik 135633, xiv
Keenan, John, 222
'Keep On Keepin' On', 100, 206
Kelly's, Manchester, 130
Kilburn & the High Roads, 98
'Kill, The', 63, 92, 156, 213, 297
Killing Joke, 240–1, 242, 285, 287
King George's Hall, Blackburn, 226
King's School, Macclesfield, 29, 30, 31
'Komakino', 287, 289, 296
Kowalski, 240
Kraftwerk, xiv, 109, 140, 158
Kray twins, 25

Lamar, Foo Foo, 42, 91
Lancaster University, 216
Last, Bob, 68–9, 81, 92, 93
Lawrie (fan), 286
Lea, Stephen, 71
'Leaders of Men', 74, 92, 94, 126, 127, 130,
    211, 212, 221, 222, 225, 228
Led Zeppelin, 14, 25
Lee, Belinda, 51
Lee, Danny, 24, 25, 46, 51, 66
Leigh Open Air Festival, 174, 221
Les Bains Douches, Paris, 197, 231
Lesser Free Trade Hall, 15, 16, 35, 36, 41,
    87, 216
Level 42, 119
'Licht und Blindheit', 188, 189, 287, 297
Limit Club, Sheffield, 217
Locarno, Bristol, 121, 133
Lori & the Chameleons, 221
'Lost', 92
'Love Will Tear Us Apart', 106, 135, *135*,
    145, 150, 162, 163, 189–90, 225, 227,
    228, 229, 230, 231, 245, 253, 266, 273,
    277, 282, 283, 284, 285, 287, 288, 289,
    290, 291, 293, 297
  12-inch version of, 295
  video, 83, 141, 263, 264–5, 293

Ludus, 219

McCall, Davina, 214
McCartney, Paul, 150
Macclesfield High School for Girls, 30
McCormick, Oz, 106
McCulloch, Ian, 68
McGarry, Steve, 130
McLaren, Malcolm, 31, 36
McQueeney, Danny, 17, 19, 25, 58
Magazine, 29, 47, 48, 70, 109
Maher, John, 195
Maida Vale Studios, BBC, 231
Malvern Winter Gardens, 290
Man Alive, 22
Manchester Evening News (MEN), 35, 39,
    65, 82, 203
Manchester Musicians' Collective (MMC),
    105, 108, 127, 131, 212
Manchester Polytechnic, 29, 93
Manchester Rains, 65
Manchester Ship Canal Company, 20, 21,
    50, 97
Manicured Noise, 217
Marquee, London, 211–12
Marr, Johnny, 206
Martin (fan), 132
Mason, Eileen, 64
Mason, Terry, 36, 38, 58, 63–4, 66, 67, 87,
    88, 90, 137, 149, 172, 174, 181, 183,
    217, 222, 243–5, 252, 257, 259–60,
    269, 302
  bad behaviour of, 192–7
  becomes New Order's tour manager, 49
  drugs and, 230
  easy-going nature of, 49
Mathan, Chris, 215, 296
Matlock, Glen, 37
Mayflower Club, Manchester, 76, 105, 111,
    127, 161, 219, 223
Mazel Radio ('Mazel's'), 39–40
'Means to an End, A', 231, 278, 282, 283,
    284, 285, 289, 293, 296, 297
Mechanicals, 143
Meecham, Charles, 296
Melody Maker, 25, 31, 39, 41, 160, 163
MEN Arena, 205
*Messthetics #106: The Manchester
  Musicians' Collective 1977–1982*, 108
Middlehurst, Mick, 131
Middleton College, 53
Mighty Wah!, 68
Millins, Kevin, 214

Mills, Russell, 127
Minny Pops, 258, 260, 282, 284, 290
Moines, Des, 224
Monkees, 37
Monochrome Set, 221
Moon, Tony, 59
Moonlight Club, London, 289, 297
Morley, Paul, 35, 55, 73, 98–9
Morris, Gillian (Steve M's wife), see Gilbert, Gillian
Morris, Stephen ('Steve'), 49, 65–6, 69, 76, 82, 99, 103
    bad behaviour of, 192–7
    birth of, 31
    closed-off nature of, 66, 67
    driving 'skills' of, 121–3
    drumming abilities of, 115–16
    education of, 31
    first gig of, 92
    first gig as Joy Division, xv–xvii
    French-language skills of, 197
    Gillian marries, 84
    girls/girlfriends and, 198
    Ian's death and, 269, 270
    ill health of, 77
    jobs taken by, 66, 160
    RCA deal and, 100–1
    'Shakin' Steve' sobriquet of, 119
    'Son of Forsyth' sobriquet of, 66
    songs written/produced by, 153, 189–90, 211, 229
    tank collection of, 121–2
Morrissey, Steven, 35
Moscrop, Martin, 221
Motörhead, 79
Mountain, 37
Mountford Hall, Liverpool University, 224
Movement, 150, 151, 153, 154
Movement of 24th January (M24J), 126
Murray, Pauline, 27
Music Force, 28, 61

Nagle, Chris, 152, 154, 155, 215, 245, 246, 296
Nashville Rooms, London, 25, 30, 31, 170, 173, 220, 222
National Front, 81, 129
Needle Time, 79
Negatives, 59, 73, 89, 98, 99, 108, 126
Nervous Breakdown, 93
'New Dawn Fades', 74, 202–3, 212, 213, 215, 216, 220, 225, 226, 230, 282, 284, 293, 297

New Electric Circus, Manchester, 133
New Hormones, 28, 112, 135
New Musical Express (NME), see NME
New Order (formerly Joy Division, q.v.), 9, 35, 106, 139, 151, 181, 206–7, 214, 239, 246, 277, 279, 280, 283
    Australian tour of, 265
    awards won by, 24–5
    Bernard's threats to leave, 50
    beginnings of, 67, 141, 269
    book of, 20
    first album of, 150
    Gillian joins, 197
    Ian's death and, 67
    lack of confidence within, 154–5
    school photoshoot of, 13
    song titles, inspiration for, 284
    splits up, 161, 240
    tensions within, 69, 229
    Terry becomes tour manager of, 49
    trademark lighting of, 182
    videos, 264–5
    writing songs for, 188
New Osborne Club, see Factory II at
New Romantics, 144, 147
'New Rose', 88
New York Dolls, 56, 57
Nice 'N' Easy, Manchester, xiv
Nico, 27, 280
1966 World Cup, 8
NME, 12, 13, 25, 31, 41, 54, 55, 73, 79, 99, 109, 160, 163, 168, 170, 209, 214, 219, 244, 254
'No Love Lost', 74, 80, 94, 126, 127, 130, 212, 217, 229
Nolan, David, 35
Nolan, Mike, 178
Norman, Neil, 254
Nosebleeds, 70
Nottingham Playhouse, 210
'Novelty', 51, 71, 92, 126, 162, 163, 216, 219
Nuffield Theatre, Lancaster, 216
Nuttall, Stephanie, 217
Nuttall, Tony, 30

Oakey, Phil, 217
Oaks, Chorlton, 65
Oasis, 12
Object, 112
Ocomin, Martin, 212
O'Connor, Hazel, 254
Odeon, Canterbury, 132, 215
Odeon, Manchester, 162

Odeon Theatre, Birmingham, 226
Oldham Tower Club, 84–5, 164
One Show, The, 23
'Only Mistake, The', 156, 212, 215, 228, 297
Orchestral Manoeuvres in the Dark
    (OMD), 115, 214, 215, 217, 218, 220,
    221
Orme, Stuart, 293
Otway, John, 121, 133
OutKast, 181
OZ PA, 49

Palmer-Hughes, 1, 40
Panik, xv, 29, 65, 70, 94, 103
Parker, Alex, xiv, xvi
Parker, Ian, xiv, xvi
Passage, 108, 133, 213, 287
'Passover', 231, 277–8, 282, 285, 289, 291,
    293, 296, 297
Paul (Pennine engineer), 63, 76
Pauline (punk), 62
Peel, John, 139, 164, 189, 190, 209, 231
Penetration, 55, 58, 89, 90
Pennine Sound Studios, 63, 73, 92, 94, 130,
    215, 245, 282
Pet Shop Boys, 31
Pete Wylie, 68
Phil (fan), 290
Phoenix, Pat, 159
Piccadilly Radio, 160, 215
Pickering, Stuart, 294
Pils, Dave, 30, 149, 172, 173, 181, 183, 185,
    193, 196, 197, 211, 213, 221, 229, 244,
    260, 270
Pink Fairies, 79
Pink Floyd, 246
Pink Military, 112
Pinky's, Broughton, 262, 264, 270, 292
Pipers, Manchester, 93
Pips Discotheque, Manchester, xiv, 22, 49,
    76, 94, 97, 104, 126
Plan K, Brussels, 185–8, 225, 283
Platty (friend/roadie), 67, 98
Polydor Records, 255
Poor, 289
Pop Group, 108
P-Orridge, Genesis, 227, 248, 249, 263–4,
    266
Porter, N. F., 100
Prefects, 70
Presley, Elvis, death of, 92
Primal Scream, 240
Prince of Wales Conference Centre, 219

Psychedelic Furs, 168
Public Image, 222

Quadrophenia, 179
Queens Hall, Leeds, 222

Rabid Records, 28, 81, 89, 103, 104, 112,
    127
Radar Records, 143
Rafters, Manchester, 56, 57, 60, 89, 90–1, 93,
    94, 97, 98, 99, 103, 126
Rainbow Theatre, London, 193, 195, 230,
    254, 256, 258, 289
Rainy City Records, 65
Rainy Days, 94
Ranch, 42, 73, 91
Rare Records, 30, 100
RCA Records, 99–100, 206
'Reaction', 92
Reade, Lindsay, 257, 260, 261, 290
Record Mirror, 133
Red Hot Chili Peppers, 205
Reed, Lou, 100, 101, 266, 280
Regent Road Primary, 8, 12
Reilly, Vini, 128, 160
Revenge, 240
Revolution Club, York, 134
Rezillos, 93, 120–1, 132, 133
Rich Kids, 127–8
Right Said Fred, 128, 217
Riley, Sam, 45
Risk, 105, 106, 127, 130
Riviera, Jake, 98
Rock Against Racism, 81, 130
Rock Garden, Middlesbrough, 92
Rocos, Cleo, 128
Romulus Club, Birmingham, 220
Roots Club (Cosmo Club), Leeds, 128,
    217
Roseberry, Anne, 144
Rossi, Mick, 41–2
Rotten, Johnny, 37, 38
Rotters, 22
Rowland, Kevin, 220
Rowntrees Sound, 22
Roxy Music, 24, 49, 76
Royal Family, 254, 289
Royal Manchester College of Music, 58
Royal Standard, Bradford, 129
Royalty Theatre, London, 215
Rushent, Martin, 144–5, 147, 211
Russell Club, Manchester, see Factory at
Ryan, Tosh, 27, 81, 104

Sad Café, 83, 84, 210
St Ambrose College, 29
Salem, Charles, 222
Salford College of Technology, 71, 93, 133
Salford Grammar School, 9, 10, 29, 46
Salford Jets, 83
Santana, 16
Sarge (friend), 180, 182–3, 195, 225
Sargeant, Bob, 209
Sargeant, Rex, 167
Savage, Jon, 299
Saville, Peter, 29, 61, 107, 112, 114, 117, 131,
    141, 157, 215, 223, 253, 291, 296
Sawyer's Arms, Manchester, 108, 113
Scala, London, 222, 263, 292
Scanlon, Craig, 212
Schoetens, Marc, 283
Scritti Politti, 221
Searling, Richard, 100
'Sebastian', 24, 25
Section 25 (band), 115, 218, 231, 254, 257,
    258, 259, 260–1, 284, 285, 286, 287,
    289, 290, 291, 292
Sedaka, Neil, 150
Sex Pistols, 22, 25–6, 31, 35, 36–9, 43, 45,
    47, 48, 51, 64, 76, 81, 87, 170
  film about, 269, 295
  Joy Division inspired by, 35, 36–9, 41–2,
    44–5, 158, 280
'Shadowplay', 106, 110, 126, 129, 140, 148,
    205, 211, 212, 213, 215, 217, 218, 219,
    220, 221, 222, 223, 224, 225, 226, 227,
    229, 230, 231, 282, 283, 284, 286, 289,
    293, 297, 299
Shelley, Pete, 35, 47, 53–4, 90, 120–1, 180,
    225, 229
'She's Lost Control', 106, 148, 152, 166, 175,
    204–5, 209, 211, 212, 213, 215, 217,
    218, 219, 220, 221, 222, 223, 224, 225,
    226, 227, 230, 231, 282, 283, 284, 286,
    287, 288, 289, 290, 291, 296
Short Circuit: Live at the Electric Circus, 70, 71,
    81, 93, 109, 127
Shy, Steve, 55
Shy Talk, 55
Sidebottom, Frank, 28
Sievey, Chris, 28
Silk, Doctor, 66, 176
Silverton, Peter, 45
Simonon, Paul, 111, 112
Simply Red, 35
Sinatra, Frank, 153, 207, 288
Siouxsie and the Banshees, 30, 65, 97, 162,

168
'Sister Ray', 212, 259, 283, 289, 297
Skin Two, 128
Slaughter & the Dogs, xv, 28, 29, 41, 42, 44,
    59, 65, 70, 71–2, 87, 89, 92, 93, 103,
    104
Slaves of Venus, xiv, 80
Smiffy, 83
Smirks, 241, 242
Smith, Mark E., 35, 38
Smith, Patti, 29, 30
Smith, Robert, 254
Smiths, 35
Snyde, 93
So It Goes, 28, 88, 98, 107
Solamar, Steve, 112
Solstice, 35, 37
Something Else, 175
'Something Must Break', 163, 215, 216, 297
Sordide Sentimental, 189, 224, 287, 297
Soul Boys, 289
'Sound of Music, The', 221, 227, 229, 230,
    231, 282, 283, 285, 289, 296–7
Sounds, 25, 45, 46, 59, 81, 99, 109, 134, 224
'Soundtrack', 211
Spandau Ballet, 147
Split Beans, 90
Squat, 42, 45, 58, 89, 90
Stadgarten Studio, 240
Staff 9 (band), 212
Stage 2 (band), 128
Starr, Ringo, 17
Steel Pulse, 70, 127
Stephanie (Steve M's ex-girlfriend), 67, 198
Sterling, Linda, 29
Stiff Kittens (later Warsaw, then Joy
    Division, then New Order, *q.v.*), 42, 45,
    48, 55, 89
Stiff Records, 143
Stiff Test/Chiswick Challenge, 98–9, 103,
    108, 126
Still, 265, 285, 289, 293, 296
Stone Roses, 150
Stooges, 248
Stowell Memorial School, 5
Stranglers, 42, 112, 254, 256, 258, 289
Strawberry Studios, 145, 150, 162, 202, 213,
    219, 245, 246, 288
Strummer, Joe, 121
Stuff the Jubilee, 59, 89
Stuff the Superstars, 219
Sturridge, Charles, 28
'Substance', 212

Suicide with the Actors, 128
Sumner, Bernard ('Barney') (formerly
    Bernard Dickin), 36, 39–43, 53–4, 58,
    64–5, 70, 230, 291
  a.k.a. Bernard Albrecht, 118, 127
  bad behaviour of, 197
  band formed by, 39, 45, 87, 88
  'Barney Rubble' sobriquet of, 10, 59
  becomes a skinhead, 12
  birth of, 29
  comic nature of, 12
  'economical' playing of, 150
  education of, 29
  exams taken by, 14
  first gig as Joy Division, xiv–xvii
  girls/girlfriends and, 193
  gran's organ borrowed by, 160, 189
  graphic design skills of, 73, 77, 80, 103,
    156
  guitar-playing skills of, 82
  Ian close to, 67
  Ian's death and, 269
  Ian first meets, 51
  ill health of, 25, 122–3
  infamous sleeping bag of, 90, 123, 238
  jobs taken by, 50, 160
  parents indulge, 22
  Peter praises, 82
  Peter meets, 9, 10
  Peter's arguments with, 69
  PM falls out with, 66
  press/media and, 157
  pubbing/clubbing of, 22
  RCA deal and, 101
  scooter owned by, 16, 22
  Sex Pistols inspire, 44–5
  songs written/produced by, 229, 276
  Sue marries, 67
  Terry's relationship with, 49–50
  threatens to leave New Order, 50
  WWII obsession of, 81
  see also Dickin, Bernard
Sumner, Sue (née Barlow) (Bernard's wife),
    36, 38, 244, 249
Sunshine Valley Dance Band, 31
Surbiton Preparatory, 6
Surgical Supports, 133
Swan Records, 100
Swan, Salford, 50, 88
Swell Maps, 220
Swing Out Sister, 47
Swingin' Apple, Liverpool, 85, 94
SX, 213

Syd Lawrence Orchestra, 150

T. J. Davidson's ('TJ's'), 83, 90, 103, 140, 165,
    167, 170, 190, 192, 264, 293
T. J. M. Records, 167
Tabac, Toby, 55, 59, 90
Tanz Der Youth, 129
Teardrop Explodes, 68, 168, 219, 221, 223
10cc, 150, 155
Tennant, Neil, 31
'Tension', 92
Teret, Ray, 293
Tester, Nick, 134
That'll Be the Day, 17, 18
'The Drawback (All of This for You)', 126
'These Days', 215, 216, 217, 225, 229, 230,
    231, 282, 283, 284, 285, 287, 291
'They Walked in Line', 126, 156
31G-350125, 70
Thrills, Adrian, 219
Throbbing Gristle, 74, 108, 109, 114, 189,
    227, 248
Thunders, Johnny, 56, 57
Tiffany's, Leicester, 22, 63, 92
Tiller Boys, 108, 127, 131
Time & Place, 49
Time Out, 35
timelines:
    May 1948 to April 1976, 27, 27–31
    June 1976 to December 1977, 87, 87–94
    January 1978 to December 1978, xiii,
        125, 124
    January to December 1979, 208–17, 208
    January 1980 to October 1981, 281–97,
        281
Time's Up, 90
TJM Studios, 299
Today, 45, 88
Tonay, Don, 107
Top of the Pops, 23, 24, 28, 36, 139, 265
Top Rank, Sheffield, 226
Topping, Simon, 258
Touching From a Distance (Curtis), 99, 161,
    234, 262
Toyah, 254
'Transmission', 95, 105, 106, 126, 140, 145,
    148, 150, 161, 162, 163, 175, 188, 202,
    209, 211, 212, 216, 217, 218, 219, 220,
    221, 222, 223, 224, 225, 226, 227, 229,
    230, 231, 282, 283, 284, 286, 289, 291,
    293, 297
Trident Studios, 79
Tschichold, Jan, 29

Turmel, Jean-Pierre, 189
24 Hour Party People (film), 35, 36, 45, 123
'Twenty Four Hours', 223, 224, 225, 227,
    230, 231, 279, 282, 283, 284, 285, 286,
    287, 289, 290, 293, 296
Twinny (Karl) (roadie), 66–7, 88, 105, 121,
    132, 137, 149, 158–9, 165, 172, 176,
    177, 181, 184, 186–7, 192, 197, 217,
    222–3, 229, 230, 238, 243, 244, 256–7
  Ian's death and, 269
  injured at Bury gig, 259–60, 261
  piles suffered by, 90
  resigns/unresigns, 178
Twinny (Paul) (friend), xiv, 66–7
Twisted Wheel, 68

Ultravox, 147
Undertones, 120, 132, 133
United Artists, 92
Unknown Pleasures, 63, 74, 141, 142, 151,
    156, 163, 199–207, *199*, 218, 244, 245,
    248, 278, 280, 296, 297, *301*
  recording of, 151–8, 213
  release of, 160, 164, 215
'Untitled', 220
Ure, Midge, 128
U2, 252–3, 255

Velvet Underground, 35, 82, 101, 109, 140,
    205, 248
Vicious, Sid, 210
Virgin Records, 65, 70, 71, 93, *125*, 127, 214
Visage, 147
V2, 65, 93, 167

Waiting for the Siren's Call, 151
'Walked in Line', 212, 213, 227, 228, 297
Walker, Geordie, 240–1
Wall, Mick, 99
Walthamstow Youth Club, 173, 211, 213,
    221
Ward, Dave, 12
Warner, 147
Warsaw (formerly Stiff Kittens, later Joy
    Division, then New Order, *q.v.*), xiv, 31,
    47, 55, 63, 64, 68, 80, 81, 92, 127
  'A Talent Contest' entered by, 91
  band members take turns to manage, 73
  billed as Stiff Kittens, 89
  bootlegged tape of, 93
  final Electric Circus performance of,
    70–1
  first recording session of, 63
  first-ever gig of, 55–6, 89
  first-ever review of, 89
  formed, 35
  last gig of, 94
  manager and roadie of (Terry), 49, 54,
    63–4
  'Mary Whitehouse-odometer' rating of,
    89
  Middlesbrough gig of, 68–9
  Nazi associations dog, 93
  only live recording of, 92–3
  Ranch bars, 91
  reviews of, 59
  Steve B joins, 59
  Steve B leaves, 65
  Steve M joins, 65–6, 92
  tensions within, 70
  Virgin Records sign, 71
  Warsaw Pakt hampers, 79
  'Warszawa' inspiration for, 55
'Warsaw', 70, 74, 94, 126, 127, 130, 212,
    224, 229, 231, 283, 284, 286
Warsaw 'Live in Middlesboro', 93
Warsaw Pakt, 79, 129
Waters, John, 164
Weller, Paul, 175
Westwood, Vivienne, 31
White, Barry, 80
Whitehead, Malcolm, 148, 212, 222
Whitehouse, Mary, 89
Who, 37
Wiggin, Paul, 261
'Wilderness', 205–6, 213, 215, 219, 220,
    221, 222, 223, 224, 225, 227, 230, 231,
    282, 283, 284, 286, 287, 289, 290, 291
Williams, Robbie, 188
Wilson, Mr (work colleague), 15, 16, 18
Wilson, Tony, 20, 28, 29, 38, 54, 58, 88, 89,
    98, 99, 107, 110, 112, 116, 117, 126,
    129, 143, 147, 150, 153, 168, 188, 257,
    260, 261, 286
  birth of, 28
  Corrie siren started by, 159
  drugs and, 159
  Joy Division relationship begins, 105
  'Mister Granada' sobriquet of, 113–14
Wilson, Tony (producer), 231
Windscale Festival, 90
Wise, Alan, 133
Witts, Dick, 108
Wolff, Bernard Pierre, 296
Wood, Greg, 17, 24, 66–7
Wood, Ian, 214

Woodhead, John ('Jack') (Peter's dad), 3
Woodruff, Deborah ('Debbie'), see Curtis,
    Debbie
Worst, 59, 70, 89
Wreckless Eric, 98
Wroey (trial singer), 45, 46
Wythenshawe College, Manchester, 209

X Factor, The, 98
XL5, 291
X-O-Dus, 254, 289

X-Ray Spex, 68, 92

Yachts, 93
Year of the Child, 218
YMCA, Tottenham Court Road, 168,
    219–20
'You're No Good for Me', 63, 92

Zero, Martin, 28, 65; see also Hannett,
    Martin
Zyklon B, 218